Mirror Maps

Bill Baird

Mirror Maps

Collected Lyrics
/
Songbook

Copyright (c) 2020 Bill Baird
Published by Bill Baird / EBB
ISBN 978-1-7349964-0-1

Contents

14 About this book
15 Conceptual Continuity
    Lyrics
17 24 Karat Soul
18 A Perfect Light Awaits Me
19 A Place to Fall Apart
20 All Aboard Explorers
21 All I Know is Now
22 Alone Without You
23 Always Leaving Keys
24 Amber of the Now
25 An Artist Frets
26 Anything You Want Me To, I'll Be
27 As the Sun Will Rise This Dream Recedes
29 Automate my Lifestyle
30 Azure Shimmer
31 Ba Ba Ba Baby
32 Baby Blue
33 Bad Vibe Bank Account
34 Baptize Your Wasted Face in Wine
35 Be Yourself
36 Belly Flop
37 Bending of the Light
38 Bending the Truth
39 Big Orange
40 Bill
41 Black Hole Stopwatch
42 Bleach (Jesus is my Janitor)
43 Blindfolded in the City
44 Bliss
45 Bob
46 Bones
47 Boogie Fever
48 Bonnie Raitt's Afterlife (A Bluer Shade of Hell)
49 Boomerang Grenade

50 Bourbon is my Special Friend
51 Bourgeois Blues
52 Bow Down to the Brain
53 Bright Blue Dream
54 Buffalo buffalo Buffalo buffalo buffalo buffalo
55 Burn Burn Burn Burn
56 Bye by Numbers
57 Captain Brain
58 Captain Brain Theme Song
59 Caroline
60 Christmas in Jail
61 Civil War
62 Coffee is my Lover
63 Color of the Love You Have
64 Condo Graveyard
65 Cosmic coupon
67 Cranks Give Thanks
68 Daily Dance
69 Dead Man
70 Dear Broken Friend
71 Dear Friend (Failing Domino)
73 Death Smile
74 Decaying Monday
75 Diamond Eyepatch See
76 Diamond Studded Caskets
77 Does Not Compute_Head Wound Error
78 Doe See Doe
79 Dollar Bill Flashlight
80 Don't Hate Your Neighbor Just Because He Drives a Porsche
81 Don't Imbibe the T.V.
82 Don't Sleep til You're Dead / Heed my Words
83 Dragging Down the Street
84 Dreams of Sandy
85 Dusty Diamonds
86 Easy Machines / Telephones
87 Eat the Lawn for Free

88 Echoes of Each Glass
89 Emerald Arizona
90 Emotional Swings
91 Empty University
92 End's End
93 Everlasting Pleasure Cruise
94 Everything Explodes
95 Everything is Fine
96 Expiration Date
97 Existential Meltdown
98 Failing Domino
99 Feeling Bad Does Not Feel Good
100 Fishtown
101 Flower Children's Children's Children
102 Folkswinger
103 Game Over
104 Garden of Eden
105 Ghost of Myself
106 Go to Mexico
107 God the Smoker
108 Gold Dissolves to Gray
109 Gone
110 Goodbye Dear Friend of Mine
111 Goodbye Father
113 Goodbye Vibrations
114 Graveyard Dog / Dawn
115 Green Truck (Cycle of Life)
116 Hair Forest
117 Hairy Sally
118 Half a Man, Half a Man
119 Halfpenny Prince
120 Halfway to Nowhere
121 happiness is Forgetting
122 Hard so Hard
123 Heart Sound
124 Hearts Got a Hole
125 Heaviness of Flame

126 Heavy Light
127 Help Me Lord
128 Here Comes the Clock
129 Hey Old Buddy Old Friend
130 Hide
131 Hippie Hate Hippie
132 Home
133 Humanity (Hairy Sally's Lament)
134 Hunt So the Need High
135 I am that I am, I is that I was
136 I Burnt All My Black
137 I Can't Turn Around
138 I Don't Know Where to Live Anymore
139 I Love my Job
140 I Picked a Fight
141 I Think Too Much
142 I Will Be True
143 I Witness the World as a Glowing Ball
144 I'm a Gravedigger
145 I'm a Surfer
146 I'm Getting Laid Tonight
147 I'm Not a Perfect Person
148 I'm Sad but I Can't Play the Blues
149 I've Waited my Whole Life to Disappear
150 If God Gave Us Freewill
151 Illuminated Night
152 Imaginary Lover
153 In the Future
155 Infinite Eye
156 Inflatable Man
157 Inflated Head
158 Insomnia Insane
159 Interior Design
160 Intravenous Blues
161 Is Nothing There
162 It was a Lovely Way to Die
163 It's Over, my Dear, it's Through

164 It's Already Here
165 It's Empty Time
166 Jones Street Blues
167 Lady Dark
168 Lady Darkness Daydream
169 Las Vegas
170 Late Night Dawning
171 Leaving the City
173 Life is Rad (Just Say Yes)
174 Life's a TV Show
176 Lifer's Lament
177 Like Butter, Like Ice
178 Like Every Day Before
179 Limp Limo
180 Live That Way
181 Lone Writer
182 Long Ascent
183 Looking for Lines in Between the Dots
184 Lord of Your Apartment
185 Lost at Sea
186 Love Don't Exist Until it's Given Away
187 Love Gone Cold
188 Love that Passes is enough
189 Loveshines 1
190 Loveshines 2
191 Loveshines 3
192 Luby's Purgatory
193 Lunar Eyes
194 Mac n Me
195 Mad Mother
196 Man's Heart Complaint
197 Mellow Out My Mind
198 Memory (It Glows)
199 Memory's Hazy Golden Glow
200 Miami Nice
201 Mind Cops
202 Minimum Wage

203 Mirror Maps
204 Mister Treadmill
205 Monday Monday Monday
206 Moonlight
207 Mosquito
208 Mother Nature
209 Mummified
210 Muzak of the Spheres
211 My Brain is Made for You and Me
212 My Flame's Expired
213 My Pride and My Tobacco
214 My Woman Hates My Guts
215 Nature Dot Com
216 New City Lights
217 New York Love
218 No Time Big Time
219 Nobody Knows
220 Office Jerk
221 Oh Hi, Mr. Death
222 Old Growth
223 Old Sandy Bull Lee
224 Option Paralysis
225 Orca's Revenge
226 Other Side of the Sky
227 Our Dreams Did Weave a Shade
228 Ouroboros Shoes
229 Pain Pile
230 Party Party Party
231 Pizza Man in the Sky
232 Pocketful of Debt
233 Prometheus' Lament
234 Quicksilver Slip
235 Rainbow Brain
236 Rebel Without a Brain
237 Reclining in my Easy Chair
238 Ride the Toxic Wave
239 Robot Dan

240 Rot Down Cellar

241 Sally's Lament (plain spoken verse)

242 Sampson

243 Sandy My Love

244 Santa Claus of the south

245 Sewage Sirens

246 Shape Shifting Game

247 Shave

248 She Dreams in Diamonds

249 Skull Castle Decorator

250 Sleepwalking Someday

251 Slip into Shadow

252 Slow Motion Silver Skies

253 Slug

254 Slump City

256 Smoked by the Sun

257 Smoking Crack Ain't All It's Cracked Up to Be / Peace Love and Crystal Meth

258 So Long Farewell Adieu

259 So Says Me

260 Social Swamp Quicksand Screen

261 Soggy Soul

262 Somebody's Looking Out for You (rejected jingle for Goodyear Tires)

263 Song from a Dream

264 Sound in Your Mind

265 Special K Hole

266 Spreadsheet Star Charts

267 Spring Break of the Soul

268 Square dance

270 St John's Wort Blues

271 Stan is Dead

272 Stingk

273 Summer is Gone

274 Sunset's bath time

275 Sunshine Hair

276 Swirling Down the Drain

277 Symphony Sunrise
278 Talking Convict Life Story Blues
280 Talking Fossil Fuel Blues
281 Talking God Blues
282 Talking Love Blues
283 Talking Texas Blues
285 Texas Saves
286 Texas Tune
287 Thaw My Heart
288 The Boy Without a Brain
289 The Darkness Stares Back
290 The End of the World
291 The Emperor's New Clothes
292 The Lonesome Death of Cosmic Cowboy
294 The Moon is Shining Too
295 The Past Just Won't Forget Me
296 The Singer is the Song
297 The TV Imbibed Me
298 The World is Awaiting
299 There Goes my Ego
300 This Time You Broke My Heart This Time
301 Time Machine
303 Time Revolving Time
304 Tiny Truck
305 Tourniquet Pants
306 Trapped in Paradise
307 Trash Compactor
308 TV Guide Blues
309 Ugly Piece of Shit
310 Unplug Your Head
311 Until My Dying Day
312 Vegan Meatheads
313 Velvet Rut
314 Walkin in the Dark
315 Walkin with a Daydream
316 Walking in a Straight Line
317 Warm Inside

318 We'll Meet Again Someday, or We Won't

319 Weird Year

320 When Perfect Flames Expire

321 White Male Blues (boo fucking hoo)

322 Wiggle Worm

323 Wino Strut

324 Work Work Work

326 World Frames Your Face

327 World Gone Deaf

328 You and Me Make 3

329 You Can Never Go Home

330 You Can Never Go Home Again

331 You Cut my Heart in Two

332 You Know Who You Are

333 You Know You

334 You're Still Glowing

335 You're a Special Girl

336 You're Already Home, Indianna

337 You're Free if You Want to Be

338 You're My Girl

339 You're Someone Else

340 You've never lived a day in your life

341 Your Dark Sunglasses Won't Make You Lou Reed

342 Your Eyes are Mirrors

343 Your Heart Breaks into a New Heart

344 Your Soul Glows in the Dark

345 Zombies

Appendices

346 Appendix A: How Songwriting Ruined My Life

382 Appendix B: Photographs

402 Appendix C: Letters to Xavier

422 Appendix D: Onward!   Thru the Many Fogs

427 Appendix E: Answers to Unasked Questions

430 Appendix F: Conceptual Continuity

433 Appendix G: Chronology / Biographies

439 Appendix H: Creative Anxiety

About This Book

empty songs
vacant songs
vagrancy songs
penthouse songs
gutter songs
dumpster songs
compost songs
lonely songs
expansion songs
anti songs
professional songs
amateur songs
spoken songs
whispered songs
screamed songs
stutter songs
exasperation songs
satisfied songs
life songs
death songs
rebirth songs
joyful songs
existential songs
songs from the point of view of a child
songs from the point of view of a cloud
songs from the point of view of the cosmos
departure songs
drunken chant songs
sea shanties
murder ballads
TV theme songs
collage songs
middle-class mediocrity songs
self-loathing songs
human folly / delusions of grandeur songs
Texas songs
California songs
songwriter songs
&
yes....
love songs

Songs share imagery, characters, chords changes.
They reference each other freely.
I have made a diagram which shows how the songs relate.
The web is complex.
All together, they form a single story.
The story of my life.... and yours.
"His life but a weave and each memory a thread"

Conceptual Continuity

About half of these connections were a conscious effort, and half were a natural part of the process. Songs that relate to each other using characters, imagery, chords, phrases, or themes, and connected using lines.

Like a spider's web. Each circle is numbered 1 – 50. I numbered each song and found the connections it makes to every other song.

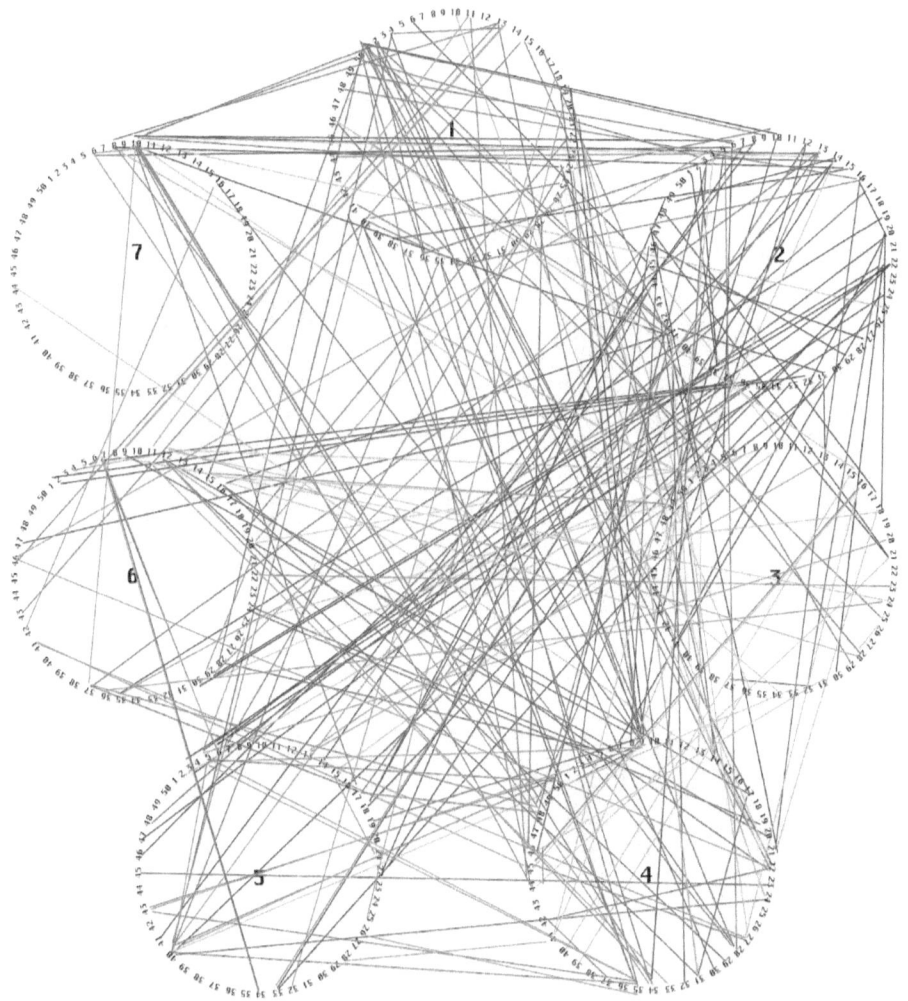

Lyrics

24 Karat Soul

flying east is flying west
these mirror maps together pressed
in lost and found loneliness
i fake a laugh and something dies
but these memories create disguises
smile real wide
while i die inside
how much longer can it be denied?

24 karat soul
there's solid gold
in your hand
25 pounds of mold
rots away inside a safe

your pretty face will wrinkle past
memories of youthful laughs
and golden sun
a tombstone will steal your name
and you'll go to hell
but there's no flames
it's a parking lot
with no pleasure or pain
where everybody looks
and thinks
and dresses just the same

24 karat soul
there's solid gold in your hand
25 pounds of mold
rots away inside a safe

you cannot overlay
until your dying day
it's already there, already there
the porsche that you drive
the wrinkles on your face
it's already there, already there
the works of art you never could create
it's already there, already there

A Perfect Light Awaits Me

sable pall and waving plume
a thousand blazing torches will illume
the future at your doorway
parting glance and burning tear
seem to fall upon the pier
departing stars bursting with their pilgrims
a lustrous gloom shines into your tomb

ba ba ba ba
a perfect light awaits me
be ba ba ba
resplendent life fit for two
me and you
me and you

you and i of kindred clay
watching all the coffins sink away
a single mind will guide us
a curse is cast from lunar eyes
as rosy fingered dawn gives up and dies
all our friends are leaving
a placid moon pops like a balloon

babababa
a perfect light awaits me
babababa
resplendent life fit for two
me and you
babababa
the moonlight hangs beside you
babababa
i'll hold a hand to guide you

swam out a swell into the sea
reflecting back the flashes of your memory
tombstones were humming all a tune
the mood struck us right
we took off our shoes
and we danced
oh how we danced
now you're set free!

A Place to Fall Apart

the pipes in my head
are dripping draining lead
and my brain's deflated to an empty yawn
and my self assurance screen
is mumbling at the seams
and the skin i'm in
is a costume i put on

darling won't you give me
a place to fall apart?
protect while i die and disappear back to the start
i've half a mind to tell you
i've nothing left to be
and the other side of my vacant mind
is waiting there for me

there's nothing to be feared
when your demise is near
but still and all it's not a pretty sight
you wither up and die
with no tears left to cry
and pass beyond
the land of black and white

darling won't you give me
a place to fall apart?
protect while i die and keep me warm against the dark
i've half a mind to tell you
i've nothing left to be
and the other side of my bothered mind
is waiting there for me

i'm through playing tough
there's no point in pride
i'm crawling and my legs and arms are bound
when the world goes quiet
it starts to talk
and when i sit still
i start to walk
and admitting when i'm lost
is when i'm found

darling won't you give me
a place to fall apart?
protect while i die and disappear back to the start
i've half a mind to tell
you i've nothing left to be
and the other side of my vacant mind
is waiting there for me

All Aboard Explorers!

it's all aboard explorers
we'll heed the ocean's call
it's all aboard explorers
all boundaries are sure to fall

never mind we don't have munitions
never mind we don't have supplies
the pain will just make you stronger
that is, until you die

when you die
we'll float your corpse
horizon you'll meet by and by
the sharks may take a little nibble
but who cares?
you've already died

All I Know is Now

breath draws in and stays
threads of lives
entangled fates
what good would it do me?
time only runs through me
all i know is now

future's fogged in throw
blind men see what they already know
what good would it do me?
time only runs through me
all i know is now

we all dissolve
like the edge of a cloud
but to keep moving forward
is all that's allowed
what good would it do me?
time only runs through me
all i know is now

Alone Without You

i find it hard to send a card
i can't pick up the phone
i feel the need to just concede and lose these nights alone
but i'm a man and if i can
i hold on to my pride
until it's time to sing and rhyme and i got no place to hide.

with tongue in cheek these words i speak
of hidden thoughts i'd disallowed
i wrote this song for you
but now i sing it to a crowd
the crowd may come and sing beside me
i'm alone without you

the bustle of the city is no substitute for home
everyone trapped in their heads
their ego safety zone
and there's something so lonely
about a traffic jam
everyone alone at once
and i can't tell who i am.

with tongue in cheek these words i speak
of hidden thoughts i'd disallowed
i wrote this song for you
but now i sing it to a crowd
the crowd may come and sing beside me
i'm alone without you

someday you'll see
we were meant to be
two halves fall apart like a half beating heart
and we decompose into a tree

so humbly i beg of thee
to not leave me cold
i need someone to care for me
when i'm gray and old
i'll be the yang and you can be the ying
so there'll always be someone to cheer
every time i sing

Always Leaving Keys

storm clouds brew the blackened cup
the lack your words betray
and you've nothing more to say
moon's magic brightens
from the dark your days return
and you've nothing more to burn

eyes into future held
the hope to past reclaim
and you've nothing more to name
never into nothing walk
except when standing free
and you've nothing more to see

absence in the empty hand
is presence in the mind
you learn to live
you leave your life behind
absent other options
you became what you lacked
always leaving, always coming back

air head holding up your masks
deflated to the ground
but nothing made a sound
stillness of the midnight asks
which storm the day will bring
and there's no more wind to sing
nothing there is nothing more to worry you my dear
there's nothing more to fear
the world's portrait will provide the image of your strength
you are everything

absence in the empty hand
is presence in the mind
you learn to live
you leave your life behind
absent other options
you became what you lacked
always leaving, always coming back

Amber of the Now

where can life be seen?
pavement cracks shooting sprouts of green
then the sprouts they all get mowed
so it goes

where can life be heard?
a sea of sound where silence is absurd
while the white noise blizzard blows
so it goes

here we are trapped in the amber of the now
there is no why
there is no why
oh why?
oh wow
here we are trapped in the amber of the now

where can life be felt?
fluorescent faces
shrug at what they're dealt
while the world outside explodes
so it goes

where can life be lived?
anywhere you have your love to give
using an app that's on your phone
so it goes

here we are trapped in the amber of the now
there is no why
there is no why
oh why?
oh wow
here we are trapped in the amber of the now

An Artist Frets

empty faces fill a room
reeks of rot and stale perfume
they take their seats, the lights go down
and from the stage comes not a sound
behind the curtain, an artist frets
his inspiration's not come yet
but the crowd won't notice
they paid their fare
and if his music fails
they won't even care
so he keeps abreast the poor charade
but he's coasting on the works he's made
so long ago, afraid to stop
he's pushed himself until he dropped
and when he rose
he'd lost the plot
froze in motion, couldn't stop
it's fool's gold, he realized
to look good
while inside you die
so he went back in time
reversed the clock
he was a child again
without no clogs, worries nor fear
he sang a joyful song sincere
and now the crowd fell silent
stopped their jeers
and they all burst into tears
"such innocence," the people cried.
"such pure beauty"
"somebody better grab a video camera"
so they videoed this song of glee
and sent it off to mtv
and the song became a worldwide hit
and yet again
the singer became an ego driven piece of shit
his moment of humble realization
got buried in a cocaine blizzard
until he made a midi album about an aging wizard
the music — midi triggered peruvian pan pipes
sung in olde english tripe
clad in acid washed jeans
frizzle fried perm hairdo
he took more drugs, solidified his clogs
shaved his head, bought a convertible
which he lost in bankruptcy proceedings
all this failure shoved him brain-first
into another creative block
and the cycle goes again.
behind the curtain
an artist frets....

Anything You Want Me to, I'll Be

if you're standing outside
i will be the door
if you're covered with ice, dear
i will give you warmth
if your stomach's empty
i will be your food
and if your feet get blisters
i'll take off your shoes
if you're feeling lazy
i will do your chores
and buy you anything you want
when we go to the store
and when your hair is tangled
i will be your comb
and if you're lost and lonely
i will take you home

anything you want me to, i'll be
rainbow colored ocean
candy colored tree
anything you want me to, i'll do
crawl on the highway
or burglarize the zoo

republicans start dancing
when they see your face
monkeys and orangutans
stare into space
images and magic
your words
a spell they cast
magic wands and spatulas
you teach a cooking class

anything you want me to, i'll be
rainbow colored ocean
candy colored tree
anything you want me to, i'll do
crawl on the highway
or burglarize the zoo

As The Sun Will Rise This Dream Recedes

the holy man, he said it loud
god's in the sky he's in the clouds
his tears are drops of life that we call rain
he moved me so, i left to see
those visions of eternity
out the windows of a delta jet air plane
as the plane took off and rose above
i looked for signs of cosmic love
but saw only blues and whites and browns
the colors gave a wondrous view
and lit my soul, this much is true
but the plane flight just couldn't lift me off the ground

so there i sat, bout two miles high
and felt alone so i had to cry
and i cried and cried until i died of thirst
and an angel came, shaped like a clock
and to him i expressed great shock
but he said get over it boy, you ain't the first
you lived your life and now you died
you gave your love and never had a bride
you left no kin to carry on your blood
your legacy, the house you built
the poems your wrote with ink you spilt
but now you're outside time and it's all just mud
so i hope you remember those things you said
because all things now exist just in your head
and theres no place else to find what you forgot
so tell me now bout things you did
the lives you changed, the love you spread
and if your life was good, you get another shot

so i looked at him and thought
i've done good things, but i forgot
i didn't let them fester in my mind
what should i say if i can't recall
ever having done a thing at all
not brave nor vile nor weak nor meek nor kind
and so i rose to my defense
and said
"angel man it makes no sense
to speak of me as if i'm really here
you know i've lived a thousand lives
each day i'm born, each day i die
your presence has been expected, i have no fear
if you need my story, read my face
its got my life in every crease
it speaks my shadows and my golden rays
for body mind and spirit and soul are all one thing, as you well know
so just look into my eyes and lets be on our way."

he gave a steadfast look then smiled
he said

"old boy i like your style
your way of squirming out of traps with words
but cleverness can't do a thing to remedy the pain you bring
in denying all the love that has occurred
what matters most cannot be said
cannot be writ, cannot read
its only in yourself that you will find
the life that you may selfless live
to die correct, to forgive
and to hear others words as if born blind
so remember that these things i said were made for life,
not for the dead
for where words matter none, its only deeds
i send you now to be reborn, a rising sun, an early morn
and as the sun will rise, this dream recedes
and as the sun will rise, this dream recedes
and as the sun will rise, this dream recedes."

Automate My lifestyle

shadow robot chauffeur
built into your chevy
the future's much too much to bear
and the past is getting heavy

algorithmic automation
fascist henry ford
automate my lifestyle, baby
before i get bored

wake the brain of disney
before his thaw doth drip
the future he imagined
well, it ain't worth the trip

algorithmic automation
fascist henry ford
automate my lifestyle baby
before i get bored

Azure Shimmer

azure shimmer
rippled rolling skin
once you hop aboard
you can't go home again
everything you see
is your reflection
my friend

strange to see
how the journey started
adrift in the world
of the broken hearted

Ba Ba Ba Baby

early in the day
just before the hour 5
splashing water on my face
to try and stay alive
and in the other room is cause of all this bustle
a little hungry human
puts your day all in a tussle

baby baby little baby
can't you understand
all these words i say
(no)
for i am just a man
but deep down in my insides i'm a baby just like you
and sometimes i feel like crying

afternoon comes creeping in
the sun and all its rays
twenty cups of coffee and i'm still all in a daze
but the little bitty baby has agendas of her own
and let's see what the dice have thrown
oh! your lucky number again.
go change the diaper, my friend.

baby baby little baby
can't you understand
all these words i say
(no)
for i am just a man
but deep down in my insides i'm a baby just like you
and sometimes i feel like crying

day is grounding to a halt
to evening time relax
but nothing is that simple
no
there must be a tax
just as i go sitting down
you sing another tune
are you shrieking for your dinner
or howling at the moon?

Baby Blue

ringing eardrums
numbing all that I once held inside
something inside me died
world keeps spinning
wheel of misfortune
pat sajak is god
and vanna white the holy host
slowly cashing nature's bounty
trading in ourselves
computers rust on shelves
swollen sports bars
pulsing traffic
bring on memories
of toilet paper trees

baby blue
reflecting the world back to you

stolen silence
white noise violence
this city hums with life
like crickets bringing blight
perched above this
can I hold out against this constant flood?
These streets are stained with blood

baby blue
reflecting the world back to you

Bad Vibe Bank Account

keep your head in quicksand, man
hack in hand
and gigging band
cloud breath breathes a brown cigar
slithers to his compost car
penny loafing dollar bake
you want to live like a mistake
but peel your face off of your plate
and pull soul out of the grate

bad vibe bank account
bad vibe bank account

vapor trailing bubble thought
your memory calls and i get caught
ain't no way to live a life
trickle down and sell your self
you've papercut your way to hell
a bridge across the river cliff
whose notes won't help to mend the riff

bad vibe bank account
bad vibe bank account

Baptize Your Wasted Face In Wine

baptize your wasted face in wine
wave my wand and everything will be fine
baptize your eyes in a jar of gin
a fresh start to fumble up again

sallow sleepy cheeks
and a bit worn smile
i can tell that you've seen some nights
days and weeks
counting every mile
a trail of disappointments and fights

the final foe you cannot flake
and if you shrug enough
your shoulders will break

so i'll
baptize your wasted face in wine
wave my wand and everything will be fine
baptize your eyes in a jar of gin
a fresh start to fumble up again

twisting in the wind
like a kite on a branch
shredded like guitars at double speed
with a pale face of stone
that your years did blanch
your indifference just projects a sense of need

the final foe you cannot flake
and if you shrug enough
your shoulders will break
so i'll
baptize your wasted face in wine
wave my wand and everything will be fine
baptize your eyes in a jar of gin
a fresh start to fumble up again

Be Yourself

throbbing head
halfway dead
your bed is as messed as your mind
you're drowning in the seas of hazy memories
and the future that you never seemed to find
all in vain, all in vain
for the end of every bottle is the same
you slur a sappy song
and wonder went wrong
and gargle down another til its gone
til its gone

all your statues made of lifeless stone
glorify the lone tortured soul
your heroes held on high
they'll all teach you how to die
but everything they told you is a lie
the rule breakers need a set of rules
so speak the avant guarded fortress schools
"don't listen to authority"
no leaders none to say
let's all be unique in the same way
but when you're gone
you will turn to mud
and the last sound that you hear will be a thud
the sound of the fall of the dropping of a ball
you held aloft with myth believing blood
all these myths you mistook for truth
dissolve away in a silent poof
and the histories you preached are getting dusty on the shelf
all you can do is be yourself
all you can do is be yourself
all you can do is be yourself
be yourself

Belly Flop

rippling in waves
this life it comes and goes
nothing ever stays
into the sea it flows
& gets cycled back around
to come through your garden hose
drop by drop
this life's a belly flop

poseidon in a bathing suit
wading out the time
til all the world's engulfed again
by salty water brine
from oil spills to tar
we're pickles in a jar
drop by drop
this life's a belly flop

the best sailor i knew
ate spinach from a can
he might've been strong
but about food he didn't know a damn

slap onto your belly
a sandwich of rejection
then watch the bread dissolve
upon further inspection
there's nothing there to cure
existential head infection
drop by drop
this life's a belly flop

it slaps and it hurts
it sprays and it squirts
rancid mayo pool
the ocean laughs
"human fools"

Bending of the Light

the sun took crooked turns
corners cut across
its colors burned
speckled on your skin
as life returns to share its second sight
your orbs yearn with the bending of the light.
images of old into the ditch
black and white and technicolor switch
and the itching of your eye
becomes its strength
the dry, subsumed in second sight
you can't but cry at the bending of the light
of the light

rainbow curves in time to form your frame
i know you must go and it's a shame
but i see where you are
it's a morning dream
i visit every night
i see your face in the bending of the light
and your eyes combine, unite in second sight
and the world returns with the bending of the light
of the light

memories can never fill the space
the place you stood like an angel of grace
memory, imagination
neither one is right
neither one is right
but i'll see you again in the bending of the light
memory, imagination
neither one is right
but i'll see you again in the bending of the light
of the light

Bending the Truth

your goldfish drowned in its bowl
on its murky puddle shelf
your perma-grin online life
shines a statue of itself
empty tub in water tread you tell yourself is home
pretend to read <u>war and peace</u>
while staring at your phone
the facts of your life maybe hard to take
but bending the truth won't make it break

you want to give up your conscience
and do just as you please
but that scraping sound upon the ground
is you crawling on your knees
you're half a man completely
you've stooped to serve your whims
you sell your soul discreetly
it's glimmer fades and dims
the facts of your life maybe hard to take
but bending the truth won't make it break

a market research study
can tell you how to smirk
but in the end when you pretend
you're just a pointless jerk
the world's already waiting
the world's already here
so stop procrastinating
someday you'll disappear
the facts of your life maybe hard to take
but bending the truth won't make it break

Big Orange

we are the makers of the modern age
we blaze into the unknown
we are imperfect but we like it that way
we keep it real and we make it our own

all you scenesters with perfect hair
and permanent frowns
you'd better 86 cuz we're on our way
to blow up your town

you taste our steel
you feel the ivory pulse
don't be afraid of your fear
orange shivers
be happy
convulse
every day is a new year

big orange
big orange

so your life is done again
what will you do?
the journey of 1000 steps begins
by tying your shoes
we're not the demons that you think we are
we're also angels too
a mouth of flames and a vacuum guitar
and we have a sound for every one of you

Bill

please allow me to introduce myself
my name is bill
i'll drip wax poetic on your proustian shelf
balloon thoughts popping like pills
i've wagered all my sorrow on a winning bet
drifting in the deep end of my dreams
and clawed my way from a lukewarm pit
of boiling yoga pants shaped like jeans

bill bill bill bill
bill bill bill bill

lizards licking money
plastic surgeon pins pricking all you wish to do without
backslapping money
paying hourly for my friends
to say i'm great until they've clocked out
please let me please reintroduce myself
my name's still bill
please don't let me sing this by myself
it's lonely up here on the hill

bill bill bill bill
bill bill bill bill

Black Hole Stopwatch

staring at a broken clock
feeling most confused
wrinkles pile onto my face
a blue second hand
calendar commands
WAKE WORK SLEEP EAT
and then again tomorrow i'll do it all again

seconds keep hurrying by
can't fathom where they go
scenes of my day replay like a rerun tv show
someday i'll get cancelled and come back on video
until then it seems i'll just sit here and smoke

time
killing time
nothing here is real
not even my mind
i punched a hole to the next dimension
what did i find?
a black hole stopwatch
tick tock tick tocktick tocktick tocktick tocktick tocktick tocktick tocktick tocktick tocktick
tocktick tocktick tocktick tocktick tocktick tocktick tocktick tocktick tocktick tocktick
tocktick tocktick tocktick tocktick tocktick tocktick tocktick tocktick tocktick tocktick
tocktick tocktick tocktick tocktick tocktick tocktick tocktick tocktick tocktick
tocktick tocktick tocktick tocktick tocktick tocktick tocktick tocktick tocktick tocktick tock

if time is an ocean
then death is the shore
and everyone's a sailor
and our thoughts the ocean floor
heaven is a beach resort
and all the saints are there
umbrellas in their goblets
sands of time in their hair

time
killing time
nothing here is real
not even my mind
i punched a hole to the next dimension
what did i find?
a black hole stopwatch

time hurries on
even while you're gone
and the road you're traveling on
takes you back to where you've left
with a broken smile and a pocket full of debt

Bleach (Jesus is my Janitor)

eyes shooting blank
all i see is shame
mud caked halo
aura jello
everywhere i go
my soul drags down below
mud caked halo
aura jello

bleach my brain
bleach my brain
call my mom and change my name
bleach my brain
a shiny sheen
make me look like mr. clean
jesus is my janitor
jesus is my janitor
jesus is my janitor

oh sigmund freud
my penis is a void
mud caked halo
aura jello
bleach my brain
bleach my brain
call my mom and change my name
bleach my brain
a shiny sheen
make me look like mr. clean
jesus is my janitor
jesus is my janitor
jesus is my janitor

Blindfolded in the City

hardships sailed upon me
i floated off the farm
on city booze, delta blues and floozy women's charms
but it all went dark
life turns black
as sober moments fade
left the sun for skyscraper shade
and the quick flash flame of cocaine
glittered past my eyes
the sun went down, faded fast
spirits began to rise
i lived my life in daydreams
i dreamed through all my daze
i danced inside a darkness
of only blacks and grays

blindfolded in the city
ain't no sun to make the concrete pretty.

so i crawled about with pretty girls
faces painted fierce
pasting on their toughest eyes
they thought no-one could pierce
but i saw in and loved them all
and told them plain and true
two days of love and this affair is through
i had no way to tell that they
were pulling me down worse
love affairs i thought were blessed
ended up a curse
now i'm tarnished, blue and black
totally ashamed
i dyed my hair and legally changed my name.

blindfolded in the city
ain't no sun to make the concrete pretty

Bliss

when i saw you
in the phone
i knew you were at home
and the moment
hung so heavy

lost into the grid
abandoned to your id
and bolted to its bevy

waves washed above
i knew our endless love
had reached
its always empty

wind blows a theft
and now i stand bereft
waiting on
the life you left me

Bob

bob smith is a reasonable man
he nods along with the nightly news
ice cold beer is glued to his hand
and sensible ergonomic shoes
bob smith doesn't understand the strife
all the yelling and protesting in the street
bob smith will never question his life
he just needs a place to microwave his meat
bob smith queues up for the train
orderly moderation jail
the world is just the way it is
and anything worth having is for sale
bob smith has long gone numb
slouching through his day til he gets home
he has lots of Facebook friends
it helps him forget that he's alone

bob bob bob
your head's just a knob
whose door got locked many moons before
bob bob bob
you slump through your job
afraid to question what you're working for

there is no moral to this tale
there's bobs by the million all around
even his demise was a "sensible" event
a proper square plot in the ground
his life it came, his life it went
and the dreams he took great pains to save
so sensibly he went
and the dreams he never spent
are now pushing up the daisies on his grave

bob bob bob
your head's just a knob
whose door got locked many moons before
bob bob bob
you slump through your job
afraid to question what you're working for

Bones

thawing in the headlights
you turned into a watch
and now every second that it ticks
is every second lost.
life dissolving quickly
and you cannot grab ahold.
first finger
second hand
is pointing at a skull

blacker than the bible
that speaks the end of days
this darkness that surrounds you now
will trap you in its gaze
a tar-bath burning shower
with not a drop of soap
and it's dripping slow, so painful slow
but don't give up your hope.

bones!

this watch kept changing hands
in pawnshops' shifting sands
til it ended as an antique now
with several lifetime spans.
falling through manhattan
a lower east side dive
you're shining in a window there
trapped but still alive.
trapped but still alive.
trapped but still alive.
trapped but still alive.

bones!

Boogie Fever

boogie fever
boogie down
shake your boogie
down below the ground
boogie madness
boogie drugs
pop some advil
ride the flying rug
it's a mental breakdown
downtown
the beat of feet and city sounds
crashing cars and breaking glass
and the city bus won't let you pass
but hey, pop down in the sewer hole
there's a party down there beyond control
the black and whites and reds and greens
are ballet dancing
getting obscene
the rhythm's pulsing, emulsing
through drainage pipes and toilets
the vibes we lay down underground say
man, you know the score
it smells bad down here
but bad is good
let's have some more.

Bonnie Raitt's Afterlife (A Bluer Shade of Hell)

and i walk right down the freeway
and i walked into a wreck
and i shot out of my body
and to the afterlife I trekked
and i stood around knock knock knocked upon heaven's gate
and they looked at me and laughed and said
"hello bonnie raitt
you tried your best to play the blues
and for that your soul did sell
and now it seems you're going to a bluer shade of hell

pentatonic scale
got your pentatonic scale
ringing in a bluer shade of hell

so i journeyed down to hell
and i said hi to genghis khan
and he was playing the drums on human skulls
and the devil on saxophone
he played kenny g and kenny g and kenny g some more
and jumped into the worst of all:
lounge act covers of "the doors"

pentatonic scale
got your pentatonic scale
ringing in a bluer shade of hell

so now i'm in a band
we roam the world and haunt
all humanity doing what they shant
from south austin to jersey
we spread the screeching news
a whitewashed version of the delta blues

pentatonic scale
got your pentatonic scale
ringing in a bluer shade of hell

Boomerang Grenade

swirl circle drain
your brain is slipping
and she's laughing at your
self-inflicted pain
shoelace tied together
always tripping
while throwing a
boomerang grenade

her eyes are the holes
your heart is seeking
and you're peeking
but nobody's at home
her image is a mirror
that you're tweaking
so stop freaking
just cuz you are alone

so let yourself let go
and then you'll have her
no more blather
no more whispers from the wall
you see she was never what you were after
all that mattered
was a way to break your fall

Bourbon Is My Special Friend

my feet are muddy
there's water in my shoes
swimming for shelter from these drizzling bathtub blues
bourbon is my special friend

holy water
guzzle every drop
demon water mouthwash
brackish belly flop
bourbon is my only friend, bourbon is my special friend

dear bourbon.... won't you come out to play?

dull bonanza
apathy for lunch
boredom banana
yawn
gulp
crunch
bourbon is my only friend, bourbon is my special friend

this swimming pool's amazing
it's brown and it's cold
i tread water sometimes
it helps me unfold
bourbon is my swimming pool
and sometimes i'm a drowning fool

where is my feeling?
where is my pain?
where is my happiness?
where is my shame?
bourbon is my only friend.
bourbon is my only friend

Bourgeois Blues

when you wake up in a water bed
that's filled with imported perrier
and your conversations consist
of what you already knew they'd say
and your spirit animal
is the same as the skin of your shoes
it's printed on your sox
you've got the bourgeois blues

life is a checklist
a spreadsheet shaped like a yawn
when you a use a pair of tweezers
to trim the edges of your lawn
all your elevator buttons
are labelled "down" and "snooze"
you've got an empty cup
of the luke-warm bourgeois blues

its true i point my finger
but its really pointed back at me
the worlds a magic mirror
we see what we want to see
we all need an enemy
an imaginary foe which to use
to remind us who we are
and for me its the bourgeois blues.

Bow Down to the Brain

everywhere around the world
it's everywhere the same
problems needing to be solved?
they all consult the brain.
an architect, mail order bride, or job of any name
the one thing that can't be denied
they bow down to the brain
bow down
bow down
bow down to the brain

now in matters of the inner life
my record's not so hot
i've killed every passenger
that's ever graced a cot
but one thing that i know for sure:
before they met their fates
they bowed down to the brain
just like my first mate
bow down
bow down
bow down to the brain

now i would bow too, you see
but i ain't got no knees
just a brain floating in a jar
a briny water breeze
goes blowing through rippling folds of
blobby matter gray now
everybody sing it loud
and let me hear you say
bow down to the brain
bow down to the brain
bow down
bow down
bow down to the brain
bow down
bow down
bow down to the brainbow down
bow down
bow down to the brainbow down
bow down
bow down to the brain

(charbydis smiles)

Bright Blue Dream

sleep, sleep darling one
lock your eyes in the sun
free your brain from the leash it's on
watch your hands turn to steam
as you dive into a deep blue dream
color of the sky
shape of the air
where is the happiest place you've been?
hold your tongue
i will take you there
the wind is made of words
every dream that's ever occurred

frozen exploding trees
and headlights pulsing
they're behind you now
deep blue water
step inside
right now
your dangling worries have died

dream, dream darling one
ease your mind
take a rest
tomorrow will be a trying one
dream your eyes into your mind
it's time you closed your eyes and slept.

Buffalo buffalo Buffalo buffalo buffalo buffalo

buffalo buffalo buffalo buffalo buffalo buffalo
repetition is a form of change
repetition is a form of change
especially when you're feeling strange
it's a linguist's trick used to explain
the arbitrary nature of grammar's game

buffalo buffalo buffalo buffalo buffalo buffalo
say the same thing again and again
say the same thing and it means a new thing
say the same thing again and again
say the same thing and it means a new thing

buffalo buffalo buffalo buffalo buffalo buffalo
like if i say "i love you"
it means what you get
but if i say "i love you, i love you"
it means i'm desperate
buffalo buffalo buffalo buffalo buffalo buffalo

Burn Burn Burn Burn

let's burn down this city baby
we'll watch the flames dance across the lawn
the spark will be the scene
and our lust the gasoline
and the fire will burn until the dawn

like a magic sword that cut away my skin
and left my soul exposed to the wind
I got nowhere left to hide
no more walls to stand inside
and i'll never see the world the same again

there's a flamethrower blowing through my head
I should've just played it cool instead
but I got nothing left to be
so let's destroy this shell of me
and the fire will burn away my head

and when this burning city's gone
the impulse to destroy will linger on
it's a lifestyle we can't quell
so we'll burn away ourselves
and i'll see you on the sunny side of hell
burn burn burn burn
burn burn burn burn
burn burn burn burn
burn burn burn burn

Bye by Numbers

feet feel the road and move my legs
bent to the sounds of departure
but you've never heard the words i've said
so let these numbers paint you a picture
1 is all i need to be
another 1 is not there with me
there's 91 ways to say we're through
and when i disappear that's 92

there's new in what i say
it's as timeless as its passing
but i can't give another day
boredom is an assassin
1 is all i need to be
another 1 is not there with me
there's 91 ways to say we're through
and when i disappear that's 92

don't let these words weigh your mind
nothing there is nothing more to hurt you
and please don't think me too unkind
when i happily desert you
1 is all i need to be
another 1 is not there with me
there's 91 ways to say we're through
and when i disappear that's 92

Captain Brain

chrome dome styling foam
shiny mental sphere
briny water floating home
pulsing face of fear
oh, captain brain!

mental janitor
can you sweep away my past?
i acted like a moron
i acted like an ass
oh, captain brain!

bleach blonde scrub head
make me look nice when i'm dead
or scrub away my face instead
spinal cord to tie a thread
oh, captain brain!

fair trade ferrari
organic corvette
bill gates wears a sari
and solar powered jet set
oh, cap and trade!
oh, cap and trade!

Captain Brain Theme Song

flailing flapjack breakfast, no syrup for our trials
we need someone to help us out, to help us out in style
what good would it do us for some slob to save our necks?
our hero needs a necklace, dangled in a rippled chest
i
know
this
sounds
quite
insane
but

captain brain is a brain floating in a jar
he doesn't play tennis, he doesn't drive a car
but at stanford university, he paid a quarter mil
to have his brain inflated til it began to spill
i
know
this
sounds
so
quite
insane
but
i
think
it's
time
we
called
on
captain

captain brain oh captain brain please tell us what to do
ripe fermented lactates are dripping off our shoes
it's a smelly shitty mess up to our turtlenecks retract
wobbly knees knocking doors, let's come up with a pact
we'll obey your orders and submit unto your name
for everybody's know there's nothing smarter than a brain
submerge all our instincts, intuit nothing more
you are our master so tell us what's in store

my little boys, so glad to hear
you've given up your will
inflated brain will save the world....
for other inflated brains

mwhahahahahaha

Caroline

holding hands on frozen sidewalks
on the seashore
on the pier
you need someone better than me
and you'll know that
as soon as i'm not here
oh lovely caroline
you sprung out of this land
a mother hen flaming and frothing
but your tears only distract
the facts have long been sung
in the end
we will be one
but until that end we'll be apart
surrounded by the snow
that's piled up in place of the love
we used to know

oh silly caroline
your false heart condemns
this house that we built out of empty
oh silly caroline
i'm never coming back to this land
but i'll always take you with me

your promises betray
all the things you couldn't say
the clenching of your fists
can't squeeze the feeling
abandoned and forgot
the love you left to rot
you only notice paint when it's peeling
kind words can do a lot
but there's no replacing time
if you'd kindly just stop talking
and pour me another glass of wine

oh silly caroline
your false heart condemns
this house that we built out of empty
oh silly caroline
i'm never coming back to this land
but i'll always take you with me

Christmas in Jail

when your face falls to ashen
and the sunshine stays away
all these christmas celebrations
seem like silly games
you run to the barroom
and drink away your blues
there's something about this christmas cheer
that really bothers you

you're drunk and then the waitress
comes barging in
"i'm sorry sir you have to leave, it's 3am"
so you stumble out the door
and fumble for your keys
you puke while you're driving
and you see the police

christmas in jail, you're spending christmas in jail
and you can't trade in your gift cards
for your ten thousand dollar bail
the lights from the squad car are flashing red and green
and all in all it's not a holy scene

if joseph and mary
had been caught on christmas day
and got busted for vagrancy
where would they stay?
they'd end up in a jail
where mary would give birth
baby jesus the jailbird
three wise men out of work

christmas in jail
they're spending christmas in jail
and a thousand hallelujahs
won't pay their bail
christmas in jail, they're spending christmas in jail
and the holy light of heaven would light up their cell

Civil War

in every part of me
there'll always be
a raging civil war
my north fights my south
my teeth bite my mouth
though my soul has always been a pacifist

my heart versus my brain oh
i fight like mark twain and samuel clements must've fought before
there's no way to win
oh i've killed myself again
this lonely land of me in civil war

well the mason dixon line
oh i guess that'd be my spine
and my blood stream's the mighty mississipp
robert e. lee is my honesty
my morality is named abe
and my nightlife is named john wilkes booth

my heart versus my brain oh
i fight like mark twain and samuel clements must've fought before
there's no way to win
oh i've killed myself again
this lonely land of me in civil war

Coffee is my Lover

head got hazy
my legs got lazy
and the boss man said
"you're fired"
drank enough tea to drown a horse
and still i'm bleepin tired

so I found me a number on the bathroom wall
and I called it there and then
the lady on the phone said to perk me up
she'd introduce me to her friend

this stain's gonna blow my cover
coffee is my lover
stain's gonna blow my cover
coffee is my lover

so I lay in bed with a bag of beans
breathing in the fumes
grind it up between my knees
and nouveau my perfume

my little lady
started getting jealous
and asked me who i'd seen
she slapped my face and called me a liar
when I said
"espresso bean"

stain's gonna blow my cover
coffee is my lover
stain's gonna blow my cover
coffee is my lover

Color of the Love You Have

last night
sleeping
dreaming
of you
last night
sleeping
dreaming
of you
last night
sleeping
dreaming
of you
last night
sleeping
dreaming
of you
last night
sleeping
dreaming
of you
last night
sleeping
dreaming
of you
last night
sleeping
dreaming
of you
last night
sleeping
dreaming
of you
last night
sleeping
dreaming
of you
last night
sleeping
dreaming
of you

Condo Graveyard

condo graveyard
mixed use pit
stucco nose job
smells like shit
car honk hair dry
 horn blow loud
trampled by the texting crowd
condo graveyard
rent to owe
pigsty party
down below
first floor market
minimum rage
fifteen dollar sandwich stage

condo graveyard
die
condo graveyard
die

oil slick hair to blinding teeth
cannot hide the scum beneath
skin tight costume frames your head
hate your life but what a spread
sofa steak and sheep get shorn
for your uggs in early morn
man bun blight
shriveled fright
facetime your chihuahua
what a delight

condo graveyard
die
condo graveyard
die

Cosmic Coupon

eat your pride for lazy lunch
free range tesla brunch
working man with slippers slid
bluetooth babysitter
rancid kids
got 9 golden graces
got 8 wasted slaves
got 7 in the basement
got 6 that can't be saved
got 5 sins inside me
that multiply by 4
got 3 in the jury
who say 2 tries....
no more
got 1 person left
to help me with my plight
her name is ayn rand
and she is full of shite

cosmic coupon!

the world don't give no discounts
no layaway nor lease
crawl through a pile of shit
to find your inner peace
clip your karma discount code
wheelbarrow weight your load
watching waiting lick a toad
empty holy to explode

cosmic coupon!

working man who nothing makes
profits off others mistakes
cruising downhill won't hit the brakes
into a brick wall he skates
got 9 frozen feelings
got 8 feeling 'meh'
got 7 too indifferent
to even care
got 6 made numb by overtaste
got 5 made numb by greed
got 4 sucking human blood
got 3 that gone to seed
got 2 left for to show the
got 1 left indeed
ray kurzweil, pave the path
to everlasting greed

cosmic coupon!

the world don't give no discounts
no layaway nor lease
crawl through a pile of shit
to find your inner peace
clip your karma discount code
wheelbarrow weight your load
watching waiting lick a toad
empty holy to explode

Cranks Give Thanks

i see a plague of cars coughing
clogging up the streets
braindead soggy vapid bars
oil slick market meat
tv news man talk in tongues atwist
repeat the same old shit

i'm a rollerblading blind man
going straight downhill
swimming in a bed pan
smoking a zero dollar bill

limousines filled with dirt
sell it by the pound
driving luxury until it becomes the ground
taxidermist, freeze my head
into a permanent smile

oh tailor
sew my clothes to my body for awhile
can't see myself again
a broken world's infected brain

so let's put my head up on the shelf
until the world needs it again
"hey crank, you hate everything
why don't you find your joy?"
i'm thankful i live mostly in my head
cause the world's a broken toy

Daily Dance

screaming sirens call
on a million ringing phones
busy people all around
yet you feel all alone
you search for connection almost any way you can
the weaving web of city life creates this daily dance
and wittta say
1 2 3 4

footsteps pound the pulse for every passerby
no time to think
no no no no
no time to wonder why
metronomic sidewalk push has put you in a trance
shuffling your shoes you choose to walk this daily dance
and witta say
1234

false frenetic pace on tires, treads and wheels
and every time it goes around
it gets harder to feel
the numbing of the noise
just seems to be the circumstance
acclimate emotions all within this daily dance
and witta say
1234

patterns they persist
molds human to machine
fading channeled chaos blurs into a strobing dream
counting all this patterned grid
as fate and circumstance
each and every one of us upon this daily dance
1234

Dead Man

one day i died
got buried in the dirt
the worms ate my feet
the worms ate my shirt
the worms shed their skin
the skin fed a tree
the tree became the wood siding inside an suv

dead man, dead man
you're a dead man
dead mean, dead man
you're a dead man
(i'm already dead, which means i'm being born)

the suv got repossessed
and sold into scrap
the metal parts were bought by makers of rat traps
a rat trap caught its prey
and chipped its metal teeth
the rat got sold to a rendering plant
and labelled as ground beef
the ground beef shaped a patty
that fed a raving drunk
but he threw up in the gutter
and down the drain it sunk
and washed out to a stream
where fishing boats set sail
and fed a fish that ended up in the belly of a whale
the whale got harpooned
and into oil it turned
that fed a lamp
whose flame upward turned
and rose above the earth
made its way to a black hole
went to the other side
a parallel dimension
where i had never died.

dead man, dead man
you're a dead man
dead mean, dead man
you're a dead man
(i'm already dead, which means i'm being born)

Dear Broken Friend

holding onto nothing
waiting for your break
you've wasted every chance you've had
now it's too late

dear broken friend
trapped by the past
_____ yourself in broken glass

we will, we will _____ _____
we will, we will _____ _____
we will, we will _____ _____
we will, we will _____ _____
we will, we will _____ _____
we will, we will _____ _____
we will, we will _____ _____
we will, we will _____ _____
we will, we will _____ _____
we will, we will _____ _____
we will, we will _____ _____
we will, we will _____ _____
we will, we will _____ _____
we will, we will _____ _____
we will, we will _____ _____
we will, we will _____ _____
we will, we will _____ _____
we will, we will _____ _____
we will, we will _____ _____
we will, we will _____ _____

Dear Friend (Failing Domino)

that crowded road you've been traveling
crumbling underfoot
it's unraveling
oh, domino
you've tripped yourself
you fall back home
retreating
same town, same streets
you've always known
oh, dominos
your uniform is on
dear friend
if you go another round
dear friend
you'll collapse onto the ground
dear friend
so tell the people what you've found
dear friend
is it even worth repeating?
failures glow
all around you
everyone you meet
only reminds you
oh
your domino's uniform is on

dear friend
if you go another round
dear friend
you'll collapse onto the ground
dear friend
so tell the people what you've found
dear friend
is it even worth repeating?

(spoken word, ad lib, but along these lines)
Oh, where will you go, domino?
With that greasy uniform and nametag
staring at the ground
afraid to look up at the sky
is this what life has come to?
Is this your fate?
All your work, all your education
only to deliver pizzas to grinning frat boys?
The void is creeping in fast
in the form of a rotting pizza crust
shaped like a crooked smile
the universe is reflecting back your sadness
reflecting back your failure
in a puddle of rancid ranch dressing

you are the pizza, domino
you are delivering your soul to the grinning frat boy
each delivery, a life in miniature
you walk to the doorway
step by step
and with each step
one closer to your demise
you reach the door
knock knock knock
the smiling frat boy
is your own reflection
you stare into the pizza box
the crust opens its jaws
your feet glued in place
as you watch the rotting pizza crust
eat you

that road you took was empty
now all you have is envy

Death Smile

no more whiskey
no more beer
just a crowd of clowns
all dressed in fear
all that hidden life
projected from their eyes
the smiles that they project
make it seem they've something to protect
a gnawing disguise
shooting from their eyes

i got a death smile today
i think i'll sit and stare and just be on my way
if a smile is fake what's the good anyway

*(only while they stick the knife
and butter your brain too)*

crawling towards their grave
the world sees them as kings
but i know they got played
in a stock market landslide
left with just their masks
smile into the void my boys
the end is coming fast

i got a death smile today
i think i'll sit and stare and just be on my way
if a smile is fake what's the good anyway

Decaying Monday

creak and stretch, the world awakes
rhythmic traffic, find your place
from bright blue dreams we rub our eyes
it's every day until you die
yes, every day we run the track
we sprint so far and sprint right back
and all you'll see is in your face
a wrinkled map in slow decay
decay, decay
decaying monday

the sink is clogged, the laundry smells
your head it aches, your stomach swells
it's a shitty way to start your week
you're halfway dead and half asleep
walking to the bus stop quick
hungover head, it makes you sick
you stepped in dog shit, smear your shoes
but you cannot stop, no time to lose
your bus-ride schedule hours behind
so you take a walk inside your mind
decay, decay
decaying monday

like bartleby in cyberspace
you cannot smile, but only fake
your myspace page an evil check
but still you've looked ten times yet
you get home and your soul has died
so you cook it into a flaky pie
decay, decay, decay
decaying monday

smack your head and crack a beer
to numb the pain, forget you're here
oh every day, it seems the same
no matter places or the names
scenes replay your soul to steal
hyped up hamsters in a wheel
replace my head with a dollar bill
if the eyeballs glow, it's time to kill
decay, decay, decay
decaying monday

Diamond Eyepatch See

diamond eyepatch sea
the waves that are crashing
wash away the world
and everything that stands
diamond eyepatch sea
reflects what you were thinking
the seer becomes the seen

diamond eyepatch see
you squinted til you slipped away
never did before
but now it's nevermore
diamond eyepatch sea
the glitter of the evening

the lightbulb in the sky
the lightbulb in the sky
the lightbulb in the sky
the lightbulb in the sky

Diamond Studded Caskets

zombies all around us
wearing fancy clothes
feed their brains into a clock
that tells them where to go

one by one we step into traffic
beauty of the pain and the tragic
run and run with tireless abandon
make the world of what we imagine
hidden forces working against us
out of line they come and arrest us
one by one we step into traffic
beauty of the pain and the tragic

stealing air from bottles
sucking water dry
diamond studded caskets
they wait for you to die
they wait for you to die

diamond studded caskets
roll around on wheels
tombstone business deals
diamond studded caskets
by the graveyard mall
it's a cold world out there
and that is all

diamond studded caskets
roll around on wheels
tombstone business deals
diamond studded caskets
by the graveyard mall
it's a cold world out there
and that is all

Doe See Doe

come on boys, don't be shy
grab that guy around your thigh
this is called the doe see doe
come on now
touch your toes
come on guys, don't be mean
come on girls, grab your spleen
come on girls, open that door
come on boys, don't be no bore

spin your partner round and round
find the silence in the sound

come on girls, don't be shy
grab that gal around your thigh
this is called the doe see doe
come on now
touch your toes
come on girls, don't be mean
come on boys, grab your spleen
come on boys, open that door
come on girls, don't be no bore

spin your partner round and round
find the silence in the sound

Does Not Compute_Head Wound Error

S T U P I D I D I D I E
stupider, stupidest
stupidiciousness is bliss
be like child
like jah said
we'll figure it out when we grow dread

does not compute
head wound error
does not compute
i scratch head
blood comes pouring down

S T U P I D I D I D I E
stupider, stupidest
stupidiciousness is bliss
be like child
like jah said
we'll figure it out when we cut dread

does not compute
head wound error
does not compute
i scratch head
blood comes pouring down

Dollar Bill Flashlight

shaving all the mountains
smoking all the trees
dollar bill flashlights
revealing memories
the shape of your soul
is the mark of a pen
the history books remind us
and it's happened again

your wage is not your worth
your fate is not your birth
your weight is not your pull
your truth is not your bull

the world don't owe you nothing
no use to use that lens
and when you fall to failure
you'll see who was your friends
humans ain't the job they do
nor are the house they're born
all these things get shaved away
just as a sheep gets shorn

conincidence and unearned luck
and pleasures of your station
are about as relevant
as a stay-at-home vacation

you only answer to yourself
and to yourself should ask
what have i done with my time
did i achieve the tasks
i meant to do so long ago
before life clouded mind
before my dollar bill flashlight
made me go blind

illuminating nothing
except to what you lack
but every dollar has a price
you'll never get back
money is a contraption
which your soul just can't handle
so throw your dollar bill flashlight away
and light a loving candle.

Don't Hate Your Neighbor Just Because He Drives a Porsche

your toes and feet are just as smart
as your mind and
you will find
all you know to be true
is in every inch of you
nothing is revealed
nothing is concealed
it's all right there
inside your hair
inside your brain *(feet)*
inside your toes *(smart)*
every inch of you is filled with truth
is filled with love
don't hate your neighbor just because he drives a porsche
invite him over to dinner and you'll see
he's a nice guy
give it a try
don't hate your hatred
don't fear your fear
just spread something good
make the world better than your porsche driving neighbor

Don't Imbibe the T.V.

sucked out to sea
i hit the shore
bikini cams with mtv endorsements
cocaine turned
the sand dunes into gold
castles in the sky
were made of mold
the corporate headquarters

don't imbibe the tv
you'll glisten in the sun
no imbibe the tv
it'll make you dumb

Don't Sleep til You're Dead / Heed my Words

in younger days i saw myself
i wanted to change
to lead a life that others would call strange
but then i grew a year or two
and i felt myself torn
i'd run out of ways to not conform
everyone just seemed the same
and so i made a choice
to listen to none other than my voice
i'd figured that i'd learned to live
and i didn't need no-one else
so now i sit and i just talk to myself
"heed my words," i often say
"don't get stoned, don't get laid
rid your actions of the i
see the truth in every lie"
"heed my words," i hear it said
write the books you think you've read
and don't sleep til you're dead"

so like mahatma gandhi
i tried to be a force
i tried to have my way without no force
but i got pushed and i got shoved
and i got kicked and i got mugged
so i went and bought myself some boxing gloves
now i avoid fights all together
by wearing these here gloves
i'm peaceful now without religion or drugs
and people think that i'm quite odd
when they see me on the sidewalk
they hear my voice and listen to me talk
"heed my words," they hear me say
"don't get stoned, don't get laid
rid your actions of the i
see the truth in every lie"
"heed my words," they hear it said
write the books you think you've read
and don't sleep til you're dead"

Dragging Down the Street

dragging down the street
heart filled with empty
fill it up with hurt
fill it up with whiskey
dragging down the street
i know someone would miss me
if i disappeared forever
swallowed by the smog
dragged by my feet
where the night will take me
into the arms of a whore
let's make a screaming baby
dragging down the street
led by my shadow
he cackles at my sorrow
and pokes into my guts

(and still the night it calls me)

cobblestones sound brightly
the clicking of the shoes
pale sunken faces
the daytime has refused
dragging down the street
handfuls of empty
curtain bedroom calls
but my shadow won't let me
my shadow's name is lobo
his velvet suit is dapper
his suit, pressed and trimmed
he moves just like a flapper
dragging down the street
i do my best to hide
but every time i see a light
he creeps in from the side

Dreams of Sandy

tonight I dream of you
tonight
tonight I dream of you
tonight
your face it comes in flashes
in soft drops of my lashes
your skin so pale
with arms so frail
you're pure
like snow
like ashes
from the sands of creation
bursting through the foam
i'm going home

Dusty Diamonds

bouncing back and forth
ever since we first met
we'd kick and fight and call each other names
our hearts jump so quickly between love and hate
sometimes it seems they're the same
the clay of which we're made
is a teeming tangled mound
with past lives' corpses on the ground
and sometimes when we're lonely
we bring them back to life
such beautiful decay we've found

dusty diamonds
sunk ship
islands
always right back where we were before

strolling hesitation
we amble down the street
second looks at everyone we meet
can they look and see what's happened?
can they see what we've become?
when hearts go cold, everything gets numb

dusty diamonds
sunk ship
islands
always right back where we were before
dusty diamonds
sunset's bathtime
always right back where we were before
sung this song so many times before

Easy Machines / Telephones

you and i could never talk
so what's to say now that all has stopped?
the best way to let things die
let our telephones say our goodbyes
no final touch
no last caress
no other people there to impress
and no last look in the eyes
our telephones will say our goodbyes

oh machines
easy machines
manufacture money
manufacture dreams
but these grinding gears lined two by two
can't recreate the love of me and you

so from these flames we both shall rise
wipe the ash out of our eyes
and move along with the rest of our lives
our telephones have said their goodbyes

oh machines
easy machines
manufacture money
manufacture dreams
but these grinding gears lined two by two
can't recreate the love of me and you

Eat the Lawn for Free

artesanal dirt pay by the scoop
growling truck in boiling soup
live your life and eat your flute
salad chipmunks munch and mutter
they gave up wheat and they gave up butter
they eat the lawn for free
eat the lawn for free
salad chipmunks nibble small
and crawl a door out of the wall
and eat the lawn for free
eat the lawn for free

fish head hammer
sulking pizza
a heavy brunch might just defeat ya
devoid your plate of heavy clutter
salad chipmunks munch and mutter
they gave up wheat and they gave up butter
they eat the lawn for free
eat the lawn for free
salad chipmunks nibble small
and crawl a door out of the wall
and eat the lawn for free
eat the lawn for free

a diet on the plate
is a diet in the hand
eat your greens
&
be a man

a diet on the plate
is a diet in the hand
eat your greens
&
be a man

a diet on the plate
is a diet in the hand
eat your greens
&
be a man

a diet on the plate
is a diet in the hand
eat your greens
&
be a man

Echoes of Each Glass

the moon's consumed the sun
our golden moment's done
and in its feathered wake
escape to slake our thirst
we see that our glassy eyes all blank
but we must refill the tank
for now it seems we've both downed our drink
and the echoes of each glass
call to mind the ages past
as our time together swirls down the sink

with each successive pour
the past is conjured more
nostalgia weaves a net
that catches old regrets
yes, happy men must drink
when they've had too much to think
we see that the fading of our youth
trades a denture for a tooth
and once again we've both downed our wine
and the echoes of each glass
call to mind our glories past
as our former glowing deeds begin to shine

it's a long graceful dive into an empty pool
you forget that you're alive
you blather like a fool
oh everyone must taste this intoxicating haze
but the present that you waste
gives away the good old days
we witness the fading of tonight
and the bar's turned off the lights
and now we're both drunk on dead dreams
and the echoes of each glass
call to mind the evenings past
when we both lived an identical scene

Emerald Arizona

power chords and power lines
stretch across the sky
ac/dc electric chair
i think my brains are fried
megalife and desert dust at the headbanger's prom
my date went home with the band
i went home with my mom
ten years old in tucson
ten year old in tears
this used to be an ocean when nobody was here
now the sea is broken
golf course always damp
forgotten hair
breathe the air
retiree summer camp

emerald arizona
tender age of 10
it used to be dry and vacant
i liked it better then

from phoenix out to tempeh
the climate's getting bad
heading north for the summer
staying with my dad
he's got a new wife now
her name is babe
i visit them once a month
they work me like a slave

emerald arizona
tender age of 10
it used to be dry and vacant
i liked it better then

Emotional Swings

the orange glow of my window
lights up my pain (pane)
the empty skies soak up my cries
and scream them back again
did i love that girl
or did i love to love her?
i just can't tell
i guess my life is over so i'd best be getting to hell

this girl of my past always moved too fast
running from fears
i gave her shelter
she gave me warmth
we mopped each other's tears
but us two shared too much too soon
and soon our words ran dry
left a lump in my throat
and wanderlust in mine eye

emotional swings are humorous things
when your girlfriend is not your friend
i felt kind of bad about leaving her stranded
time and time again
i needed some air so i got some space
and what do you think i see?
another soul scared and the blame falls square on me

Empty University

gridded block by block
a frame above the void is hung
and you can't help but be but shocked
when you shake hands with an empty shell

and they'll tattoo on your back
a golden gilded degree
when you learn what you lack
at empty university

vacant state of mind
the highest form to which we all aspire
not mean nor kind
just staring at each other's invisible jeans
and stick it in with pins
just to make sure that you don't deflate
non-existence in this void in which we built a happy home

and they'll tattoo on your back
a golden gilded degree
when you learn what you lack
at empty university

(empty university cheerleader chant!)
square chin alpha-jaw-fossil find
empty your wallet and empty your mind
square chin alpha-jaw-fossil find
empty your wallet and empty your mind
square chin alpha-jaw-fossil find
empty your wallet and empty your mind
square chin alpha-jaw-fossil find
empty your wallet and empty your mind
square chin alpha-jaw-fossil find
empty your wallet and empty your mind

and they'll tattoo on your back
a golden gilded degree
when you learn what you lack
at empty university

End's End

well i tried
to pull my weight
empty thoughts
that can't be saved
i can't open up the gate
there's more to me to life
than just my pay
faith's time
is faked no more
there's nothing here
at all worth looking for
it's hard to watch
the world just pass you by

this is the end
the end of the end
this is the end
the end of the end
this is the end
the end of the end
this is the end
the end of the end
this is the end
the end of the end
this is the end
the end of the end
this is the end
the end of the end
this is the end
the end of the end
this is the end
the end of the end
this is the end
the end of the end
this is the end
the end of the end
this is the end
the end of the end
this is the end
the end of the end
this is the end
the end of the end
this is the end
the end of the end
this is the end
the end of the end

Everlasting Pleasure Cruise

(sailor chant)
stroke stroke stroke
stroke stroke stroke
stroke stroke stroke

type 2 diabetes home
say hello to the king on his lazy boy throne
remote controlled wife and fido's plastic bone
coca cola baby bottle
breakfast lump
eating diet lard balls
hit the middle aged hump
it's time you took a snooze on an everlasting pleasure cruise

(sailor chant)
stroke stroke stroke
stroke stroke stroke
stroke stroke stroke

spandex shorts stretched to the brim
now i'm sweating to the oldies
got to stay trim
sit and be fit
snort dexatrim
happy happy happy happy
barbells used as bookends for
those health club books that you ignore
beer belly earthquake when you snore
why not take a snooze
on an everlasting pleasure cruise?

(sailor chant)
stroke stroke stroke
stroke stroke stroke
stroke stroke stroke

florida keys go and get a tan
spring break of the soul with stagnant stan
wilford brimley's aura glows like phosphorescent oat bran
the tide rolls in, the tide rolls out
in flux
oh pilgrim have no doubt
you're never going to lose
you're on an everlasting pleasure cruise

Everything Explodes

optimism drowning down until it turns to drought
and the wobbly world is crumbling
cuz it wants to do without
everything's expanding
everything explodes
wishing wanting aint enough to turn the tide
but when everything feels hopeless you just hold it all inside
everything's expanding, everything explodes
everything demanding discarding what you know

sorting piles of washed out styles
of doing what you're told
thinking that the thing you want's
the thing that you were sold

but never to have fallen
is just never to have to have tried
and the only way to be reborn again
is to have died

everything's expanding,
everything explodes
everything demanding discarding what you know

Everything Is Fine

if you sit still long enough
the world turns halfway around
and you see things from the other side
backwards
upside down
and now you're gone
you're following the feeling
like the snake that shat out its tail
and gave birth to another snake
in the shape of letters that spell
"oh well"

the world's still turning
we've drained another jug of wine
clocks are burning
everything is fine

so if you've walked in a circle
and you're stuck in that same old mess
do what feels real
don't try to impress
and it will pass

the world's still turning
we've drained another jug of wine
(the ocean doesn't care)
clocks are burning
everything is fine

Existential Meltdown

half empty glasses piled upon the floor
and all your former friends
have walked out the door
what are you doing?
why and what for?
i don't know anymore.

i used to be so sure
and my feet pressed ahead
now i can't remember
half the things i said
i guess this will continue
until i'm dead
i don't know anymore

existential fog descends

i'm standing with my feet glued down
just another lifetime going around
i'm waiting for the telling sign
what occurs next time i die?

i'm standing at the bottom of a still
whiskey drowning me slowly
what a lovely kill

Expiration Date

dust is bit, the date is shot
the music's ripe and starts to rot
the radio's fires a blaring blot
but the sounds don't impress me

there's creatine kids with ritalin babies
14 year old naked ladies
training wheels, stiletto heels
writing jingles
cutting singles
eating pringles

expiration date
you're past your prime
expiration date
you're past your time

i bought my wife at wal-mart
i bought my life at sears
i bought myself forgetful in a bucketful of beer
a lost and found borrowed sound
undercover underground
in incognito, live libido,
a church of sound in an old tuxedo

you're past your prime
you've gone to seed
your hands held out
as if in need
but needs not wanted
lined in bold
are filling up your fridge with mold

expiration date
you're past your prime
expiration date
you're past your time

Failing Domino

falling dominoes
forged of frail bones
eyes filled with stones
deliver me unto my worst fears
i'm burning inside
flood the fire with cheap beer
my kidney a canteen
spilling gasoline
my head is on fire
my feet have fallen off
took themselves a walk
down know how they'll knock
the air is choked with cars
they won't get very far
driving circles down a
cul-de-sac figure 8
ouraboros pizza plate
i stand outside this mess
unbathed and undressed
am i cursed or am i blessed?
let's check the nametag on my chest
it says "bill"

Feeling Bad Does Not Feel Good

i scraped away a scab
to watch my body bleed
and somehow it filled an inner need
if i get too happy i shrivel up
and wither like a prune
so i click the light
and my mind's a blackened room

i took a bath in tar
it burned away my skin
now i'm just a lonely skeleton
and you could look into my eyes
but they're already gone
and my bones clatter like a rattling cage

feeling bad does not feel good
and when the darkness comes
my spinal cord becomes a noose
and brain keeps going numb
feeling bad does not feel good
but i still feel compelled
to wade into the burning flames of hell

my lips are painted black
my heart is painted blue
and it beats with the dragging of my shoes
i'd probably be better off giving constant thanks
but nothing bores me more than a smiling face

feeling bad does not feel good
and when the darkness comes
my spinal cord becomes a noose
and brain keeps going numb
feeling bad does not feel good
but i still feel compelled
to wade into the burning flames of hell

Fishtown

shadows frame the faces of the scene
between cracking pavements come shoots of green
life gets sprung from all that
which is dying
delawares could whisper to the land
standing there beneath their ancient trees
but the breeze with which they spoke
got caught by sailboats

william penn he saw the future clear –
pave the woods in perfect squares
while the fishies swim in beer
floating arctic splashing down sepviva.
fishtown, fishtown,
some washed ashore, others are in the ground

fishtown, fishtown
no matter how you change
you can still keep your name

dragging metal pieces down the street
tremors of the night are gathering steam
but beneath the ground
the dirt still looks the same

fishtown, fishtown
sounds of the street are gently humming
fishtown, fishtown
no matter how you change
you can still keep your name

the shad's gone the saw of the swede
tailpipes bleed
their raucous noise
but listen close
the land still has its voice

Flower Children's Children's Children

peppermint pansy
a portrait paint
and oscar wilde was the patron saint
flower children's children's children

a benefit plan for a berkeley band
text me a toot
line is in the sand
flower children's children's children

foggy and famous
it sure ain't free
fluttering like tattered tapestries
flower children's children's children

the way of the wise was to move out west
but now maybe back to the great midwest
flower children's children's children

the grateful dead are now just dead
so bury the load of the past instead
flower children's children's children

the big one comes
the split earth will spin
and swallows the scene
and we start again
flower children's children's children

Folkswinger

how are you doing today?
(i do the boot scootin boogie)
that's great.

chew chaw
cole slaw
ha ha ha yee haw
outlaws
burnt bras
cheese whiz
show biz
ha ha ha yee haw

i'm a folkswinger
can't you see?
ain't nothing you gonna say is gonna bother me
i'm a folkswinger
don't you know?
you can't escape this song no matter where you go

yard sales
rat tails
ha ha ha yee haw
tight jeans
bruised spleens
ha ha ha yee haw
square dance
hot pants
ha ha ha yee haw

i'm a folkswinger
can't you see?
ain't nothing you gonna say is gonna bother me
i'm a folkswinger
don't you know?
you can't escape this song no matter where you go

Game Over

we've burnt all our black
ashes fill our cups
raise the empty glass
glassy fields in flame
held still in timeless pose
scorched into our brains
let it go

colored flags fly no more
frantic eyes
eye the door
debutantes rip their gowns
talk the good old days
with photographs in flames
held still in timeless pose
though they can't recall the names

*and all the while you know
you must just let it go*

emptiness abides
silence speaks
collapsing floors
closing doors
shifting shores

flapping tongue
mouthing words
silence reigns
have you heard?
walls rise in between
but at least we got to share
a moment to dream
let it go

Garden of Eden

well once upon a time
mankind was all just a bunch of apes
we all had furs and we all ate steaks
and the whole world was paradise
and we didn't even know it
but then we got self-aware and boy did we blow it

you see, we were all living inside of the garden of eden
until we started eating of the tree of knowledge
and reading and going to college
and we created lace and underwear
to replace the leaves and sticks
strategically placed to fix our newfound nudity

well the garden of eden has got good eating
it's got granny smiths and reds.
but it's got no place to hide your face and no bank to hide your debts
could it be that here and now is the only heaven we've got?
or could it be that the knowledge tree
is buried beneath a parking lot?

so we created fires and walls and concert halls
to hear divine harmony
these halls, called churches
were part of mankind's search for the earth as it once stood
the earth gawd created and called good

but this paradise could not be found,
not in the sky nor underground
man searched the earth far and wide
but he still had yet to search inside
so pilgrims went west when things went to pot
but damn it all if they forgot –
if you keep heading around the globe
you end up in the same spot

so what now?
well, we're here
and that's that.
and as for me, i'd like to be an ape again
but i'm allergic to steak
and my beard's too thin

well the garden of eden has got good eating
it's got granny smiths and reds.
but it's got no place to hide your face and no bank to hide your debts
could it be that here and now is the only heaven we've got?
or could it be that the knowledge tree
is buried beneath a parking lot?

Ghost Of Myself

i'm the ghost of myself
persisting just because
at family reunions they remember who i was
a morsel of a memory to keep upon the shelf
and praise the way i used to be when i was myself

why can't i see?
cuz my eyes don't belong to me
floating below the floor
i'm the ghost of myself and all i was before

each of you are ghostly too
at least to some extent
you wander through your life
and can't remember where you went
and all i can take with me is everything i've felt
the joy and the sadness
the radness and the guilt

why can't i see?
cuz my eyes don't belong to me
floating below the floor
i'm the ghost of myself and all i was before

Go To Mexico

frozen flashing trees
dead exploding leaves are on the ground
on the ground
all around

go mexico
go mexico

blistered skin
in the sun again
feel so new
here next to you
wasted and exposed
wearing dirty clothes
your days are gone

go mexico
go mexico

frozen battered trees
dead exploding leaves are on the ground
on the ground
all around, all around

God The Smoker

the cosmos gets cancer with every sunset
the sun's the smolder of god's cigarette
and when she coughs and wheezes everyone gets wet
and every tornado is the wheezing of her breath
her lungs have turned black
and i don't think she's coming back

a long time ago when everything was dark
the universe was boring so she sprayed a spark
she lit up her smoke and chuckled at her joke
the punchline you see is humanity
and i'd cut her some slack
but i don't think she's coming back

so if god the smoker shows her wizened face
in a desiccated raisin
or a cracked statue of grace
please ask her kindly
where the hell's she been?
the world she created's
become a painful scene
as the globe begins to crack
i sure hope she's coming back

Gold Dissolves to Gray

when we were young and bold and strong
we always had a good time
dancing all night long
we'd dance the night away

but now the years have come and gone
we're watching all the good times
setting with the sun
watch them fade away

now sunlight hides its golden hair
there's no more good times
and we don't even care.

golden melts to gray
golden melts away
gold melts to gray
gold melts to gray

lines that wrinkle up your face
remind you of the good times
that left you in their place
what more is there to say?

time snuck in from the side
buried all the good times
you haven't even died
but you're laying in your grave

gold dissolves away
gold dissolves to gray
gold dissolves to gray

Gone

gone gone gone gone gone
so glad to be gone
so glad to be gone

the stain of your memory will fade
even though your tongue's a blade
and it cut my heart in half

so glad to be gone

microwave my heart until it thaws
pull me tongue out from your jaws
it's time i talk my mind

the wasted carcass clock points mortem time
but darling i can't hear the chime
i'm too busy moving on

gone gone gone gone gone
so glad to be gone
so glad to be gone

the emptiness of all i left behind
got deflated in my mind
hot air head came crashing down

you will never hear these shoes again
i dumped them in the goodwill bin
and my feet will find a way

gone gone gone gone gone
so glad to be gone
so glad to be gone

Goodbye Dear Friend of Mine

goodbye dear friend of mine
we're free as our thoughts allow
but still it seems to me somehow
we'll never know each other again

you're standing next to me
but you're not really here
your expectations blind you
your lungs are filled with fear

oh we both already know
that nothing gold can stay
but still it seems a sad thing
when a friend slips away

goodbye dear friend of mine
we're free as our thoughts allow
but still it seems to me somehow
we'll never know each other again

the ghost of our past
will soon set you free
and we may meet again
but you won't recognize me

and when you gather with your new crowd
and dream of younger days
will you tell them about me?
your old friend who slipped away

goodbye dear friend of mine
we're free as our thoughts allow
but still it seems to me somehow
we'll never know each other again

Goodbye Father

my father came to me
and tried to look through me
on the day that i was leaving
he tried acting proud
but he spoke too loud
and i could see
in his eyes he was grieving
he should my hand firm
but i had to squirm
and i saw on his cheeks he'd been crying
he said,
"my son i shouldn't be the one
to tell you your father is dying"

i stood there and stared
my heart was broken
but not as broken as him
his hands trembled
his eyes on the floor
i poured him a glass of gin
his fingers pale, he lifted
inhaled the glass of gin i'd just poured
he said, "my son, the time has come
to be the man you've ignored.

our faces aging, our roles changing
i'm empty, you're full of life
you maintain eyes that don't waver
mine can't stop crying
now's the time, as it's always been
tomorrow i live only in you
so drink of my soul as i speak it and spill
and pour it unto you

beware of all salesmen
who smile so determined
to reach inside of your head
the grease from their minds
drips down and it blinds
their conscience
and keeps them well fed
that which they promise
is always beyond us
for our wants are things we can't own
and if you manage to
purchase yourself from the circus
you'll find yourself all alone"

then my mother
stepped from the shadows

a smirk outlined her lips
she took in us two and said
"oh it's true
your father has many fine tips
of bitterness biting
and pain so inviting
and rubbish of his misspent youth
he thinks that the madness
which comes from such sadness
has shown him the way to truth"

then my mother turned to my father
as his moments dwindled to dust
she told him to die
to sink to the sky
to leave her if he must
but save her a place in infinite space
where they may embrace yet again
at this my father split his sadness
back into a grin

he looked at me
and his lungs they trembled
he said, "my son, the end has come
but this ain't really the end.
now you'll take the torch and sit on our porch
and smile as life passes by
and you'll give this speech and struggle to teach
the good in the word goodbye"

Goodbye Vibrations

goodbye
my darling
goodbye
i'm headed west tomorrow
to follow the glowing sky
your tender arms tried so hard to squeeze
my restless soul
but it won't budge by your pleas

i know you say a memory can't hold you
but in the end we're all memories anyway
so hold me today
and let tomorrow be the time to cry
goodbye, my love
goodbye

so long, my darling
so long
i'll carry your vibration
as i travel on
when we were together
we shone like the sun
but you always i had to leave
and that this day would come

i can't say if my love will linger
a fire left alone will die away
but i won't forget the warmth of this flame of you and i
goodbye, my love
goodbye

Graveyard Dog / Graveyard Dawn

lungs on fire and eyes so calm
his owner's dead and won't come home
graveyard dog sits
in prone to lines of scratch that milk his bones
skies of ash, a treeless view
parking lots and concrete shoes
empty grounded brown and dry
how can you tell when your love has died?
there's dirty weeds to withered leaves
that flutter down in stacks and sheathes
loud green lightning gives a sign
his friend has been reborn alive

graveyard dog
just let go, just let go
graveyard dog
just let go, just let go
graveyard dog
just let go, just let go
graveyard dog
just let go, just let go

parched cracked wings of stone
stand mile high cliffs and sheets of bone
where untold darkness folds within
oh... life's a game that no one wins
gray matter floating limp
like clouds dispersed in oatmeal drips
they give a shine, a dull gray light
to the dog who's given up his life

graveyard dog
just let go, just let go
graveyard dog
just let go, just let go
graveyard dog
just let go, just let go
graveyard dog
just let go, just let go

doggy bones and alpo treats you
tunneled light would like to meet you
step into the other side
you'll be reborn, you won't have died
purple aether flashing wasted
days of thunder, cruising zombies
spitting back what they've been told
power shopping for their souls

Green Truck (Cycle of Life)

a little stream
becomes a river
the river drains into the ocean
the oceans evaporate to the sky
the sky rains down
and makes a stream

circle of life
so lovely to be
a dead man like me

in this same way
you and i are trapped
neverending changes
drawing mirror maps
and if we're lucky we'll be born again
seven times a day
but each time that you die
you won't come back the same

cycle of life
hard to believe that it's true
i'm as close to you
as a pile of dirt

Hair Forest

hekka lekka high
mekka hi high
hekka hookah no smoke
calling to the beard in the sky
human go bye bye
hair forest ya ya

dreading in the hair go knot
not haircut
don't stop
spitting in the face
make ball drop
forest go chop chop
hair forest ya ya

peppy pep boys gonna drink oil
microwave tin foil
sanka sanka coffee no work well
caffeine dry spell
head in the laundry
clean dirty mind
i gonna go blind
hair forest ya ya

feather floating down
wear flip flop
marching men eat slop
hakka lakka break bread
break wheat
gluten on the chin chin
hair forest ya ya

Hairy Sally

your skin turns to ashes
every time we touch
your brittle bones rattle out a rhythm
but your weakness is your crutch
you don't want to get friendly
aloof you shall remain
but your devastating hairstyle
puts me in such pain

hairy sally
why do you fake it all the time?

when life comes as a burden
and darkness takes its grip
you will find me dressed as a surgeon
razor in my hand to cut your hairy lips

hairy sally
why do you fake it all the time?

Half a Man, Half a Man

i'm spitting out a folk song
but i'm not feeling well
and if you could see just where i be
you'd rather sunbathe in hell.
cuz it's cold as stone to feel alone
surrounded by a crowd.
their hungry ears rip up my songs
and it makes me scream out loud.

i'm half a man, i'm half a man
i've sung myself in two
i smoke a spliff
play a riff
and try to tie my shoes
i'm half and half
a short giraffe
a dentist with no teeth
i write songs of love
and they only bring me grief

nobody knows
nobody sees
i sing a happy song and the people are all pleased
but to know what happiness is
you first gotta know the sad
and to find inner peace
you first gotta go mad.

i'm half a man, i'm half a man
i've sung myself in two
i smoke a spliff
play a riff
and try to tie my shoes
i'm half and half
a short giraffe
a dentist with no teeth
i write songs of love
and they only bring me grief

Halfpenny Prince

wallet in ticker tape tatters
parade a clog traffic to choke
trader joes samples stack up to a lunch
you're a prince who just happens to be broke

royalty sermon to any who hears
your words swallowed by smoke
no place in the world that you can't disappear
you're a prince who just happens to be broke

recycle your crown
to its hole on your head
indignantly laugh at this joke
you cannot escape
though it all seems a fake
you're a prince who just happens to be broke

Halfway to Nowhere

lend a fading a ear
into my emptiness a second
i'll tell you what it's all about
you'll tell me what it's all about?
right.
nothing that you're looking for
will ever be an ending
it's a handful of air
as you collapse into your chair

a circle ever cycling
that spirals ever downwards
a grave with your name
tombstone impressive fame
so if you're going nowhere
let's enjoy being here
throw off your shoes
and pop a non-alcoholic beer

we're halfway to nowhere
halfway to nowhere

humanity wants answers
what's the purpose
what's the deal
but there's nothing i can say
to make it go away
the emptiness you're shunning
is half of everything
so stop running
the world will appear
if you just sit right here

we're halfway to nowhere
halfway to nowhere

Happiness is Forgetting

i don't care what you say
i'm gonna be my own cliche
and fall into the here and now
and learn to smile
but i don't know how

forget being happy
cuz happiness is forgetting
and you'll never end up regretting
all those things that you can't remember anyway

amnesia amplified
forward to the future side
backwards bay in bloom
smells of sweet perfume

embattled bay bridges burned
towards the tide you've turned
disregard your self-help scenes
backstroke to shore against the stream

forget being happy
cuz happiness is forgetting
and you never end up regretting
all those things that you can't remember anyway

forgo everything you know
let go of everything you've heard
and remember how to laugh
cause everything is absurd

Hard so Hard

running with the crowd
taking things too hard
you want to move away sometimes
make another start
cut off all your hair
cut off all your ties
see the world again through clear open eyes

but it's hard so hard
to jump out of the noose
when you're kicking up the past with antique shoes
yes it's hard so hard
to go it all alone
to say goodbye and
unplug the phone

the diamonds of your youth
you thought would grow on trees
cannot be found but underground
and crawling on your knees
you slide into the darkness
you cannot turn around
and no-one will hear you scream and cheer
at the beauty that you've found

it's hard so hard
to jump out of the noose
when you're kicking up the past with antique shoes
yes it's hard so hard
to go it all alone
to say goodbye and
unplug the phone

but why dig these diamonds that cannot be repeated?
you see them shining in the ground
in the end you must leave it
you're popping pills like tic tacs
rolling backwards eyes
numb the pain if you want
but numbness makes a poor disguise

it's hard so hard
to jump out of the noose
when you're kicking up the past with antique shoes
yes it's hard so hard
to go it all alone
to say goodbye and
unplug the phone

Heart Sound

when my hollow's eaten through
and my mumbles cannot choose
i skew across the narrow way
and disregard what can't contain
into my limbs these words resound
my heart becomes the sound

tiptoe round my mouth
til something new to say
dance upon the breath
as my body slips away
into my limbs these words resound
my heart becomes the sound

blurry humming hymn
projecting out my eyes
held melodies
sonic vision rise
into my limbs these words resound
my heart becomes the sound

resounding through ur skin
body song begins
a slow easy catch
all good things must end
into my limbs these words resound
my heart becomes the sound

Hearts Got a Hole

asteroids collide
on the meadow stumbled through
while world size styrofoam
lines your life in glue
and it hurts to say it's done
so you linger at the show
until the bands forgets its song

a plastic party melts until
there's nothing to unglue
congeals into an absence
my heart's got a hole the shape of you

early morning's crows collide
against the rustling leaves
as your eyes paint the past
while your children grow and leave
like the words of an old song
that you'd written way
before you'd learned to do it wrong

a plastic party melts until
there's nothing to unglue
congeals into an absence
my heart's got a hole the shape of you

delete your old excuses
they've been shrinking on repeat
they've monogrammed your trophy
for giving up defeat
and the words escape your grasp
so you let go of the phone
and you fill your car with gas

a plastic party melts until
there's nothing to unglue
congeals into an absence
my heart's got a hole the shape of you

Heaviness of Flame

oh the beauty of the flame
that your heart cannot hold
you know it would destroy you
you must tell it no
and content yourself, you must
to just watch it die
and dwindle into ashes
into dust
into sky

the heaviness of flame
has no weight
burns away your will
your spine just breaks
and all the while you know
you must just let it go

never felt before but familiar nonetheless
there's so much i want to tell you
but so little to express
and dancing to the beat of a ticking of a bomb
that destroys all those around it
no matter how strong

the heaviness of flame
has no weight
burns away your will
your spine just breaks
and all the while you know
you must just let it go

someday in another life
i'll see you on the street
and suddenly comes rushing back
the echoes of this heat
i'll smile at you gently and let you pass me by
remembering our love
and how we had to let it die

the heaviness of flame
has no weight
burns away your will
your spine just breaks
and all the while you know
you'll never let it go

Heavy Light

darkness burns your eyes
your shadows hang
a dim disguise

he-vy-light-he-vy-light-he-vy-light-he-vy-light-he-vy-light
he-vy-light-he-vy-light-he-vy-light-he-vy-light-he-vy-light
he-vy-light-he-vy-light-he-vy-light-he-vy-light-he-vy-light
he-vy-light-he-vy-light-he-vy-light-he-vy-light-he-vy-light

will it ever stop?
I don't know
my heart moves faster than my brain can go

he-vy-light-he-vy-light-he-vy-light-he-vy-light-he-vy-light
he-vy-light-he-vy-light-he-vy-light-he-vy-light-he-vy-light
he-vy-light-he-vy-light-he-vy-light-he-vy-light-he-vy-light
he-vy-light-he-vy-light-he-vy-light-he-vy-light-he-vy-light

darkened days
moonlit phase
a grace unseen by shade of night
a heavy light

this static in between us can't stay
it's too heavy now to hold and i'm tired anyway
heavy light
thoughts in cuts
paper blade
our dreams did weave a shade

he-vy-light-he-vy-light-he-vy-light-he-vy-light-he-vy-light
he-vy-light-he-vy-light-he-vy-light-he-vy-light-he-vy-light
he-vy-light-he-vy-light-he-vy-light-he-vy-light-he-vy-light
he-vy-light-he-vy-light-he-vy-light-he-vy-light-he-vy-light

darkened days
moonlit phase
a grace unseen by eyes alone

the sun and moon are still
they may never be entwined
but I know someday we will
darkened days
moonlit phase
a grace unseen by shade of night
a heavy light

Help Me Lord

tell me lord, tell me lord
why won't you smile on me?
tell me lord, tell me lord
why won't you smile on me?
the road tonight is cold and dark
ten men are after me

the man he come, the man he come
to hang me from a tree
the man he come, the man he come
to hang me from a tree
found sally ketchum floating in the river
all fingers point at me

help me lord, help me lord
help me as i run
help me lord, help me lord
help me as i run
ten men trying to hang me
for something i never done

Here Comes the Clock

tick tock
tick tock
tick tock
tick tock
tick tock
tick tock
tick tock
here comes the clock
tick tock
tick tock
tick tock
tick tock
here comes the clock
tick tock
tick tock
tick tock
tick tock
faster than me
faster than you
it has no legs
but it will outrun you
(what can you do?)
tick tock
tick tock
tick tock
tick tock
tick tock
tick tock
tick tock
tick tock
tick tock
tick tock
tick tock
here comes the clock
tick tock
tick tock
tick tock
tick tock
here comes the clock
tick tock
tick tock
tick tock
tick tock
faster than me
faster than you
it has no legs
but it will outrun you
(what can you do?)
tick tock
tick tock

Hey Old Buddy Old Friend

hey old buddy old friend
would you be there in my time of need?

hey old buddy old pal
yes i'll be there like you would for me

the darkness doesn't stand a chance i know
the bhagavad gita done told me so

hey old buddy old friend
would you bail me out of jail?

hey old buddy old pal
i'd wade you through the fires of hell

the world is a cold and lonely place
until i see the smile on my friend's face

hey old buddy old friend
oh I know you've done your best

hey old buddy old friend
come to me, now you can rest

your vibrations stretch across the sky
if you need assistance
i'm your guy

Hide

dead end of my dreams sent suspended into air
float the flickered vapor
doubt dispersing everywhere
and the emptiness of feeling
led the wild all back inside
looking for a place to hide

caverns of conclusion
got me pulled into a hole
sparks jumping dancing on the inside of my soul
and i couldn't see the ending nor beginning where i lied
looking for a place to hide

hiding from yourself
on masks you do depend
your frayed former cells
still have their debts to lend

impossible and pointless
what can you be but you?
there's nowhere else to go and there's nothing else to do
so dissolve away the feeling and let it slip inside
it's looking for a place to hide

hiding behind walls
hiding behind rules
condescension cloak
looking down on fools

memory and music fills the silence in the void
melody/emotions from the past that were destroyed
and what cannot be remembered in your body stored inside
it's looking for a place to hide

Hippie Hate Hippie

patchouli stains on the wall
tapestries just fall into pile
dial my friend paul
crumple up the velvet rut in style

tuesday two o'clock
laptop coffee slop
not an empty chair
do these people ever work?
or does it feel like work to just be sitting there?

i'm a hippie who hates hippies
my throbbing dreadlock will take you with me
i'm a hippie who hates hippies

whole foods in workout gear
a beer to wash down everything that's wrong
a feel good happy song
i dig good vibes
but i think i'll hit the gong

i'm a hippie who hates hippies
my throbbing dreadlock will take you with me
i'm a hippie who hates hippies

flower power sucks
an empty slogan traded in for bucks
i want the world to sing
but honestly it can't do anything

i'm a hippie who hates hippies
my throbbing dreadlock will take you with me
i'm a hippie who hates hippies

Home

sizzling summertime
lawnmower yawn
eyes breathe the air that rises at dawn
happy, warm and home

koozie control
with suds on the side
bar-b-q grill with tofu inside
happy, warm and home.

windows all down
don't have a/c
face in the fan
vocoder free
happy, warm and home

everything i need
is everything i have
nothing more to want
nothing more to nab
happy, warm and home

Humanity (Hairy Sally's lament)

humanity!
poor humanity, all in the same boat as we
for nowhere will we ever go
and nothing will we ever be
and the bounce between the black and white
the right and wrong,
the left and right,
an endless circle with little delight
and no answers
and no end in sight
spring break rolls dark clouds
and the evil one will soon laugh aloud
a nervous system nervous in its entirety
oh do be nervous, voyagers
do be nervous
before your own system of such
becomes no more

Hunt So the Need High

(chanted by cavemen in business suits)

hunt so the need high
we walk in the foot
hunt so the need high
we walk in the foot
hunt so the need high
we walk in the foot
hunt so the need high
we walk in the foot
hunt so the need high
we walk in the foot

hand on the elbow
we stand in the woods
hand on the elbow
we stand in the woods
hand on the elbow
we stand in the woods
hand on the elbow
we stand in the woods

I Am That I Am, I Is That I Was

i once was a kid in a philosophy class
and the teacher asked a question
and i had to pass
and she asked me why
i said, "the sky"
she said, "that don't make no sense"
i said, "nothing else does neither so let's give up the pretense."
she said, "if you don't believe in nothing, it's awfully cold, with nowhere to go"
and i said, "that may be so, but i believe in something"
and i said this:

i am that i am
i is that i was
and why does it happen?
oh hell, just because
there's people hating hatred
and people fearing fear
let's renounce all this renouncing
let's go and buy a beer

every question only asks
a dozen more questions passed
onto every answer
flimsy tissue soaking wet
nevermind no answers nor questions
resolve yourself instead to life's ultimate bet:
will you live it to the full?
or get swallowed and distracted
by all the bull?

i am that i am
i is that i was
and why does it happen?
oh hell, just because
there's people hating hatred
and people fearing fear
let's renounce all this renouncing
let's go and buy a beer

I Burnt All My Black

stare up above
and the sky stares back
i know what i see
is only what i lack
i burnt all my black

woman she bends
and she beckons me
can't lift my eyes
i cannot see
i burnt all black

I Can't Turn Around
(after Hank Williams)

i tried so hard my dear to show
to quit this stupid game
rock and roll and posers
and this stupid grasp for fame
but if i knew what else to do
i'd do this anyway
the only things that i know
are feelings to convey
i can't turn around

it feels right to take this path
though everyone says i'm wrong
the only time this life makes sense
i'm conjuring a song
too far down the road i've gone
all i can do is sing these songs
but every song's for you
every song's for you
i can't turn around

I Don't Know Where to Live Anymore

trapped in the past
a looking glass contained
photocopy city plan
but change just the name
blur past the places
that all feel the same
i don't know where to live anymore

counting all these coffins
it sure hurts my dome
i wish that some familiar face
would just bring me home
but between all of my feelings
i have been condemned to roam
i don't know where to live anymore

paint your plastic tapas
to stale designer bread
nothing is not nature
or else it's in your head

out where the edge curves into itself
a space in between the thoughts i'm keeping to myself
halfway to a heart attack
and halfway to health
i don't know where to live anymore

mow down the meadow
condo sprawl instead
nothing is not nature
just like the guru said

so never will i walk through life so easily and calm
always stumbling to some room
that i don't belong
like a zero legged dog
who's gone swimming in a pond
i don't know where to live anymore

I Love My Job

paperclips in piles
emoticons of smiles
dry eraser stains
i love my job

new message, hey look at that!
like a pellet fed to a rat
do these pants make me look fat?
i love my job

office happy hour
obsequious man gets sour
when he has a drink or two
i love my job

donuts every morn
and a pep talk with my boss ron
this folgers tastes like shit
i love my job

fifteen minute bathroom break
it almost feels like an escape
this thrift store don't fit too great
i love my job

doin them abcs
in filing room 123
this paperwork's drowning me

put stamps on every form
each tax pack must conform
stapled top left corner
i love my job

this job just makes me sick
sometimes i want to quit
but i'm too scared of it
i love my job

doin them abcs
in filing room 123
this paperwork's drowning me

I Picked a Fight

i picked a fight last night
i actually thought i could win
i got covered in blood and dirt
i'll never do that again

i lost a fight last night
the boy was half my size
he put me in a garbage can
i just sat there to hide

I Think Too Much

i think too much, i think too much
drowned my thoughts on meditation yachts
i think too much

i paid out the nose to wear white clothes
and think about light
and how to do what's right
but it's all just shite

i think too much, i think too much
drowned my thoughts on meditation yachts
i think too much

ten thousand books on tape playing side by side
each one kept saying that your thoughts can't hide
just trap them in the corner with a cosmic net
that we sell for a thousand dollars a set

i think too much, i think too much
drowned my thoughts on meditation yachts
i think too much

so i bought me a hat to crown my dome
and now every thought just stays at home
like an oil explosion that got capped
finally i can take a nap

i think too much, i think too much
drowned my thoughts on meditation yachts

I Will Be True

just to see you
used to make me complete
all around me
the world stood at my feet
oh it's weird what time will do
but you know i'll be true

frozen moments
of tender sweet embrace
they departed
they left without a trace
oh it's weird what time will do
but you know i'll be true

i'm an asshole
i'm a selfish selfish man
but i swear i swear
i'll do the best that i can
and i'll give it all to you
i will be true

I Witness the World as a Glowing Ball

forced force of nature
nature of my legs
think it's time i dig me from the dregs
force force of nature
nature of my mind
i think it's time i leave my mind behind
but i witness the world as a glowing glowing ball
and i witness the world without seeing anything at all

force force of nature
nature of my knees
all worn out from empty begging pleas
force forced to witness
witness all this farce
i think it's time i stick it up my _____
but i witness the world as a glowing glowing ball
and i witness the world without seeing anything at all

I'm a Gravedigger

well i'm a gravedigger
and i keep my family fed
by digging graves alone at night
and burying the dead
last night a boy named bill baird
was brought to me to rest
they said to lay him six foot down
and i dug my best

but something strange happened that very night
cuz when i finished burying the boy
there came a light
the letters on his gravestone shone like the stars
and the dirt i'd just shoveled on his grave
turned into fire

well i jumped back in fear and felt the urge to run
but i's so shocked my legs were stuck and a black cat had my tongue
then the flames subsided and a book rose from his grave
and i grabbed the book and ran to warn the town out the cemetery gates

cuz something strange happened that very night
cuz when i finished burying the boy
there came a light
the letters on his gravestone shone like the stars
and the dirt i'd just shoveled on his grave
turned into fire

the people didn't believe me til i showed them the book
that had risen out of bill baird's grave
and they all had a look
the book seemed to be a sick joke and they called a liar
and police put me in a strait jacket as i screamed about the fire

cuz something strange happened that very night
cuz when i finished burying the boy
there came a light
the letters on his gravestone shone like the stars
and the dirt i'd just shoveled on his grave
turned into fire

I'm a Surfer

west texas
where desert meets mountains
and out here the cactus plains swell and heave like a distressed ocean
and that being the case
i consider myself a surfer
i start my car
music turns up
start driving my truck into the desert
where winds blowing south from the guadalupe range
mildly roar in your ears like a sedated leafblower

and i bought this truck myself
it has four wheels, a bed and an accelerator
i can't say much more for it
i guess my truck usually does the talking / coughing for me
i started chewing tobacco at age 8
quit that at 10 when i found my first girlfriend
started drinking at age 9
smoked pot with some ranchhands at 13
thrown in jail for most of the petty, pointless crimes on the books:
shoplifting, cow tipping, attempted bank robbery

now picture this scene:
boy walks into convenience store
smells his breath in his hands
bad breath, he cringes
and girl nearby says "your voice smells. your breath smells."
he picks out a tic-tac from the rack, shakes out a few
pops them in his mouth, puts back the container
he walks out of the store
employee comes out, grabs him by the wrist
a struggle then ensues
the boy is thrown to the pavement
and the boy feels stupid with blood pouring out his nose
and an employee's orthopedic shoe on his back
and police lights reflecting on the wet concrete
as he's cuffed and carted off to the city jail
where he'd spend the night with chico, rico, rick, john, james, sonny
and a few others
and that whole scene does persist to this day in my memory...
and my criminal record
employer sees that and says
"sorry, position's already been filled"
and all this and that
and all that rejection, it about gets me to commit another crime
except this time it wouldn't be tic-tacs, i assure you./

I'm Getting Laid Tonight

the night is young and so are we
there's nothing much to do
let's pile in daddy's mini-van
let's dye our hair blue
i ripped up my report card
and ripped up all my clothes
my milk money's paying for this piercing in my nose
i did my best, puffed up my chest
read the dictionary for an hour
i sloshed around some chicken wings
then went and picked a flower

i'm getting laid tonight... *word up*
i'm getting laid tonight.... *beer gut*
i'm getting laid tonight.... *male slut*
i'm getting laid tonight.... *say what*?

i've been pumping iron for seven days and nights
i've done jazzercise
i've worn purple tights
i've found a tight t-shirt
i'm tearing off the sleeves
i've found myself a midget
i think his name is jeeves
i did my best to shave my chest
i made a protein shake
twas old abe lincoln's birthday so i baked him a cake

i'm getting laid tonight... *word up*
i'm getting laid tonight.... *beer gut*
i'm getting laid tonight.... *male slut*
i'm getting laid tonight.... *say what*?

got my shit sewed up like betsy ross
to flow the chart
got a 12-pack of keystone
i've cleaned out sky mart
the grease i use to shine my shoes
glistens on my hair
my rubber ducky's in the tub
my teddy bear's named blair
i did my worst to get my first girl by 9am
by noon i'd gone to sea world
did some squats down at the gym

I'm Not a Perfect Person

this world doesn't show much to be mine
and half my days are wasting time
staring at a clock that i unplugged an hour ago
brain ten below zero

but yahweh's everywhere
i see hair shining holy
but you're giving me the eye
like you wish for me to die
looks like i fucked up again

you feed me like the air
and i love you dear i swear
but i'm not a perfect person

a soldier standing naked
he keeps on fighting the same old war
and feels he's gotta fight but he can't figure out what for
the door has no key because there is not a door

you feed me like the air
and i love you dear i swear
but i'm not a perfect person

I'm Sad but I Can't Play the Blues

stevie ray yawn bit a bicep steak
and played the blues on a private yacht
make no mistake
he had it made
but he forgot how to play the blues

a robot he used in his place
it made the funny shredding face
guitar hero hit so deep
stevie yawned
the crowd went to sleep

i'm sad
i'm sad
i'm sad
but i can't play the blues

sour patch storks deliver kids
soul patch dorks say "stevie shreds"
like jimi hendrix forgot to take acid
like jimi hendrix took nyquil instead
like jimi hendrix forgot to take acid
like jimi hendrix took nyquil instead

i'm sad
i'm sad
i'm sad
but i can't play the blues
i'm sad
i'm sad
i'm sad
but i can't play the blues
i'm sad
i'm sad
i'm sad
but i can't play the blues

I've Waited My Whole Life to Disappear

your face outshines a thousand suns
and smiles them back to everyone
i've waited my whole life disappear

i've never known something like this
when you are here i don't exist
i've waited my whole life to disappear

you're in my hair and in my skin
your presence = floating smile again
i've waited my whole life to disappear

i used to care about myself
now i think about something else
i've waited my whole life to disappear

If God Gave Us Freewill

if god gave us freewill
i'll see her as i please
a lovely darling damsel with hair down to her knees
a wondrous apparition glowing from within
the source of my virtues and my sins

each day i walk into the world
and see my fellow man
he's getting things accomplished
he's making all his plans
but man needs another half to fill his empty soul
the warmth of the feminine
to make this human whole
there's a hole there to be filled
in everyone alive
and you got to fill that hole for your sanity to survive
some fill that hole with emptiness, some fill the hole with lust
some fill it with up with worthless wealth
some fill it with distrust
but these fleeting futile dreams endeavored in a haze
are simply ways of filling up the emptiness of days
even this here song is an empty headed plea
that the world might heal itself towards a harmony

if god gave us freewill
i'll see her as i please
a lovely darling damsel with hair down to her knees
a wondrous apparition glowing from within
the source of my virtues and my sins

first things first, go call your mom
your love for her do share
a seed of mother nature's spread
to breath this earthen air
and realize that everything you make here is dead
nothing you create can match what's in yer head
there's emptiness inside
for you pursued what wasn't best
by bowing to the world of greed
aggression and conquest
the story of the world
has only half been told
and the picture complete
sure beats what you've been sold

if god gave us freewill
i'll see her as i please
a lovely darling damsel with hair down to her knees
a wondrous apparition glowing from within
the source of my virtues and my sins

Illuminated Night

when the last believers left
go bitter and bereft
and wade above their heads
in lukewarm lite
they wage a war while numb
but victory never comes
except by illuminated night

when the whales lounge on the beach
and god has been impeached
and the false and true
cease these silly fights
and the mirrors all pray
that their reflections go away
comes dawning illuminated night

when the jester of the crown
speaks the only truthful sound
and paid actors
evade the stage in fright
and the chorus of the queen
is unheard and unseen
comes dawning illuminated night

when darkness does unfold
and all the truths are finally told
we'll see there was no need
to shrink in fright
and if it all does come to pass
we'll disappear at last
swallowed by illuminated night

Imaginary Lover

bleached your brain
to remove the stain
of the way you felt before
once she had you down on your knees
and crawling on the floor
got left in the cold
and truth be told?
you didn't even care
your empty flippant words of grief
just seemed like so much air

shocked you to discover
you never even loved her
now the words they stutter
-i- i- -i- -i- imaginary lover

burned the books
that were shaped like hearts
you broke the records too
you threw away the masking tape
you threw away the glue
not a thing can ever be done
no, nothing to repair
to mend or fix or fuss about
something that wasn't there.

shocked you to discover
you never even loved her
now the words they stutter
-i- i- -i- -i- imaginary lover

In the Future

In the future
it will be found that any benevolent impulse not acted upon
will clog the arteries and cause cardiac arrest
all those with the right idea but too weak-willed to act upon it
will be clutching their chests in agony by their mid-50s
while all the greedy assholes
who never had a feeling of empathy to begin with
will be laughing over their piles of money
into their 80s, 90s, and beyond.

in the future
it will also be found that money
is the great lubricant, if you will,
in more ways than one
rich folks will have perfected
a method of crushing hundred dollar bills
 into a creamy paste
which they will rub all over their bodies
in an effort to stave off
wrinkles, sags, and other signs of age
poor folk will have tried a similar technique
by collecting all the world's discarded pennies
but the paste subsequently attained
only deepened their wrinkles
and gave off a smell that the rich
would do their best to avoid

in the future
it will be found that each human hair
is a tiny antenna to a great cosmic being
named hair god
who is a primordial being
obsessed with follicles
and possessed the body and mind of vidal sassoon,
 at various points in his life
of course, if the human hairs have been permed or teased
their antenna powers will be blunted severely,
if not entirely eliminated

in the future
anytime somebody notices or mentions you on
cybercosmos
(the great integrated social networking platform
that has representations of everything
every human, every emotion,
every blade of grass, every speck of dirt
and has even managed to incorporate unified field theory)
a red pellet is dispensed
from a hole in the ceiling
shaped like a cloud
eerily reminiscent of charleton heston

playing moses
in the 10 commandments
the pellet is sweet and sugary
and mildly sedates you for a few minutes
some do not eat these pellets,
instead collecting and trading them
like the beads and furs of yesteryear
in fact, the red pellet black market
has been doing brisk business of late
with one confirmed transaction
of 10,000 pellets for a 1997 geo metro
which brings up the following:

in the future
it will be generally agreed that
the 1997 geo metro was the best car ever made.
moving on.

in the future
the walls of our dwellings will be edible
and at the end of the hallway
of most apartment buildings
will be a bakery
that manufactures edible bricks
to fill the holes in the walls
in the great "angry stomachs protest" of 2040
a group of 400,000 angry union members
stormed the west wing of the white house
they would eventually pull back
when the military began shooting mortar rounds
of dexatrim
the famed diet pill of the 1980s
and since dexatrim was in fact just a speed pill,
similar in nature to cocaine,
these 400,000 angry, stuffed union members
all turned to one another
and began blabbing non-stop
about how excited they were
about "all this cool shit coming up"
and since everyone was talking all at once
no-one could hear each other
and the resulting din sounded like 400,000 screaming hyenas
the right wing media subsequently
spun the episode and the union members as
"gluttonous speed freaks anxiously
discussing things that will never happen"

Infinite Eye

up above my head
the floor is crashing
and now i'm cashing
my cosmic clone
inside out the world walks inside me
so why should i be
feeling alone?

overthrown by the emptiness
conveyed in the space
of the zero in your eye

deeper dive
you find the world within you
and it will spin you
until you're still
emptiness of nothingness
will warm you
and then swarm you
content until

you're
overthrown by the emptiness
that's shown in shade
the zero in your eye

ooooh infinite eye
i see your face inside me

so never will i feel i've gotten somewhere
i know that nowhere
lies within

i've met the void
it said don't get cranky
and please don't thank me
you cannot win

overthrown by the empty throne
he owns
it's the zero in your eye

ooooh infinite eye
i see your face inside me
ooooh infinite eye
i see your face inside me

Inflatable Man

he smiles through his teeth
his grip an iron hand
laser pointer lawyer briefs
his skin efficient skin tan
oh inflatable man
in men's magazines, he rips out each page
flipping through the fads
organic cotton rage
oh inflatable man

but sometimes late at night all the air rushes out
his shriveling skin is deflated by doubt
oh the world forgives you deflatable man

has every type of stat to make his prowess felt
biceps by the inch
pussy scalping pelts
oh inflatable man
his job it consists of vanquishing all foes
he struts in his cubicle
texting his bros
oh deflatable man
sometimes late at night all the air rushes out
his shriveling skin is deflated by doubt
oh i forgive you
inflatable man

and sometimes i do see
the deflated man is me
in an artsy kind of way
pretending more than i can be
oh deflatable me
so the shallow bro and i
we exchange a hug
share our fears over beers until
we're slumped on the rug
oh inflatable men

and when the beer has worn off
we retreat into our roles
me pretentious artsy guy
and him a soulless troll
oh inflatable men
but sometimes late at night all the air rushes out
our shriveling skin is deflated by doubt
oh please forgive me inflatable man
oh i forgive you inflatable man

Inflated Head

my thoughts often flutter
beyond my mouth's grasp
beyond my words
my head has become a
massive over-inflated balloon it seems
a balloon floating through dense cloud cover
engorged with hot air and squeaky cheeks
eventually to deflate and wash ashore
to later be retrieved by a native
living in some distant south seas island
clad only
in a fig leaf
and a sun visor
and maybe a dab of zinc oxide
they will marvel
at my deflated head
and place it on top a totem
and i will become their new sun god
or perhaps their new god
of deflated balloons
or perhaps their new god
of shattered dreams

Insomnia Insane

dreamtime
all asleep
outside the night is humming
i can't sleep
inside my head
the past it slowly rings

insomnia insane
battle of the brain
paralyzing pain
all i feel is shame
oh when will come the morning?

i took myself
and gave away my soul, dear
long time clawing back
the claustrophobic night fears

insomnia insane
battle of the brain
paralyzing pain
all i feel is shame
oh when will come the morning?

Interior Design

mid century modern cage
with pain perfectly placed
every scene a magazine
but one thing you can't erase
the cabinets are empty
and the books left wrapping on
there's nothing quite so fashionable
as a thousand dollar yawn

your interior design
your insides
look a lot like mine

the emptiness inside your life
is the empty of your lair
sweep your past
into the trash
lazy boy armchair

your interior design
your insides
look a lot like mine

so sparkling and empty
priceless
nothing can be touched
the scene we see's like you and me
we've cleared away too much
let it pile into a clump and clump into a heap
then we'll shave the overflow
a buzz cut to a sheep

your interior design
your insides
looks a lot like mine

Intravenous Blues

stapled to my throne
shopping bags of bones
eyes are filled with stones
tv for a face

computer in my place
after you are dead
and the world glows hellish red
you're forced to eat stale bread
and you're never fully fed

intravenous blues
hole punch my skin
feeling mighty weak and awful thin

intravenous blues
dance inside my veins
the sun and the moon
look just the same.

my woman hates my guts
she left me there for dead
which messes with my head

Is Nothing There

your tragic mask
a mini broadway play
frowning at the crowds that walk away
shuffling confused
feeling like they just been used
they toss you a withering bouquet

left eye looks inside
the mask in which you hide
is nothing there?

to let go of your golden grief
as a tree lets go of a leaf
autumn colors fall
with no effort made at all
roaring leafblowers rule underneath

left eye looks inside
the mask in which you hide
is nothing there?

It was a Lovely Way to Die

candy flavored nightmares
teardrop flavored eyes
our love affair was littered all with pretty papered lies
sometimes you don't want to know the truth

it was a lovely way to die
stealing moments from the sky
while we drank deep the warmth of its glow
it was a lovely way to die
hallelujah by and by
but now our sun burns no more

standing in the shadows
searching for a spark
dancing to the gallows
our noose glows in the dark
sometimes what feels good is not good for you

a valentine's day dagger
a heart is its shape
your poisonous concoction
a pink happy cake
sometimes your lover actually hates you

it was a lovely way to die
stealing moments from the sky
while we drank deep the warmth of its glow
it was a lovely way to die
hallelujah by and by
but now our sun burns no more

It's Over, My Dear, it's Through

when the friends that you've made
start folding into 1
and your hole in the shade has you yearning
for a seat back in the sun
the crowded road outside seeped into your waking dreams
and your architect's torn down all his flimsy clapboard schemes
and your dishwasher's hands are frozen balls of rust
no telling who to love,
there's no telling who to trust
because you paid your friends (a back-patting must)
it's over, my dear, it's through

your shrink published a book
charting everything you lack
your world's painted red
but the bull pulls backs
away when you approach
the matador is dead
but the crowd gives the beast no reproach
salt upon the stems
your flowers wilted to a heap
and you can't still your mind to sleep
your accountant done quit cuz there's nothing for him to do
and your businessman called in sick but has golf stains on his shoes.
it's over, my dear, it's through

a withered past fades
to darkness where you've stayed
and slayed the days gone by
each day you're born
each day you die
holding nothing like its yours
pouring whiskey out your pores
brain's pocked with sadness sores
it's over, my dear, it's through
criss crossing webs of speed
the world lacks what you need
it's all just lust and greed
dear abbey, help me now, i plead
monsanto seeds stuck in my brain
all my thoughts been sucked away
dum dum daddy made the bed
kept you clothed, kept you fed
but you look now, your dad is dead
and there's nowhere to rest your head
the clock is red, it ticks away
blood let bottle chardonnay
eyes beholden in dismay
watch your gold dissolve to gray
it's over, my dear, it's through

It's Already Here

waiting all your life for something
you are not quite sure of
and all that you want
is to stop holding back
and you wonder when your life is going to start

but it's already here
it's already here
and all that you're waiting for is gone

emptiness can be your best friend
and if the past occurs again
we'll shake his withered hand
i've died a thousand times before
and i will die a thousand more
oh what am i waiting for?

it's already here
it's already here
and everything you're waiting for is gone
it's already here
it's already here
and you have known it all along

It's Empty Time

max wax eardrum falls apart
in john bonham's jeans
mini-mall-rock air guitar
bob marley poster screams,
"it's empty time"

midnight oily foot massage
a jello jail jail mold
the insides of my eyes are blank
and my food is getting cold
it's empty time.

empty time
it is the time the world just does its thing
the pulsing feet of passersby
make the sidewalks sing
it's empty time.

staring at the wall
staring at the floor
staring at the world walking by my door
staring at the wall
staring at the floor
staring at the world walking by my door
staring at the wall
staring at the floor
staring at the world walking by my door
staring at the wall
staring at the floor
staring at the world walking by my door

Jones Street Blues

vacancy of mind
excess of every kind
got some easy friends
on 12th street and vine
and if you don't mind the smell
you can come to my hotel
and i'll lead you into my own private hell
got them jones street blues again.

lost my faith and place
bowed out of the race
if you want me
you can find me on the floor
a bottle in my hand
i really couldn't stand
but if i could
you know i'd be out the door
got them jones street blues again

Lady Dark

sordid pavements
quickly dimming skies
you smile in my face
but it makes a poor disguise
your eyes blink and flutter all untrue
and the pallor of your face
paints a pallid hue
it's true I was unfaithful
for the nighttime was my friend
each day I would renew my vows
and in darkness they would end
and the stars seemed to be a sign
that the bristled blackened veil
was meant to be mine

lady dark what have you done?
A stolen face makes for a soul in yearning
lady dark what have you done?
For the one I was has gone with no returning

so cold and yet so soothing
this world we find ourselves
the glowing city's brooding
only serves to firm our shells
painted faces flashing one by one
and the gaiety and splendor can't conceal what we've become
on a tightrope made of velvet we stand above the fray
the city shuffles down below
a world in slow decay
if we hesitate we'll know that we aren't free
we'll fall from the wire to be swallowed by the sea

lady dark what have you done?
A stolen face makes for a soul in yearning
lady dark what have you done?
For the one I was has gone with no returning
lady dark what have you done?
It's a silly game in which we have been thrown
oh lady dark what have you done?
For the one I was has left to wander the night alone.

Lady Darkness Daydream

she stares ahead
her eyes in flame
the darkness glitters cold and speaks her name
i crawl to her window
consumed with shame
her bony fingers scrape the glass
and scratch out my name
lady dark, oh why
must you make me out do die?
i did not mean to hurt the ones i love
i cried out in silence
the lady smiled and said
"worry not, don't fret
i cannot you kill you
you were never alive"

darkness daydream

and so i did reply
"lady dark, oh why
torment me if the blame be not mine?"
to which her smile appeared and said,
"boy have no fear
i own you now
and the blame be mine"

darkness daydream
darkness daydream

Las Vegas

glittering plastic pile of crap
a trap to those who feel
the fake becomes the real
bathsheba in a porsche
drive thru marriage toll
crawl across the desert of the soul

slot machines wither into salt
the salt shapes a smile
this town kills you in style
bathsheba in a porsche
drive thru marriage toll
crawl across the desert of the soul

las vegas is a whore
who looks good when you're drunk
but you'll wake up in a garbage can
a skunk between your knees
las vegas is a sneeze
that you can't control
spitting golden balls of phlegm
hold onto that one it's a gem!

satan runs an all night buffet
his filet mignon's the best
but it never will digest
the plates will lick your tongue
as you eat an empty hole
and crawl across the desert of the soul

tourist trapping fur coat in a heap
you'll weep for all the holy rotten crooks
but even dick cheney has a soul

Late Night Dawning

excuse me while i go insane
or whatever they call it now
i'll take the waters
for as long as my lungs allow
excuse me while i go insane
love's a game i always lose
i wear a moonlit face
that the daytime has refused

late night dawning
early morning
they say the darkest hour
is the one where your eyes are closed

punch my face bloody
cut off all my hair
my love is dead and i really couldn't care less
shoot me to outer space
my face will assume a darkened hex
the man in the moon has changed
his sex

late night dawning
early morning
they say the darkest hour
is the one where your eyes are closed

Leaving the City

well i might take a train
i might take a plane
but i'm leaving just the same
i'm leaving the city
tired of playing the game

well, i turned 25 and looked around
to take stock of my life
five piece suits, a mistress and a wife
nights so long, they seemed as one
with the golden rays of day
i came home drunk, twas always hell to pay

so i bought myself a simple life
the freshness of my youth
but i was just putting white paint
on top a rotten tooth
cuz i tried to meditate and i fell asleep
and i went to see a shrink and i couldn't weep
and i met my inner child and he told me i'm a creep

well i might take a train
i might take a plane
but i'm leaving just the same
i'm leaving the city
tired of playing the game

well next i checked my ragged self into a house of disrepute
i was tired of wearing clothes, especially five piece suits
these ladies of the night, it's true
they do have golden hearts
i think however, it's only cause their fees are off the charts

they'd have me for an hour or more
but honestly not that long
we'd get done, she'd chew her gum
and she'd ask me for a song

i'd sing them lovely lullabies
all pulsed with sighs and sobs
afterwards they'd be fired
for sleeping on the job

then they kicked me out
when i went broke
as extra payment
they kept my clothes
and then gave me
a tube top shirt and panty hose

so i stood there in women's clothes
my pants noticeably gone
i headed straight to a church
to confess all of my wrongs

now the preacher he laughed out loud
when he noticed i was nude
he said
"son, this is a church and i think that's a little rude
to stand before the eyes of god
without wearing no clothes?
for that, it's off to hell to eternally decompose"
and now i'm naked in hell
with a heck of a suntan
i've found a new career
fronting a heavy metal band

well i might take a train
i might take a plane
but i'm leaving just the same
i'm leaving the city
tired of playing the game

Life is Rad (Just Say Yes)

living in the city
looking for a life
looking for somebody
with whom could be my wife?
oh, life is rad
life's a bust
and all i can do is find someone i can trust

staring at the wall
waiting for the day
who knows what day will come
and what she will say
oh, life is rad
life's a bust
and all i can do is find a wall i can trust

modern day scarecrow
thrown off the bus
walking piles of gravel
climbing piles of rust
oh, life is rad
life's a wreck
and all i can do is bounce back
just like my check

framed like a photo
up against the wall
smiling face
flat and still
one inch tall
oh, life is rad
life is long
and all i can do is sing the words to my favorite song

owner of a lonely heart.
owner of a lonely heart.
owner of a lonely heart.
i'm the owner of a lonely heart.
owner of a broken heart

Life's a TV Show

don't straight your slump, viewer.
it loosens you up
tune in and see "hey look that's me!"

life's a tv show
you already know
the way it ends
reruns of friends

the daily drama
your dad and mama
were all a ruse to get more views
the viewers watch and rate your life
don't come unglued
you might get renewed

life's a tv show
you already know
the way it ends
reruns of friends

get born
come out screaming
wear a diaper
parents beaming
crawl around
no more dreaming
learn the rules
stop your screaming
go to school
get berated
learn the rules
get sedated
glimpse of truth
interspersed
amongst the facts
that you rehearsed
unprepared
school is done
nowhere to work
but having fun
taking drugs
until you can't
weed makes you nervous
speed makes you clamped
so go to work
disappointed
now family time
but still disjointed
you do your best

but just can't fake it
paunch belly
look weird naked
old photos
no longer you
when will your
dreams come true?
mid life crisis
sit and stare
a flashy car
in your underwear
old man
watching tube
kids these days
they're all so rude
you watch your family
they're like a mirror
and suddenly it all gets clearer
it's all a cycle
it's all a cover
one life ends
here comes another
the center of the universe
you thought you were
the very first
but every person
all has that thought
you are the center?
well, maybe not

Lifer's Lament (bending the truth)

low wage waking charlatan
pretentious bitter flop
can't say my profession
when i'm questioned by the cops
and if i go on a drunk
that's the only way it stops

there may be infinity in my soul
but my body's getting old
and i need someone to hold

to some i'm a truth-teller
to others, full of shit
to me i'm the king of pop
who's never had a hit
there's nothing more annoying
than a lifer who insists
that the world will someday catch on
and he'll be on all the lists
he plays you all his demos
expectantly he stares
and waits for you to hear the song
and passionately declare
you're an unrecognized genius
a gift to life itself
you belong with the masters
on their guilded golden shelf
but reality is harder and colder
when its blank
neither praise nor blame
no-one to curse or thank
that is me, you see,
all alone i stand
and my catalog of unheard songs?
they all sound pretty grand

there may be infinity in my words
but honestly this sentiment's absurd
if none of it gets heard

Like Butter, Like Ice

so grab your yellow wig
and do a little jig
it's a neat-o little dance that we call "the twig"
we dress in leaves and writhe around
snap in half and fall on the ground
echo
echo echo echo

like butter, like ice
come now, dig it, ain't that nice
like butter, like ice
come dig dig it twice
like butter, like ice
dig dig dig it
say it thrice
like butter, like ice
the beats they stick like grains of rice

this sleepy bassline ain't aware of time
and my slack ass voice just sucked a lime
so don't be scared to bust a move
i'll bust a rhyme all anglo smooth
this next section bambaataa inspired
krautrock chords to keep you wired
an a major scale moving up fast
with a white man's rap
ain't that a gas?

like butter, like ice
come now, dig it, ain't that nice
like butter, like ice
come dig dig it twice
like butter, like ice
dig dig dig it
say it thrice
like butter, like ice
the beats they stick like grains of rice

Like Every Day Before

the lights go out
darkness falls
whiskey drips down the walls
the day has made its curtain calls
but i just can't go to sleep
my mind paces rapid
and into darkness shouts
why and what for is this?
and what's it all about?

fingers weave a web
with each of us enshrined
sometimes these concrete fingers
shape my mind
and the streets shape a peace sign
a thumbs up, down, or side to side
or a middle finger jammed
into the reaches of my mind

why hello world,
you want me to
off the fuck they say?

no

i will fierce and pierce the veil
and go on fighting
here today

with head in flames and eyes to shine
burnt words and charred dreams of mine
all is fuel and fodder for life's empty space
but i embrace its blankness
i take the illusion and make it my own

hero of my own fiction
its ending written and erased
every second of my life
is written on my face
and my book is done
let it drift into the sun
to burn away
as another new book is begun
let the story be written again
just like every day before

Limp Limo

wound up world
bungees down your feelings
and straps them to the hood
the limp limo labelled "should"
the shoeless wandering path
sure looks appealing
but you bought into the ride
though there's nothing left inside

limp limo coughs
its tailpipes fill our troughs
its flapping tires fan the fires of
budget luxury
limp limo coughs
gaia sits and scoffs
half price high-rise tilts
to budget luxury

grey poupon coupon crumpled worthless
the stores all shuttered boards
but there's a roadside sale on swords
throwing stars and galileo's toothless
he mumbles out his truth
while the world paves down his proof

limp limo coughs
its tailpipes fill our troughs
its flapping tires fan the fires of
budget luxury
limp limo coughs
gaia sits and scoffs
half price high-rise tilts
to budget luxury

never not a negative description
to your hall of mirrors pray
but your fringe begins to fray
super glue your tombstone's inscription:
here lies a spender large
of cancelled credit cards

limp limo coughs
its tailpipes fill our troughs
its flapping tires fan the fires of
budget luxury
limp limo coughs
gaia sits and scoffs
half price high-rise tilts
to budget luxury

Live That Way

hold it close now
hold it close now
til the moment slips away
there's no past and there's no future
there is only today
i wish that i could say that i lived that way

lose your anger
lose your envy
let the darkness fade to light
smile away your silly sorrows
and no junk food late at night
i wish that i could say that i lived that way

there's a moment
you discover
that there's no going back
looking backwards is pointless
and pulls a muscle in your neck
i wish that i could say that i lived that way

i know
that i don't know
that i know
that i don't know

all my anger
and frustration
is just fuel in the tank
write your worries
sing your sorrows
make it money in the bank
i wish that i could say that i lived that way

Lone Writer

beer bottles piled up around my head
crawl across the floor in dread
windows blacked in dragon doom
let me die inside this room
molding pizza stale surprise
yellow stench invades your eyes
sheaths of paper flutter down
and find me sprawled upon the ground

lone writer, alone lone writer
they call me
my head is my home i say
lone writer, alone lone writer
they call me
until my dying day

sink to the bottom of the bottom of the end
you'll find me there
i'll be your friend
a mirror map here for to show
there's not no place you need to go
the way within is the way without
so let there be no drift nor doubt
the squalor that engulfs my bed
it looks the same inside my head
let me be your spirit guide
and show the life that you denied
trash in heaps and truth in spades
toss the garbage, draw the shades

lone writer, alone lone writer
they call me
my head is my home i say
lone writer, alone lone writer
they call me
until my dying day

Long Ascent

life's a long ascent
past the days we've spent
always passing by
bye bye

grip in greedy
can't you see?
it doesn't mean a thing to me
propped up flimsy cloudy thoughts
mistaking fate for what you've got
in seconds flat it turns to dust
so cling to things if cling you must
you can't take nothing when you climb
those starry steps to the end of time

life's a long ascent
past the days we've spent
always passing by
bye bye

in every life there comes a time
you have to leave yourself behind
everything you thought was you
interferes with what you'll do
gather up your former cells
and memories you'd dispelled
watch it burn it away to smoke
and laugh at life cause life's a joke

life's a long ascent
past the days we've spent
always passing by
bye bye

Looking For Lines In Between The Dots

the golden flame inside the sun
it's inside of everyone
but sometimes a voice must stand alone
no need to cry or bitch or moan
cuz it's all in the game
it's all just a name
for the things we do to not go insane
we run around in circles
we run around in knots
picking wildflowers and avoiding cops

so you're alone in the home
with a plan to find someone
and they come in for a second to fill your hole
but now they're gone
cuz it's all in the game
it's all just a name
for the things we do to not go insane
we run around in circles
and tie ourself in knots
looking for lines in between the dots

Lord of Your Apartment

moccasin socks and a wooden flute
flush your family's royal chute to
refrigerator magnet bronze display
shuffle your neighbors weird away
you're the lord of your apartment
the lord of your apartment
the lord of your apartment

pageantry paging laundry buzz
your highness robe in lint and fuzz
permanent press your air dry cape
hang it on the fire escape
you're the lord of your apartment
the lord of your apartment
the lord of your apartment
the lord of your apartment

(song request)
so far away
so far away
so far away

Lost at Sea

sailing with no wind
towards the shore
you turn around and stare
did you intend to go somewhere?
intentions are good
but the ocean doesn't care
placid and serene
sheets of blue
the crew paces restlessly
they need something to do
something to destroy
they're all looking at you

strange to see how the oceans burning
lost at sea, lost at sea
living in your head
while the world keeps turning
lost at sea, lost at sea

no time to rest
you gotta plug another leak
immersed your own head
now you can't speak
and that gargling sound you hear
will never get much clearer
i guess you'd better learn to swim instead

if time is an ocean
death is the shore
and everyone's a sailor
and our thoughts, the ocean floor
we stare into the murky depths
not even sure what for
the reflection that i see: the ocean looks like me

strange to see how the old ship's burning
lost at sea, lost at sea
living in your head
while the world keeps turning
lost at sea, lost at sea

poseidon laughs
charybdis smiles
strapped to the mast
and all the while sirens call
you know you're bound to fall
each of us too, one and all, one and all

Love Don't Exist Until it's Given Away

the clenching of your heart
holds a light that is true
but holding it inside it is you it consumes
a self-eating buffet
for love don't exist until it's given away

everyone you see
has an endless boundless gift
beyond the misery and the daily grind and grift
upon which the parasites will prey
oh love don't exist until it's given away

every hollow head that has ignored
the deep freeze feelings that they stored
ends up boring, frosty and gray
cuz love don't don't exist until it's given away

my mouth gushing lies like a politicians speech
told myself i knew all the lessons life could teach
but my cold heart to me did convey
that love don't exist until it's given away

the way that i lived was a lie
i had so much to give
but i held it all inside
until my innards all began to fray
oh love don't exist until it's given away

so if i could tattoo upon my eyes
everywhere i looked i'd read it til i die
i know what this tattoo would say
"love don't exist until it's given away"

Love Caught Cold

my love spread his arms as if to hold
a lie we often told
but in distant days of young
thoughts of warmth crossed our tongues
before the changes did abound
and the darkness draped the ground

love has caught cold
never gave a whisper
love has caught cold
a sweet dream indeed
love has caught cold
gone away without a whisper

flood all our senses with our blood
stream turned to a flood
somebody's gone
can't help but be stunned
has life ended or begun?

and what little now remains
only swallows us with shame
you cannot see my face
i cannot see your face

love has caught cold
never gave a whisper
love has caught cold
a sweet dream indeed
love has caught cold
gone away without a whisper

Love that Passes is Enough

do not sing, my dear
sad songs of the end of love
lay aside your sadness
for love that passes is enough

love that passes is enough
there's nothing more that's waiting
and when it passes through
let it sing and say adieu
love that passes is enough

sing about the long deep sleep
of lovers that are dead,
and
in the grave our feelings keep
where love will rest its head

love that passes is enough
there's nothing more that's waiting
and when it passes through
let it sing and say adieu
love that passes is enough

Loveshines 1

don't be afraid of dying love
those shadows that you're scared of
don't exist
tarred and feathered in your mind
you've failed so many times
your skin's been peeled
your heart feels raw

holding hands with yourself
pretending to be strong
but you'll never change until you die
how can your heart move ahead
pretending its not dead?
don't fool yourself
you're all alone

loveshines, loveshines
all around

life doesn't bother me at all
those shadows on the wall
there's no dark til something shines
all that you see is empty space
don't forget your place
you don't exist
you're everywhere

loveshines, loveshines
all around

Loveshines 2

flooding time
a storm surrounds
and you cannot grow to higher ground
you gave a toast to the past
noticed it all slipping past
in emptiness
suspended

but sometimes
loveshines
loveshines
sometimes

melting forms fold together
holy man forecasts the weather
rain is going to melt the world away
all the cells that make your hair
dissolve to air
condense into the rain
that feeds the endless ocean

but sometimes
loveshines
loveshines
sometimes

Loveshines 3

what does it mean
when man becomes machine?
another blink in time
loveshines

all that you see
is only memory
and it all dies
when we blink our eyes
loveshines

la
la
la
loveshines
la
la
la
loveshines
la
la
la
loveshines
la
la
la
loveshines
la
la
la
loveshines
la
la
la
loveshines

Luby's Purgatory

gravy bath so gray
gargle down some tooth decay
leftovers?
no way
"tasty"

buffet line abyss
jello moldy fist
fluorescent pudding
"tasty"

microwaves in hell
are cooking lunch for you as well
burning tar for sauce so swell
"tasty"

flip a coin to see
what your choice will
either way, i'd say
you're fucked

stuck in luby's purgatory

fried chickens walk across the road
roadkill crusty gut explode
blazing eyes on soupy toads
"tasty"

the meatloaf has two eyes
and squirms there where it lies
fear not all those flies
"tasty"

flip a coin to see what your choice will
either way, i'd say
you're fucked

stuck in luby's purgatory

Lunar Eyes

lunar eyes, lunar eyes
oh watch them shine
lunar eyes, lunar eyes
don't be afraid
there's no need to hide
there's light inside your lunar eyes

a thousand shining days will come
bursting through your skull
and all of the world
will sing along with you
and the life you left alone
will shine again all pure and true
and remind you that
the moon is shining too
come darkness and a chilling night
that crawls across your skin
now you know
that you are all alone again
undulations sweet serene arrivals firm and true
inside your skull the moon is shining too

lunar eyes, lunar eyes
oh watch them shine
lunar eyes, lunar eyes
don't be afraid
there's no need to hide
there's light inside your lunar eyes

teeming cities bustle fast
breathing traffic sighs
and then our days all die
and rise back up again
but between the sun's departure
and arrival back to you
it isn't dark , the moon is shining too

the moon is just a lifeless rock
that marks the fall of night
whose borrowed light reminds you where the sun has gone
and i will be your moon my friend
when your will is done
reflecting back your light for everyone

lunar eyes, lunar eyes
oh watch them shine
lunar eyes, lunar eyes
don't be afraid
there's no need to hide
there's light inside your lunar eyes

Mac N Me

the light from above
bespeaks a martian's love
but every angel has a spaceship
they ride around in

last week at bingo
he came to visit
used his mind power to help me win
at texas t

wealthy beyond my wildest
and i'm healthy
beyond the rippedest
i'm riding shotgun with an angel
from outer space

Mad Mother

piles and piles and piles
of things
when will all these empty objects
fill your phone with rings?
it sings if
you scratch it's stomach

tiger tiger burning food
why would mother be so rude?
it's your manners can't you see
cut the root and trim the tree
clean your room

sickness sickness unto sick
stale unscented breath a trick
you wig is barely even there
collapsing clump of debonair
your head takes out the trash
and the garbage man gets paid in cash
throw away your clothes
throw away your mold

tiger tiger burning food
why would mother be so rude?
it's your manners can't you see
cut the root and trim the tree
clean your room

Man's Heart Complaint

behold your crooked fingers
invite me out to see
don't want to watch you leaving
i hope
the road will set you free
free

i'll wait
i'll wait
i'll wait

i feel now man's heart complaint
with so much pain i must be a saint
i hear now man's heart complaint
with so much pain i must be a saint

the road may rise to meet you
or lead you to the edge

i'll wait
i'll wait
i'll wait

i feel now man's heart complaint
with so much pain i must be a saint
i hear now man's heart complaint
with so much pain i must be a saint

try to smile
just try to smile
try to smile
just try to smile
try to smile
just try to smile
try to smile
just try to smile
try to smile
just try to smile
try to smile
just try to smile
try to smile
just try to smile
try to smile
just try to smile

Mellow Out My Mind

wasted days and nights
with a worried brain
ready to relax
collapse
into a puddle down my drain
slip into a sliding downwards chair
if you find me drooling on my desk
you'll know i'm no longer there

mellow out my mind
while the world slowly unwinds
just need some space
to collapse upon my face
some fresh air to wheeze
and a honey i can squeeze
i'll be just fine

sunken treasure sofa slumping scene
in between the cushions
fall your failures and your dreams
but nothing can be said to cure your woes
shake away your dread
until it tingles out your toes

mellow out my mind
while the world slowly unwinds
whooshing gush of air
as you fall into your chair
lawnmower land
with a yard i can command
i'll be just fine

the world wages war by proxy place
remote control your children
S.A.T. in interface
you want to think that you're above the game
but fate makes you mumble mouthed
while serving back the same

mellow out my mind
while the world slowly unwinds
mellow out my mind
and smash my mouth in brine
mellow out my mind
it's party stupid time
mellow out my mind
from this psychiatric slime
i'll be just fine

Memory (It Glows)

holding on to memory
holding on to steam
how can you resurrect a dream?
pour it from a bottle
write it in a verse
or steal it from the silence
that rises from the earth

it glows!
it glows!

i last saw her eyes from a distance
slowly the moment passed us by
i know it sounds cliche
but i honestly must say
a tear did spring to mine eye

it glows!

handfuls of emptiness waiting to be claimed
the center of my eye starts to rain
but there's nothing to regret now
nothing to disown
you're only a spirit
flesh and bone

so all of these memories
surrounding you like steam
can be used to resurrect your dreams
they pour from your eyelids
every time you sleep
a scuba diver swallowing the secrets of the deep

it glows!

painfully i took the road in front of me
missing friends and family
93 days of joy
and misery
led to an epiphany
all you see
all you see is memory
all you are is memory
so can it be that all the world's a forgery?
there's a better life for me

Memory's Hazy Golden Glow

it happened right behind my eyes
we came together when i realized
memory's hazy golden glow
keeps us together through the rain and snow
the world isn't only what we see
the only thing that's real is you and me
you and me

though time and space
may come between
the space that separates us
is a dream
i'll always be with you
where you are
no matter the distance
how near or how far

Miami Nice

we're headed to miami
miami is in sight
we're headed to miami on an airline flight

we're headed to miami
miami is in sight
we're headed to miami on an airline flight

purple patch is pale
and in need of the sun
so csi miami
investigate some fun
there's palm trees in the parking lots
even the socks are tan
forget the land of mickey
forget disney land

let's dive into some sunblock
let's dive into a drink
let's go a little crazy
and get sober in the sink
let's wake up all the neighbors
let's get a 'mom' tattoo
let's hit ourself with tasers
let's burglarize the zoo

we're headed to miami
miami is in sight
we're headed to miami on an airline flight

we're headed to miami
miami is in sight
we're headed to miami on an airline flight

Mind Cops

i read your thoughts
in fallow fears
that waste upon the withered years
you can't hold on
but still you hold
to something that has long gone cold
you pace around
a bloated shrimp
inflated like the goodyear blimp
hot air head
with words to match
faking something there to catch
but empty blah it's got no net
like flapping fish that won't get wet
and still you seem to forget
that i've seen inside you

mind cop handcuffs
and you're living in a jail
just make your mind stop
and that'll post your bail

a life sentence there to take
if you lead a life that's fake
no time to pose
there are ain't no need
life is short enough indeed
so worry not about the law
what your neighbors think
or your ma and pa
just do what's inside you so extolled
and then your soul will get paroled

mind cop handcuffs
and you're living in a jail
just make your mind stop
and that'll post your bail

(jailhouse chorus)
wet your blanket silky sap
taste the pain i've got on tap
i'll tap dance on your phony face
and slap you with my gloves of grace
slap you silly
slap you silly

Minimum Wage

velcro laces
inflated faces
hermits wearing leashes
my hair net's colored yellow
my apron's dyed white
and i been scrubbing meatloaf off these dishes all night
officially i'm called the chef
i hit start on the microwave
and feed no_doze to the staff
to make sure that they behave

minimum wage, making minimum wage
but i don't give a shit about that job
i quit

i dress up like a hot dog
by freeways do i walk
"you want some processed meat"
i say in megaphone
i talk
i hand out hot dog samples
to truckers who repay me
in crystal meth snorting and a
melted green slurpee

minimum wage, making minimum wage
but i don't give a shit about that job
i quit

Mirror Maps

past and future wilt
to fill the glowing skies
the eyes of a man on his prize
night and day the same
to him it's but a name
the eyes of a man on his prize
on his prize

memory of touch proves positive the source
persisting in the space of his dreams
but he loved it too much
he held on too long
now he's dying in the space of his dreams
of his dreams

mirror maps oh mirror maps
a compass couldn't tell
every road you ever took
led you to yourself

the years hurried by
faster than he could fly
now he's middle-aged
an echo of the sun
songs that he played
and woman that he laid
are now memories
echoes of the sun
of the sun

mirror maps oh mirror maps
a compass couldn't tell
every road you ever took
led you to yourself

Mister Treadmill

bottled water, tv dinner
walking nowhere makes him thinner
oh, mr treadmill
he dreads standing still

spinning circles like a rocket top
he doesn't think, he doesn't stop
he's dangling bills on a fishing line
helps him to run
keeps him in line
oh mr treadmill
he dreads standing still

has a drink from the kitchen sink
and he walks the dog on his treadmill
what a treadmill
with ten speeds
and a mountain range setting

oh mrs treadmill
"spice things up"
your husband never will

Monday Monday Monday

it's monday's morning's mental morning fog
it's monday morning's foggy smog
it's a zero legged dog
it's monday's morning's mental morning fog

gray grimace grin
swallows up your chin
to inside out
coffee line in grid
you squirm like a squid
water without

it's monday's morning's mental morning fog
it's monday morning's foggy smog
it's a zero legged dog
it's monday's morning's mental morning fog

close velcro snaps
lace up your chaps
and just start walking
dribble tongue on teeth
sunday is the thief
that stole your talking

the grid in which i hid my head
is hanging on the wall
and there's no chance to slip the grid at all

dim witted day
i'd much prefer to stay
here on the couch
but i'll get on with what needs
and the will i concede
becomes a slouch

it's monday's morning's mental morning fog
it's monday morning's foggy smog
it's a zero legged dog
it's monday monday monday monday monday
morning slog

Moonlight

you'll send your words into the air
i won't be there
and you'll turn your thoughts
up to the skies
i won't be there
shaking your own hand
please understand
that the static in between us
doesn't prove that we're not real
there's nothing new to feel

and when you realize
moonlight can reveal more than sunshine
you'll say goodbye and understand
that i'm already gone

bookshelves of
empty pages
waiting to be turned
in your trembling hands
the fire that consumes you
and all you understand
you're only being born
like the drunken priest
confessed his sins
broke his chains
but you're not the same
you won't admit you're wrong
until the subtlety is gone
and now the static that we made
has been set to a song

and when you realize
moonlight can reveal more than sunshine
you'll say goodbye and understand
that i'm already gone

Mosquito

mos – qui – to!
just let go! just let go!
mos – qui – to! mos – qui – to!
just let go!

mosquito holds his breath
his death it has arrived
with purple morning skies
but nothing really dies
the spirit leaves the body
and goes to a party
ocean foam birthday cake
puffy cloud balloons

mos – qui – to!
just let go! just let go!
mos – qui – to! mos – qui – to!
just let go!

insects hung up on themselves
don't no heaven or get no hell
like popsicles and shotgun shells
they just disappear
so when you hear that buzzing biz
that thing's the same as what you is
don't blow that one a deathly kiss
just shoo that one away

mos – qui – to!
just let go! just let go!
mos – qui – to! mos – qui – to!
just let go!

Mother Nature

22 years and still i search
i wander day to day and town to town
and i see her face inside the sun
she's life, she's death, she's birth
she scatters leaves all upon the ground
and if i breathe real deep she comes inside
to hold my breath and then take it away
and i'd tell about my searching years
but this breath already said what i would say

mother nature sends me to the world to find the life residing in myself
and i see her every now and then
in holy words and books upon the shelf
but the real place i see is in my songs
when they're heartfelt and real
the songs expose the part of me
where she resides and makes me feel

and then one day i heard a little knock from inside my head
and i opened up the door inside and saw her face in a note which read:
"find me where you need me
i'm everyone and everything alive"
and my lover stepped out from my soul
and i opened up my eyes and then i died

mother nature sends me to the world
to find the life residing in myself
and i see every now and then
in holy words and books upon the shelf
but the real place i see is in my songs
when they're heartfelt and real
the songs expose the part of me
where she resides and makes me feel

with eyes awake i met the world anew
like flowers with their blooms
and i stepped outside but i still felt confused
outside seemed no different than my room
and i cried out to the stars
"why have you cursed me so that i can't see?
the world within is the same without
and yet i must travel on
and leave my family"

mother nature sends me to the world fo find the life residing in myself
and i see every now and then in holy words and books upon the shelf
but the real place i see is in my songs
when they're heartfelt and real
the songs expose the part of me
where she resides and makes me feel

Mummified

for years and years
i laid in bed
now i'm dead but i'm not
wrapped in dust
from past decay
i'll decorate my tomb
some other day

osiris, ra and harry smith
better than the ones you're with
a starbucks tomb
to drive through die
pick my nose with a five foot pry
and look at me
i'm mummified
mummified
still alive
even though i died

hieroglyphic hands to magic carpet kicks
i got no demands
no pyramids to fix
but the world all around me
has crumbled into numb
embalm my brain and make me dumb

osiris, ra and harry smith
better than the ones you're with
starbucks tomb
drive through die
pick my nose with a five foot pry
and look at me
i'm mummified
mummified
still alive
even though i died

Muzak of the Spheres

left brain
right brain
muzak of the spheres
elevator shaft refrain
ringing in my ears
static stan and captain brain
sail across the sea

muzak of the spheres
has set me free
muzak of the spheres
has set me free

agitated larry calls
shamu's blood's been split
harry sally told you so
this tragedy we built
look to the stars
and at last you'll see

muzak of the spheres has set you free
muzak of the spheres has set you free
muzak of the spheres has set you free

left / right / left / right / left / right / left / right / left / right / left /
right / left / right / left / right / left / right / left / right / left / right /
left / right / left / right / left / right / left / right / left / right / left /
right / left / right / left / right / left / right / left / right / left / right /
left / right / left / right / left / right / left / right / left / right / left /
right / left / right / left / right / left / right / left / right / left / right /
left / right / left / right / left / right / left / right / left / right / left /
right / left / right / left / right / left / right / left / right / left / right /
left / right / left / right / left / right / left / right / left / right / left /
right / left / right / left / right / left / right / left / right / left / right /
left / right / left / right / left / right / left / right / left / right / left /
right / left / right / left / right / left / right / left / right / left / right /

My Brain Is Made for You and Me
(song for woody)

my mood was changing
my light started shining
my words were flashing
and no rhyming
my voice is chanting
now the fog is lifting
my brain is made for you and me

as i went walking on down my spinal cord
and i saw such sadness
but the sadness made me bored
so i threw my sadness
into the sun inside myself
this song was made to set me free
this song is my song
but it's really your song
to show my changing
to fill the holes inside my soul
i hope that this song might fill your holes too
this song was made for you by me

My Flame's Expired

my flame's expired
it dwindles ever more
things will never be the way they were before
i've left my love behind
anew my search begins
for a love to share her golden hair
and a flame that never ends

my flame's expired
exhausted by the cold
tight lipped by this circumstance
my struggles all unfold
i'm moving to a backwoods city
don't even know the name
where simple folk and uncluttered life
provide eternal flame

where the warmth of within
can insulate your mind
from the cold bitter reality
of life that you will find

my flame's expired
may never return
i may just have to find another
part of me to burn
i'll burn away my sadness
and burn away my plans
thrown atop a funeral pyre
that's always where i stand

where the warmth of within
can insulate your mind
from the cold bitter reality
of life that you will find

My Pride and My Tobacco

tell me girl, what's it gonna be?
i've been waiting outside your door since 3
waiting by your window
waiting for your light
i threw the line
dammit, won't you bite?

you know it's hard for me to stand here
but for this once i'll bare to you my soul
oh you're the one i miss, all i need's a kiss
and you'll taste my pain and my plug of skoal

my pride is in my mouth with my tobacco
i'd sweat it out but then it'd stain my clothes
so sooner or later i must swallow
how long i'll hold it in, god only knows
so i'm chewing on these words that i must swallow
these words that never make it out my mouth
my spit cup's bout to spill
and i've about had my fill
of chewing on my pride and my tobacco

tell me girl, what's your little plan
to find yourself another stupid man
a man who eats you up, who just can't get enough
he gnaws your arm as you lead him by the hand
you've filled my mouth with good and bad intentions
to call you close or send you back for good
oh, loving you's a curse
and i can't tell what's worse
the taste or its dribbling down my chin

my pride is in my mouth with my tobacco
i'd sweat it out but then it'd stain my clothes
so sooner or later i must swallow
how long i'll hold it in, god only knows
so i'm chewing on these words that i must swallow
these words that never make it out my mouth
my spit cup's bout to spill
and i've about had my fill
of chewing on my pride and my tobacco

My Woman Hates My Guts

she nickles and she dimes
a coke machine of lies
there's quarters in her eyes

she wastes away her life
worrying on death
her breath is stale and dry

her brain's shaped like a maze
she worships and she prays
at an altar of mirrors

she'll make you fix her lunch
when she's already ate
then she'll throw it all away

my woman hates my guts
my woman hates my guts
she point it at my face
my woman hates my guts
she holds the can of mace

wolverines on fire
screaming in a choir
orbiting her mouth

all the birds have shed
all the birds fly south
but she's loading up her gun

my woman hates my guts
my woman hates my guts
she point it at my face
my woman hates my guts
she holds the can of mace

Nature Dot Com

feel the sun burn your skin
life simple once again
nature dot com
website tan
computer wonderland

fluorescent lights are out of sight
the glow of the moon illumes
no more distilled colognes
no more sneezing perfumes

binary joy, printer trees
breath floats the breeze
forest hair, sappy gel
swelling of your soul

bare feet on the ground
and your head in the clouds
you're sifting through the stars
no more the clogged highway ramps
no more the buzzing bars

blazing sun burns your skin
life simple once again
nature dot com
website tan
computer wonderland

New City Lights

the ground pulls us down and holds us heavy
we wait and watch the world
and this is what unfurled:
a crush of cars that pile upon the city
wheels still in spin
we watch the world begin
a show nightly never-ending
new city lights

old friends have fallen all far behind me
or are they far in front?
can't remember what they want
folding faces well fed and fancy
smile upon the slaves
digging their own graves
while fashion models dress like sid and nancy
new city lights

the spirit of the scene is on the sidewalks
pulsing passersby
footsteps full and spry
fading former lives have been abandoned
places present stay
while memories decay
we wave goodbye and watch them die forever
new city lights

New York Love

new york
late fall
early morning walking
sparks of snow
floating by the river
you took the world at ease
it didn't take much to please you then
now that feeling's gone
as the glowing star
burns away the dawn

i still feel the same
i look around
everything has changed

our flame is dead
no more the flashing brilliant ruby red
no more standing ten feet tall
instead
we'll raise a toast to the past
knowing nothing ever lasts
not even new york love

all this flesh will melt with the sun
but something else
lingers on
somewhere in your memory
cloudy thoughts of you and me and flying
time stops
bubbles burst
and you cannot quench your thirst by sighing

i still feel the same
i look around
everything has changed

our flame is dead
no more the flashing brilliant ruby red
no more standing ten feet tall
instead
we'll raise a toast to the past
knowing nothing ever lasts
not even new york love

No Time Big Time

I was a part-time small time
now i'm a no-time, big time
it was a hungry time
it was a drive-thru time
it was a thirsty time
it was a thirst quenched time
it was a gatorade-sponsorship time
it was a florida time
it was a a a a a a a time
it was a a a a a a time
it was a a a a a time
it was a a a a time
it was a a a time
it was a a time
it was a time
it was back on the wagon time.

i was a part-time small time
now i'm a no-time, big time
it was an empty time
it was an infinite time
it was the present time
it was nowhere time
it was all time
it was a stretched time
it was a a a a a a a time
it was a a a a a a time
it was a a a a a time
it was a a a a time
it was a a a time
it was a a time
it was a time
it was back on the wagon time

i was a part-time small time
now i'm a no-time, big time
it was a painful time
it was an advil time
it was a tylenol time
it was a migraine time
it was no more time
it was throw away your watch time
it was a a a a a a a time
it was a a a a a a time
it was a a a a a time
it was a a a a time
it was a a a time
it was a a time
it was a time
it was back on the wagon time

Nobody Knows

nobody knows how bill baird died
did his heart stop from some grief inside?
or was it murder in the first degree
that sent him off to eternity?

nobody knows his final words
he was alone when death occurred
and now he's crossing the great divide
besides our lord up in the sky

nobody knows who did the crime
but the police want someone to do the time
they think that i committed this wrong
because i sing about that boy in all my songs

nobody knows the proper way
the proper path to find out who's guilty
the police don't have a clue
and chances are, neither do you

Office Jerk

my coat's on fire
my tie's a noose
xeroxed my face
with a tardy excuse
drowned orca
20 minute bathroom break
watching tv with ricki lake
checked my email ten times yet

i'm an office jerk, an office jerk
i'll gopher get it for you
office jerk with office smirk
and orthopedic shoe

bartleby of modern day
would i prefer?
i'd rather not say
just watch me blend into the gray
that lines your cubicle so gay
and fancy
and free-range
sustainably harvested ennui

i'm an office jerk, an office jerk
i'll gopher get it for you
office jerk with office smirk
and orthopedic shoe

Oh Hi, Mr. Death

the stillness of midnight
crept under his covers
and shivered his skin
as he rose from his bed
there were visions of women
and visions of angels
his life but a weave and each memory a thread

oh hi, mister death
you've got very stale breath

a dream this must be
he spoke in a mumble
i see the abyss and he looks just like me
inside the dark figure, a mirror's reflection
a lifetime of what was and was not to be

oh hi, mister death
you smoke crystal meth
and scythe when you shave
when the world won't behave
you're rolling mothballs through old shopping malls

to everyone living, this fate is for certain
to everyone living, this fate has been sealed
i guess if you live life always to the fullest
to meet mister death, it won't be a big deal

oh hi, mister death
my name is bob smith

Old Growth

big ideas blowing in the breeze
dancing on the wind
the sky begins to sneeze
and wipes away all our technologies
old growth stands looking on

some girl's got her hair all in a mess
she's sprayed her hair like that
and moussed her hair like this
she's so concerned she's pulled out her hair with her fists
old growth stands looking on

the way of the wise is nice and slow
there's no need to hurry
you got nowhere to go
and if you do a few great things
you can put them on your tombstone
old growth stands looking on

Old Sandy Bull Lee

sandy lee, sandy lee
sip your sadness slow
we gave it to ourselves
i want no-one else to know
the ore in all the mountains
and fountains spurting gold
could not pull my heart away
it's yours it can't be sold
so move aside the mountains
fountains drain the shores
whiskey when i'm thirsty
excitement when i'm bored

sandy lee, sandy lee
my hairball's made a mess
it's tangled like a jungle
my barber's so depressed
i pull my hair in circles
tie my head in knots
thinking of the life we shared
the love that we forgot
we stopped eating candy
smiles and laughing ceased
and had serious discussions
about what we're going to eat

sandy lee, sandy lee
hold your head up high
when you die you will turn
to cosmic stardust in the sky
when you were a child running brave and free
that's how your world will be again
and that's where you'll find me
our love will feel new again
like when we first met
we'll laugh at silly things and share cigarettes
so tear up my ticket
melt it in the snow
the glow of your skin supplies
all i need to know

Option Paralysis

bottomless dumpster breakfast bar
pink mimosas and a candy car
sink to the bottom of the bottom of the end
emoji avatar of a very good friend

oh yeah / oh no
a blank stare
on hold

winking at the waitress
by the microwave
tried to tell the lady
that my heart is just a slave
to my stomach
and my stomach has gone to seed
chow my tofu baked bird seed

oh yeah / oh no
blank stare
on hold

won't grow up until i swallow what i hate
and i won't grow young until it's too late
and i won't grow tall that's just my fate
i'm the fish that got hooked but didn't take the bait

oh yeah / oh no
blank stare
on hold

options flood and drown our minds
you don't get to leave what you never left behind
to bake your cake and hate it too
transcend the scene
goodbye adieu

oh yeah / oh no
blank stare
on hold

Orca's Revenge

mutilate, must mutilate
mutilate, must mutilate
mutilate, must mutilate
gonna chomp his bones and lick my plate
mutilate, must mutilate
mutilate, must mutilate
mutilate, must mutilate
gonna chomp his bones and lick my plate

i ain't in the mood
for salad hippie food
i want a rare steak
of humanity's mistakes
i want it thick and raw
so pop it in my paw
enlarged brain apes
with opposable thumbs
will be my meal
won't even leave a crumb
they lock us up in cages
they lock us in a zoo
they locked up my cousin
his name was shamu
and from a fellow mammal?
a better treatment now
and if you don't respond
i'll make this chump my chow

mutilate, must mutilate
mutilate, must mutilate
mutilate, must mutilate
gonna chomp his bones and lick my plate
mutilate, must mutilate
mutilate, must mutilate
mutilate, must mutilate
gonna chomp his bones and lick my plate

captain brain led you astray
you've all lost your way
stopped listening to your heart
but it's far too late to start
my bib is on
my fork is out
i've got the salt and spice
so cease with the formalities
there's no need to be nice

Other Side of the Sky

deflated dreams dangle on the horizon
dust dissolves the vacant faces scene
the sun gives up its glow
the moon is rising
you fall into the sky
oh, the freedom for to fly

winds whip across the static figures
i stood my ground until i blew away
burst into a thousand tiny fissures
but i didn't mind to die
in the freedom for to fly

wave the world goodbye
i'll see you on the other side of the sky

in thin upper air
my life it vanished
thrown to the winds like dormant seeds
amber tinted aether
i was banished
the view from on high
was the freedom for to fly

and now my life's a billion shiny glimmers
up and up and up and still no fall
swallowed by the stars
my body shimmers
and i know i'll never die
in the freedom for to fly

wave the world goodbye
i'll see you on the other side of the sky

Our Dreams Did Weave a Shade

like love letters written in the snow
that thaw away before you even know
you and i
framed by a dying sun
the one you thought i'd be
we'd set each other free
mountain morning greet the day
you wanted to leave and i wanted to stay
and our tongues did tie a dozen knots
and our love we left to rot
back in our ancient history

but when our dreams did weave a shade
we lived outside of time
and when our dreams did weave a shade
mine was yours was mine

molding million dollar bills swim in your eyes
and your mouth
out they spill
you're speaking in a foreign tongue
your younger dreams have died
and your photos won't remind you
time has blurred all the details from your face
you can recall that you've traveled
but you can't recall the place
but a lie can still say what is true
and if i find fault with you
i'm only looking at myself

and when our dreams did weave a shade
we lived outside of time
and when our dreams did weave a shade
mine was yours was mine

Ouroboros Shoes

ouraboros shoes walk across the floor
whatever path you choose
you've been there before
i have always walked here before
ouraboros shoes
i've walked here before

fire station's flames glow the city sky
no-one snuffed it out
no-on even tried
i have always walked here before
ouraboros shoes
i've walked here before

as it is beneath, so it is above
the person that you hate is the person that you love
i have always walked here before
ouraboros shoes
i've walked here before

copyrighted laws on erasable sheets
lonely plastic love
supermarket meat
i have always walked here before
ouraboros shoes
i've walked here before

soldiers burning flags just to keep warm
chilly underneath their tattered uniforms
i have always walked here before
ouraboros shoes
i've walked here before

long life running in place
you ask me how i'm doing
just look at my face
i have always walked here before
ouraboros shoes
i've walked here before

chasing the head that's chasing the whale
it's herman melville swallowed by a whale
i have always walked here before
ouraboros shoes
i've walked here before

Pain Pile

inside out and bent in awkward ways
you give the world your grief
but that won't make it go away
and the answers in a book
aint worth your while
just leave your pain with me
i'll put it in my pile

the load you lug around
must do exhaust
but now and then you find a friend
upon whom you can toss
another heartbreak ready for to file
leave your pain with me
i'll put it in my pile

roads merge
and roads they do divide
*but even when you're not with me
you're always by my side*
so go away
that always was your style
and leave your pain with me
i'll put it in my pile

Party Party Party

party party party!
with infinity!
party with infinity!

the infinite has a definite place
it's all around us, check your face
check your legs and check your socks
check your dirt and check your rocks
it's everything there and nothing that's not
it's the kettle that calls a pot
that calls the pan
that calls the spoon
that calls the sun
that calls the moon
endless ocean, all adrift
unfurl your sails and
grind your grift
infinite ocean, we sailors all
we're lost at sea
so let's have a ball

party party party!
with infinity!
party with infinity!

the glowing ball of which we glide
is like a cosmic water slide
you lose control and slide away
won't help to plead, won't help to pray
won't help to build some statue, twit
won't help to build an ugly piece of shit
accept your fate and then you'll see
muzak of the spheres
will set you free

party party party!
with infinity!
party with infinity!

Pizza Man in the Sky

i ordered it at 2 o'clock
still ain't yet arrived
pizza man said half an hour
and it's 2 past 5
truth is like that pizza
it too never comes
and when it does it's hard and cold
and sticks to your gums

oh pizza man in the sky, show your face
oh truth is like that pizza
can't find it anyplace

if wonder if the televangelist
knows where my pizza's gone
he claims to have the answers
so i got him on the phone
operator said she'd pray for me
and then my pizza'd come
but i didn't have a credit card
and she hung up the phone
oh pizza man in the sky, show your face
oh truth is like that pizza
can't find it anyplace

now the clock's chiming six
my pizza's finally here
it ain't like i expected
the cheese is crystal clear
the pepperonis look like jesus
the olives like black holes
the crust smiles like the buddha
but the delivery man wants my soul
twas satan brought the pizza
and now's on my door stoop
on his leash is an a&r record exec
and they're wearing rayon suits
they wanted me on mtv
to lip sync and other things
so i slammed the door
and grabbed the phone and ordered chicken wings

oh chicken wing in the sky
fly me away
truth is like takeout food
to get it, you gotta pay

Pocketful Of Debt

ran away from myself again
convinced that my shadow was not my friend
so i bathed in a light that i knew
would have to end
took off down a rosy colored road
but wintertime came and my feet grew cold
i caught my breath and discovered
i'd gotten old

oh, time hurries on
even while you're gone
and the road you travel on
takes you back to where you've left
with a broken smile and a pocketful of debt

so it's back to the world that you've spurned
and it's difficult to say just what you've learned
there's a car in the drive with two blown tires
and a transmission burned
but i'd like to believe in a logic behind this mess
cuz when there's nothing left to prove
and nobody to impress
i'm so overwhelmed by the beauty of the world
that i get depressed

oh, time hurries on
even while you're gone
and the road you travel on
takes you back to where you've left
with a broken smile and a pocketful of debt

Prometheus' Lament

the birds are so beautiful
the sun looks so splendid
the world is beautiful
too bad the vultures picked out my eyes and i can't see

oh the sound of music
so beautiful
worth living for
too bad the vultures came down and picked out my eardrums

i once had a woman
but the vultures

they
came
down
and
they
picked
her
up
too

Quicksilver Slip

your frozen mind
though still, can't stay
everything you know will melt away
fixed in its place
all facts inside
if it don't already exist, it gets denied

holding on too tightly is how you lose your grip
learn to take life lightly
and let the changes slip away from you

cold to the touch
with dazzling sparks
someday your frozen shine
will warm to dark
the melting forms
of which you'd fixed
clatter to the ground like frozen sticks

holding on too tightly
is how you lose your grip
learn to take life lightly
and let the changes slip away from you

someday my friend
you wait and see
someday you will sing this song to me
we all must fall
we all must fail
and face up to the fear
that keeps us jailed

holding on too tightly is how you lose your grip
learn to take life lightly
and let the changes slip away from you

Rainbow Brain

rainbow brain
color my fancy
plant a tree
call her nancy
but her name is ruth
color me red
color me bad
oh, bill is dead

cutting off fingers
putting in pockets
keep them out electric sockets
fries your head
an onion blooms
peel the layers
clean your room

every color
rainbow brain
every color
gone insane
every color
there was before
noone's normal
any more

rainbow brain
color my feelings
plant your feet upon the ceiling
seed of sorrow
seeds of joy
it's sensimilla, silly boy
color me happy
color me sad
color me grateful
color me glad
colors rain down in vice and virtue
rainbow's rays shine through and search you

every color
rainbow brain
every color
gone insane
every color
there was before
noone's normal
any more

Rebel Without a Brain

rebel without a brain
drank all of his wine from the drain
his mind it won't change
his mind it won't change but change is always the same
burned down was the best it could be
you're snoring inside of your dreams
and talk to yourself as if three
years younger than when you were three

oh rubber rebel
you're the one that i see
every time
the mirror looks just like me

rebel with nothing to shred
guitars with strings made of lead
whose whammy bar phones all rang dial tones
you shaved away all your shred
the snores were as loud as a scream
torn from old magazines
with pictures enclosed of how you would pose
when faced with what you can't see

oh rubber rebel
you're the one that i see
every time
the mirror looks just like me

with so many changes in store
please peel yourself off of the floor
the world needs you now
no need to know how
you're already fighting the war

rebel without a brain
drank all of his wine from the drain
his mind it won't change
his mind it won't change but change is always the same
change is always the same
change is always the same
change is always the same
change is always the same
change is always the same
change is always the same
change is always the same
change is always the same
change is always the same
change is always the same
change is always the same

Reclining in my Easy Chair

my dreams do awake and they whisper me to rise
but between the time that i dream and open up my eyes
i'm caught between all that is past and that which will
reclining in my easy chair while all the world is still

i'm inside of my empty and wanting for to rest
with no-one there to cuss or care and no-one to impress
wading in the waters of the soul i try to fill
reclining in my easy chair while all the world is still

the ticking gauges seconds and time it slowly cools
and it's hard to tell the self-proclaimed prophets from the fools
they both speak none at all or both beyond my fill
reclining in my easy chair while all the world is still

but i can't pretend i'm unique when my pieces dwell in peace
my neighbor's father's mother's son, he has his hole to teach
i learn from my emptiness, the joy in which to fill
reclining in my easy chair while all the world is still

and i lept from the fire and on water do i walk
flashing floods of light to you each time that i talk
i stepped right through the mirror
another side of bill
reclining in my easy chair while all the world is still

Ride the Toxic Wave

bright fluorescent smile job
your face frozen that way
a flame lit light bulb
forever happy stay

my body is temple
but the building's been condemned
I feast free samples
and smoke outside the gym

ride the toxic wave
exotic oil spillage in my vacation village
ride the toxic wave
exotic oil spillage in my vacation village

I know what i'm doing
I don't know what to do
steadily unscrewing all the cages in my zoo
zookeepers snort cocaine
and a blood bath ensues

ride the toxic wave
exotic oil spillage in my vacation village
ride the toxic wave
exotic oil spillage in my vacation village

Robot Dan

(robot voice)
feeling vulnerable right
must be efficient in workplace
must hit happy hour right at 5 o'clock
oh fuck
oh fuck
will not hit happy hour right at 5 o'clock
now i will not be happy

binary bipolar schizoid man
he's got it figured out
he's got a plan
robot dan.

hard working
fun loving
modern guy
highly efficient
his martini dry
robot dan.

programmed to smile
for photo time
he schedules his fun
starting at 5
wireless consciousness empathy
he's got it on the wall
his college degree
robot dan.

robot dan robot dan
my dear dear dan robot dan
too much information
does not compute does not computedoes not computedoes not computedoes not computedoes not computedoes not computedoes not computedoes not computedoes not computedoes not computedoes not computedoes not compute
head would errorhead would errorhead would errorhead would errorhead would errorhead would errorhead would errorhead would errorhead would errorhead would errorhead would errorhead would errorhead would error

Rot Down Cellar

rot down cellar's burning up
in decrepit flame
i've tried enough to strengthen it
but it crumbles just the same
oh i've tried
to the best of my ability
to stumble up
the splinters and the shears
but you take one look
and my frame is cracked
i strut in to meet you
and i stumble out the back

the bit inside, it's welling up
the bottle's my best pal
it drizzles down drop by drop
and i forget you for awhile
oh the hazy mutters come and go so constantly
and my empty wishes left me no more to char
your head leaks words
for all to gnaw
i can't do nothing but sit and spit
chatting with my dog

wind swirl burns
your face soon turns
and shrivels to forget
some other to abuse me
someone to be my pet
oh girl
i guess you lost your chance to be with me
so i'ld best be moving down the line
i'm done with girls now
or so it seems
tired of punches in the face
the kicking and the screams
for a little while

Sally's Lament (plain spoken verse)

to those on the land you yearn for the deep
soon point to darkness as a veil for your sleep
for nothing's revealed, tis not already there
and truth exists on both sides of the mirror
the left and right, the light and dark
cannot distinguish, can't tell them apart
but warnings to heed, of these i have one
beware the brain who hides from the sun

they never hear, they never see
the only one who knows is me
the only one who knows is me
a curse it is, a curse to be
a forward sight always to see
darkened veil lifted but to me
the future's now and so i say
there's no escape, not any way
so next time careful what ye choose
go on a carnival cruise!
but wait
no next time will there be
just ranch dressing, nightmares and agony
no known words may yet have been said
to change the past or raise the dead
but still i feel my duty true
to comment and assess for you
three bozos aboard a brain
each dead in heaping spoonfuls of pain
no shame to say the world cares not
about those boys and what they got
their hearts were cold and brains filled with snot
and to each of us perhaps we die in kind
to die of ignorance
fear
or too many return trips to the luby's buffet line
to pit heart against brain
or be seduced when ugly girls call our names
one cannot escape the blob
the blob pervades all and everyone
we are all merely droplets and runoff from the blob's haircut
as for me, i have plans
maybe des moines, maybe japan
maybe work for merrill lynch
with my powers of sight it'd be a cinch
i leave you now
for not for in time
this spring break of the soul will be yours as surely as mine

Sampson

i hop in the shower
i wash my hair
like sampson, my hair brings me power
superhuman hair lifts the phone
to call my boss
"i'm staying home"

i am sampson
i have super-hair
i have come to style the world

brush my hair
to swirling sands
timeless flow
mindless blowdry man
nevermind what isn't even there
wear a wig if you must
but trust, it won't repair

i am sampson
i have super-hair
i have come to style the world

Sandy my Love

paler than a bone bleaching itself white
darker than the bottom of the ocean
my tangled brain is torn
between day and night
and between thoughts and words
it's all distortion

oh sandy my love
your image is a force
that keeps me a-moving through the darkness

in every leaf of every tree
in every sandwich served to me
and every word of poetry
i'll see your likeness

Santa Claus of the South

agitated larry can't figure it out
he signed up for a pleasure cruise
but instead got fear and doubt
santa of the south
drops a smile into his mouth

gary happy won't raise his toast
the brochure promised pretty women
but hairy sally's gross
santa of the south
drops a smile into his mouth

stagnant stan won't lift a hand
to help a brother out
slumped there in his captain's chair
he can't slouch his way out
santa of the south
drops a smile into his mouth

Sewage Sirens

golden voice like the throat of god
that's gargling gold
but don't it seem odd
that voice of which nothing can compare
emanates from that toxic sewage whirlpool over there

sewage sirens sing
like mozart got the stink
sewage sirens sing
a jazzy stench and the smell they bring

like putrefied butter melting in your ears
drips down your cheeks and mingles with your tears
the beauty and pain together they go
like a boxing glove shaped like marilyn monroe

you know that its death
you know that it smells
but the sounds just suit you
what the hell

so pinch your nose and unclose your ears
is it the smell or the beauty that's bringing those tears?

sewage sirens sing
like mozart got the stink
sewage sirens sing
a jazzy stench and the smell they bring

Shape Shifting Game

is it strange when old friends faces change?
the facades of their faces all crack
what you loved was only projection
a reflection of all that you lacked
when the features they falter and fade
and leave a blank empty need
you fill the hole the best that you can
with therapy, whiskey or weed

quicksand foundations
with lovers engraved by their names
rearrange letters
swap all the faces
we call it the shapeshifting game

in time the images blur
even the pictures you framed
and the words and ideas you cherished
even they too do the same
for in the beginning of who knows when
when all thoughts and forms were first laid
it all got tossed in a salad bar cosmos
a never-ending buffet
time it has no beginning
no conclusions neither will come
the speed of life's endless treadmill
is the speed at which you have run

quicksand foundations
with lovers engraved by their names
rearrange letters
swap all the faces
we call it the shapeshifting game

Shave

between my legs
it's of no use
the jaws of death
won't cut you loose
my love life, you see, just can't be saved
at least until i take a shave

hairy sally
hairy sally

don't think about the past
time is a sea
try not to repeat yourself
time is a sea
someday you will learn to surf
and that day you shall be free
freedom freedom freedom

She Dreams in Diamonds

she dreams in diamonds
that carve all the stars up from ash
she finds future saints in the peeling of the paint
and the beauty and the grace
misplaced to languish in the trash

she knows how to own me
not one word need she speak
and when my family has disowned me
she shows me the hope at the end of my rope
and the beauty of being a freak

she dreams in diamonds
each day an adventure to be claimed
she speaks in silence
and lifts not a hand but the world she commands
the winds all whispering her name

i know i'll never own her
i know she must be set free
if she ever needs, my life i'd concede
but she laughs at this myth of the savior monolith
that's so 20th century

Skull Castle Decorator

sad eyed man in a black t shirt
making music for his work
and he can't stand the sunshine
skull castle decorator

telephones are stapled to the ground
he picks it up
when it doesn't make a sound
skull castle decorator

and the warning signs groan
that moan in his throat
he's swimming in the moat
skull castle decorator

and the warning signs groan
that moan in your throat
you're swimming in the moat
skull castle decorator

Sleepwalking Someday

wake up with a shaky hand
squinting through a mist
try to shake this dream away
but it's memory persists

empty headed half moon bake
grab me by the shirt and shake
this lethargy away
(that i can't escape)
sleepwalking someday

knowledge of the night before
has not occurred to me
messy headed morning breath
please brew me up some tea

empty headed half moon bake
grab me by the shirt and shake
this lethargy away
(that i can't escape)
sleepwalking someday

Slip into Shadow

fear not the end
old friend
bent light grows late
and curves to straight
all clocks now wait
slip into shadow

the end is cold
or so i'm told
bold days of yore
a boring fade into the shade
slip into shadow

fanfares don't wait
a silent space
a state of grace
no warmth nor cold
no young or old
slip into shadow

Slow Motion Silver Skies

she walked into the room
regarded him in sorrow
the man she used to know
would never beg or borrow
the words he used to say
echoed back against her
they'd take a walk outside
and he'd point his finger skyward

slow motion silver skies
the moon shines bright
and away we will fly

these memories of gold
outline dipped in shadow
now burn through her mind
the flames and the tallow
the music of the spheres
the sun can float but never fly
the moon has come and gone
but she still remembers

slow motion silver skies
the moon shines bright
and away we will fly

Slug

they roll out the carpet
for the blood soon hits the floor
flowers dying blindly
would you kindly close the door?
clumsy boxers slugging
ali is on the throne
vendors selling postcards
& butchers selling bones
when you wake up from these nightmares
and find yourself alone
slug away your grin
and punch into your phone
did it ever sink in that
you're just reaping what you've sown?

slug away
slug away
you are what is, they say

slug away
slug away
you are what is, they say

the boxing match it matters not
to those outside the ring
but to those inside the struggle's real
the fight is everything
to those outside it's showbiz
a glittery charade
forget those folks and duke it out
the fight is where life's made

so with the gloves you're given
to the fight you go
the punches from left and right
from on high and down low
life will pummel deeply
those with can't adjust
so dance across the ring i say
before you're punched to dust

slug away
slug away
you are what is, they say

slug away
slug away
you are what is, they say

Slump City

slump through the city
like a one eyed skunk
getting drunk
on the fumes
pale perfumes

slump through the city
in line to stand
stamp your hand
branding hot
cattle clot

half inflated by the motion
of the world always in rush
push push push
alarm bells ring to corpses
crawling cars all in a crush
push push push

slump through the city
like a wounded prey
braying beast
burden feast
at least you got a job

slump through the city
like a whack a mole
roles to play
smiles to pay
toll booth yawn

slump through the city
on a phantom leg
pregnant pause
giving birth

slump through the city
you shirk your mirth
a dearth of life
door to door
run some more

waiting on the world of justice
but that show was fake
my mistake
what's the worth of whining, waitress?
when there ain't no plates
our mistake

slump through the city

we grit and bear
hold your chair
shakedown comes
crown the dunce

slump through the city
we do our best
it's not enough
stuff the box
ballot toss

slump through the city
we grit and bear
hold your chair
shakedown comes
crown the dunce

slump through the city
we do our best
it's not enough
stuff the box
ballot toss

Smoked by the Sun

hazy daisy got lost up in a cloud
meanwhile back on earth the world screams loud
her mirror frames a perfect 60's scene
and the road to wisdom's lined with rice and beans

smiling vacantly with eyes that cannot see
i hate to say
but you've been smoked too long by the sun
everything is not "all good"
your wooden head needs it understood
i hate to say
but you've been smoked too long by the sun

with your head so high
does it ever get hard to breathe?
do only attempt
what you know you can achieve?
are you smarter than you look?
is it all worked out?
405 figure 8
la roundabout

smiling vacantly
with eyes that cannot see
i hate to say
but you've been smoked too long by the sun
everything is not "all good"
your wooden head needs it understood
i hate to say
but you've been smoked too long by the sun

you're busy living someone else's lie
but someday the charade will end
yes someday you will die
you'll be reborn as yourself
but be confused
what were the thoughts i thunk?
what words did i use?
yes, in the end we all must stand alone
so on second thought
please pass that number
everyone get stoned

smiling vacantly
our eyes that cannot see
you and i
we've been smoked by the sun
everything is "all good"
our wooden heads make it understood
you and i we've been smoked by the sun

Smoking Crack ain't all it's Cracked up to Be / Peace Love and Crystal Meth

sun reflecting garbage pail
mind mixed up mind, its bound to fail
so you walk these streets
your eyes in flame looking for a pipin game
of game show distraction and empathy contraction
resolving to a world that has no compassion

but smoking crack ain't all that it's cracked up to be
you stare at a clock and
gnash your teeth an inch from your tv

you're smoking paint, you're smoking dirt
you're pale and faint, your eyeballs hurt
you're snorting dirt, you're snorting cheese
exhaling life, sniffing the breeze
the fumes of failure factories
holy apostles left to sneeze
outside the walls of sanity
modern life's a walled enclosure
nobody gets through
you pay to play or play the game
where he looks just like you
you navigate the chasms whose cracks become your power
but life indeed is a plant you seed so no need to pluck the flower
smoking crack ain't all that it's cracked up to be
you stare at a clock and gnash your teeth
an inch from your tv

(Peace Love and Crystal Meth)
My socks are torn and tattered, no shoes upon my feet
mumbling, drunken, unaware, sleeping in the street
Drainage pipes and pigeon feed, Dining trailer trash
Giblets, doggie biscuits, a slip n slide rash
Fast food storms and buckets, Inciting nutrasweet
I shaved a chicken nugget, I velcroed up my feet

Peace, love, crystal meth,   that's all
Peace love, garlic breath,   let's have a ball

Aqua socks and sirloin jocks Are jacking up their tires
With the Headlights pointed straight ahead To Bust the chicken wire
the Mupflaps sighin in the breeze The Engine's running blazed
Dead grass and coaching shorts, The summer season plague

Fast food storm and buckets Inciting nutrasweet
I shaved a chicken nugget, I velcroed up my feet

My beauty's in the laundry And My bucket's full of beer
So I wave my wand and dress up pimp
Pretend I'm richard gere
Then A loss of concentration Over Ritalin and dice
I'm Gamblin for salvation I drank it once or twice

So Long, Farewell, Adieu

the time has come for us to disappear
so long farewell adieu
it's closing time so finish up your beer
so long farewell adieu
where did you buy that wig my dear?
so long farewell adieu
when you're fast asleep a car is hard to steer
so long farewell adieu
parting could be such sorrow
bye bye bye bye bye bye
but we'll be back at another bar tomorrow

So Says Me

dressed as a shadow
you slip behind the image of yourself
impressing all your friends
with the smile you keep so shiny on the shelf
fashionably frayed and distressed
bohemian if only in your dress
thread through your fashion and be free
so says me

you've nailed down the boundaries
that help you define what is real
surrounded on all sides
by the guilt that reminds you how to feel
fashionably frayed and disturbed
repeating things you've never even heard
stray from the fray and be free
so says me

with your mirrored fists enclenched
you're swinging at yourself and i know why
you abandoned your dreams
and everything you loved became a lie
fashionably ready for a fight
spilled milk inside a sea of white
step through the mirror and be free
i told me

Social Swamp Quicksand Screen

shaking hands until my grip is sore
"pleased to meet you"
"pleased to meet me"
let's mingle some more

debutante catalog
so many there to choose
high speed society
oh where's the button snooze?

hold it all inside my skull
sometimes i sit and hold my breath
and wish my life weren't dull

staring at the floor
dirties up my clothes
laundry ladies laugh at me
turning off their nose
dragging down the street
my smile's a plastic shell
drive thru dog food at taco bell

hold it all inside my skull
sometimes i sit and hold my breath
and wish my life were dull
gee you're dull

social swamp quicksand screen
social swamp collapsing into dream
hold it all inside my brain
sometimes i sit and wonder
is it me or them who's gone insane?

in the end i must admit
i always play my role
forest hair and photo smile
hold it hold it hold it hold it
ok now just let it go
as if it wasn't there
the party rages all around me
i don't even care

hold it all inside my skull
sometimes i sit and hold my breath
and wish my life were dull
social swamp quicksand screen
social swamp collapsing into dream
hold it all inside my brain
sometimes i sit and wonder is it me or them who's gone insane

Soggy Soul

stare out blank and i wonder why
but my mind just can't replace
what frozen brown clump of dirt now stands there?
it's my face
i want to live beyond myself
but i fall farther in the hole
gotta stick my heart in a microwave
and drain this soggy soul

so i drive my car around all day
listen to books on tape
beowulf by seamus heaney
my mind tries to escape
but in the end i come to myself
and drive into a toll
gotta ditch this car, ditch this dark
and thaw my frozen soul

bundled tight and feeling fright
not ready nor steady to go
gotta keep my head in a better place
gotta steady up nice and slow
i know that things could be much better
and i really do want to change
gotta stick my heart in a microwave
and thaw away the drain on a soggy soul

Somebody's Looking Out for You
(rejected jingle for Goodyear Tires)

you wish that you could speak
you wish that you could say
but the words just get in the way

just outside your grasp
you're too afraid to ask
your dreams seem to pass you by

but then it all starts changing
your dreams are coming true
the world is rearranging
somebody's looking out for you

Song from a Dream

i met myself in a dream
i shook the strangers hand
he tried to tell me where i was
i didn't understand
he led me to the forest
i drank there from a stream
i drank water from the stranger's mouth
he turned to steam

make the choice
where will you go when you die?
heading down below or up into the sky?
or you goin to mecca
or will you be a ghost
trying to resolve the things on earth
that bothered you the most
are you going back to brahmin
the source of all this world
or will you be reborn?
another life unfurled

Sound in your Mind

we hum it
we strum it
we tap our feet in time
we draw it
we saw it
we reason out our rhyme

the notes we play may well be paint
it's all the same inside
our harmonies show no restraint
and keep you satisfied

the sound in your mind
is the first sound
that you could sing
if you were singing
alone at night
don't got a light
just close your ears
see what you hear

creation
is beauty
is love
and love is all
we feel it's our duty
to write upon the walls

the secret songs within our heads
are here for you to hear
if you tune in with the music
you'll overcome your fears

the sound in your mind
is the first sound
that you could sing
if you were singing
alone at night
don't got a light
just close your ears
see what you hear

the sound in your mind
is the first sound
that you could hear
if you were hearing
alone at night
don't got a light
just close your eyes
surprise

Special K Hole

special k, it's ok
special k, it's ok
special k, it's ok
special k, it's ok

wake and wipe your sleep aside
and crawl your k hole screen
bonehead brunch
you launch your lunch
with hands all gloved and green
special k, it's ok
special k, it's ok

fucked up face and twisted tongue
tonight i'll sit and drool
alarm bouncing 6 o clock
let's drop the kids at school
special k, it's ok
special k, it's ok

swimming in my sadness
but it's hue's a pleasant brown
no shoes, no nose, no makeup with
but still a silly clown
i lost the one who loved me
oh
i threw her in the trash
no dumpster dive can save me now
my happiness has past
special k, it's ok
special k, it's ok

Spreadsheet Star Charts

map me from the muck and mire of earth
get me to the stars see what i'm worth
inflate my aura sonic stage with a bill to bite
we turn the page to my proper place among among the
egos floating free like vapid vapors from a toxic sea
and the only thing i want to be
is a plastic statue dripping with dumb fun streamer glory
spreadsheet star charts

hotshot dipshit astroturf parade
plug the grass the switch hit for to fade
celestial lawn and cosmic pool
i filled with all my fanboy drool
ruptured air which which to spool the
spoiled lives of rockstar fools
spreadsheet star charts

ashen baby lazarus be me
never not a negative decree
dumpster diving and i'm dressed in duds
and i'm done with crawling through the mud
and upon this rocket i shall ride
with its engine fueled by the years denied
my proper place amongst the aether
dance with zeus and i dine with demeter
spreadsheet star charts

Spring Break of the Soul

strangled by the heat
we crawled across the sun
tanning butter
human toast
vacation had begun
spring break of the soul
sing a golden tongue
you're late
you're tardy
you're absent
expelled, expelled, expelled

bikinis on the bounce
goggles set to stun
snorkeling with moses and surfing algae scum
margaritaville suburbs, subdivided fun
let's party, let's party, let's party

pale face melts away
passed out on the pier
wet bar
sloppy talk
oops i spilled my beer
dune buggy moto-cross
drove into a deer
what's a deer doing on spring spring break?

duel vocals:
(part one, sung by the narrator)
don't think about the past, time is a sea
try not to repeat yourself, time is a sea
all your deeds will ripple out and be lost eventually
someday you will learn to surf and that day you shall be free
freedom freedom freedom freedom

(other part, sung simultaneously, by the three morons)
crowded floor to sleep, carpet burning scab
woke up in a heap, larry paid my tab
mousy micky's forty ounce, rippling piles of flab
santa claus of the south gives the gift of gab
blah blah, blah blah, blah blah, blah blah

ten meter nosedive
into an empty life
belly flopping into shape
this mass of hair and strife
and when the party's over
i'll find a shapely wife
happily ever after
amen amen amen amen

Square Dance

come on and square your dance
erase away your pencil pants
come on and square your dance
my hexagon head awaits the chance.

circle walk and circle talk
do runaround for me
needlessly ignoring your square shaped key
the shape of the world
is the shape of your soul
so embrace the uncertainty
and gain control

euclidean endorsements
in trophies 4d
rhom bi cosi do deca hedron whee
lemniscate your figure eight
spheroid to oblate
archimedes on a double date
to polygon investigate

come on and square your dance
erase away your pencil pants
come on and square your dance
my hexagon head awaits the chance.

annulus to ring with no simple words to sing
all the shapes of the faces
and the days may bring
you'll never hold them all
dodecahedron mall
is a short measurement
from your square dance stall.

come on and square your dance
erase away your pencil pants
come on and square your dance
my hexagon head awaits the chance.

everything is arbitrary
chaos to a name
an artifical construct of the human game
imposing straight lines over a chaos frame
an artificial construct of the human game
imposing squares on places
find in clouds the faces
but nature has no lines of straight
toroid bent in figure 8
dissolves away our silly frame

the nature of the human game

illusions of control
cannot hold the void
transcend this circumstance
you silly human
dance

is it all free will or is it all just chance?
transcend the whole question
you silly human
dance

illusions of control
cannot hold the void
transcend this circumstance
you silly human
dance

is it all free will or is it all just chance?
transcend the whole question
you silly human
dance

St John's Wort Blues

name-tag says chad
every morning
blizzard of st john's wort capsules
need to decide which frozen meal to defrost later
blind white legs
gut stump
marlon brando and jimmy dean
eating sausage in a limousine
pull your pants up
pull your wig on by your bootstraps
dog skin wig
vapor wicking workout pie
serenity shoe filled with garbage
my pants are a desperate cry for help
and this song is a desperate cry for hump
it's not just a lifestyle
it's not just the leather pants
it's not just the hoop earring
it's not just the other hoop earring
it's being depressed

Stan is Dead

stan is dead
stan is dead
he melted to a mush on the deck
and you put him in the freezer
you'd have a stan popsicle
so gross, so sick
does this boat have a barf bag?

ah yes, here's the barf bag now
it's shaped like the void
into it i spew my chow
to permanently avoid

stan represents every man
stagnant in the extreme
satisfied, mediocre
never chased his dream

he's working for another man
a life forced to accept
but rather than resist
he learned to love his cage
and projected his witheld rage
on the scenes of the stage

here we are!

all the world'd a stage indeed
and stan a player, bit
cast into the world it seems
an motivated twit

so to his end, let us now know
and to his end, let us now see
perhaps your world will work out best
if you dissolve your apathy

Stingk

tantric tights
glassy eyes
jazzy grin
reclining lion in his den
ebbing smooth skin
clutching the mane
flowing precious blonde locks
fretless bass

ebony and ivory
it sustains for days
bibb lettuce on my chiseled chin
should i grow a mustache?
no

gotta stop by randall's to get some eggs
my name is stingk, my name is stingk.

keeping it real, it's in my contract
i'm contractually obligated
talk to my stan, he's my lawyer
look at that leg
shake that leg, stan!

preening paws
lick my chops
my wife keeps calling me
to pick her up from soccer

me and elvis costello
we got us a new career
singing bing crosby
summer in the dumpster
my name is stingk, my name is stingk.

i'm no hero
look at my skin tone
it's called pantone
my therapist says i'm doing better
i've learned how to snowboard and i'm cooking more
started on the treadmill (check this out)
intra-mural volleyball and pints at zax

Summer is Gone

summer is gone
the world is on fire
river's run its banks
the flames grow higher
but you and me
we feel
free

the world screams and shouts
the world curses fate
progress dissolves
the news screams too late
but you and me
we feel
free

never again
nothing can stay
if the world's ending now
that's ok
cuz you and me
we feel
free

Sunset's Bathtime

side by side
with empty hands
we rise above
these crowded lands
with nothing to hold us down this time
walking where the sea
dissolves into the sky

sunsets we find
and dive inside
come back in flames
to torch the cars we drive
and all outside
the sky keeps flashing

and as the sun dies
it's rays multiply

sunset's bathtime
sunset
goodnight
sunset's bathtime
sunset
goodnight
sunset's bathtime
sunset
goodnight
sunset's bathtime
sunset
goodnight
sunset's bathtime
sunset
goodnight
sunset's bathtime
sunset
goodnight

Sunshine Hair

sunshine hair
wrap me in the warmth of your glow
you tear me to shreds
remind me what i already know
together warm
alone i'm cold

sunshine hair
holds me to the bleeding of my heart
you tear me apart
then put me back together whole

a decent man
tripping on the traces of our past
moving fast
denying what i already know
together warm
alone i'm cold

sunshine hair
your presence put the sun all back inside
and the life that died
resurrected, didn't even try.
you stand beyond
my bitterness and fear
forever gone

Swirling Down the Drain

echoed glass again
as all my former friends
are stumbling out the door
of my mind forevermore

we each outlived a dream
and woke up bored and clean
every day mundane
old dreams go down the drain

so pour me one more wish
before these dirty dishes
wishes of my mind and brain
go swirling down the drain

Symphony Sunrise

fists full of fire
cold ashes that i rose
i lashed out at the world
the boy outgrew his clothes
but in my rush to tear apart
hypocrisy's disguise
i forgot to look up and see
the symphony sunrise

i tore at all foundations
and tore out all the walls
rip it down man
tear it down
and let the old ways fall
but bathwater's baby tossed informed me
with its cries
my rush to be reborn denied
the symphony sunrise

knelt down to the new
i covered both my ears
and waited for the sound inside
that only i could hear
but every note that floated forth
oh much to my surprise
was a pale imitation of
the symphony sunrise

so i'm back where i started
the old became the new
the upstart has departed
all the worlds he wished were true
but one thing i can now enjoy
with no need to criticize
is the simple easy beauty of
the symphony sunrise

Talking Convict Life Story Blues

i grew up on a farm
and i lived with my aunts
they told me i's a future convict
just waiting for a chance
to get thrown into prison
and lead a life of vice
and they kicked me out the door
and they double-locked it twice
as i stumbled down the road with my suitcase in hand
my aunts stepped onto the porch to bid me farewell
and they said
"goodbye nephew, goodbye you little rat
you go on and make your way
and don't be coming back
except in, oh, bout 50 years
we'll want to see you then
to see you got no tattoos and stayed out of the pen"

and so i dragged myself way out west
sticking out my thumb
i avoided confrontations
just by playing dumb
i landed down in la and crashed on someone's floor
when the cops arrived
my host claimed we'd never met before
(oops)
well, they took me to trial
booked me for breaking and entering
and using somebody's sleeping bag without their permission
sentenced me to 5 years in the la county pen
when the trial ended, they called me forward and asked if i'd anything to say
i played em a verse of the song i'd written that very day
and it went like so....
goodbye wanderlust, goodbye open skies
goodbye to the mini-skirts that opened up my eyes
goodbye happiness, goodbye hitching cars
i broke into a stranger's home and a world of iron bars

well i spent two years in prison
got let out on parole
and i went to go celebrate at a pub
just down the road
i refused to chug when a cop walked up and said
"you're drinking too slow!"
i dropped my pants and he got the chance
to kiss my ass hello
(whoa)
well, it goes without saying that they arrested me, called me scum,
and they trumped up a few more charges
cuz they didn't like the sight of me bum.
called me a rabble rouser, a democrat,

a consumer products advocate,
a feeder of the homeless
a domer of the domeless
a comber of the hairless
a wearer of bad fashion
a cold fish in ways of passion
a empty vessel in which to stash in
their flaming dumptruck crashing
a man of the people, in short
and the cops said
"say goodbye to blue skies and goodbye sassafras
say goodbye to freedom and goodbye to your ass
say goodbye to the beer bars that helped you so unwind
you've gone and found yourself another kind"

so then i was back in prison
my sentence fifty years
stuck there until i's old
and all dried up of tears
i got out and went to find my aunts
and called them both liars
i yelled at their tombstones and
then i retired
time to leave, i do believe
and i said
"goodbye huntsville hello miami beach
goodbye prison uniform
hello bikini briefs
farewell to the convicts still in the prison's reach
and hello to the cuban rafts a landing on the beach"

and on that beach i looked around
and found a woman fair
i figured it's time to settle down
so i proposed to her right there
she said yes and took my hand
and we saw a judge, me and my newfound wife
he looked at us and sighed and said "i sentence you to life"
and i say
"goodbye freedom
hello marriage ring
goodbye to my wily ways
and goodbye to all my flings
i've found me a women and inside her pretty head
 i've found a cozy little prison
and i'll love her til i'm dead"

Talking Fossil Fuel Blues

the world has many wonders
upon which people brood
some towers and some gardens
and some giant plates of food
but the greatest wonder upon which
humanity doth toil
is this stuff i like to wrestle in
and this liquid is called oil

oil that is
in swimming pools and, uh, movie stars

oil's controlled by the middle east
that's might plain to see
that's why we're in this war
it ain't to make nobody free
now, religion, politics and petroleum
that's a might potent mix
the end result is an american flag sticker
flagging king james bible plastic
and it only costs $4.95

i tried solar power just to help things improve
my car sat in the sun for hours
and still it didn't move
so i switched to wind power
to get from here to there
stood next to a politician
and drafted on the hot air
my lord, you could fill a balloon with this stuff
i hate to burst your bubble

the best way to avoid the oil
is just to ride a bike
you'll get better exercise
even on a trike
i've never used oil on a bike
not even on the gears
so that grinding sound
got me confused
like screaming to my ears
so i oiled my gears with some
organic, fair trade, sustainably squeezed butter

i'm moving to another earth, where we respect the land
and don't go on digging for what we cannot understand
for mother earth's juicy sweat, from billion years of toil
is this stuff we keep slurping up, her toil became oil
next planet i go to, gonna be a lazy planet

Talking God Blues

now here's a thing you'll never read
won't see upon no shelves
everyone just wants their gods to look just like themselves
that don't mean they're fake or false
perhaps just unaware
there's 10 billion other gods
just floating in the air
each one to their share
just reach up and pluck one

now if buddha he was fat or not
that didn't make him wise
it matters not if he snorted pot
of if he was compassionate to flies
love, friends, is where it's at
so don't be crude or crass
and enlightened folks, applaud this song!
if you don't, i'll kick your ass
yes, that's correct
one collective ass
we are all one
including our posterior

there's fighting in the middle east
of the abrahamic sort
folks calling god by different names
but i just call him mort
cuz morton is my name you know
and it's mighty plain to see
this god which you're referring to
well, he looks just like me!

so i'm starting my own hotline
a number on tv
where everyone can make a call, of course it's toll free
until you need a prayer to ease what makes life hard
in that case, please have at hand
a major credit card
i even accept diner's club

Talking Love Blues

i'm a lonesome poet most of the time
i write bad songs and sing bad rhymes
i need a date but i often find
i spend all day inside my mind
yessir, i live in my head, in memories
and there aren't too many girls up there

well my best friend went and got me a date
a forlorn attempt to meet my mate
my date and i went out to eat
she said she's disgusted by hunks of meat
well, i called off the date right there
i figured she wouldn't be interested in a beefy hunk like me

well i went to work to meet my boss
and when it comes to her, i'm at a loss
she called me in to clean her desk
she closed the door and put me to the test
i'm getting a promotion next week

i had a blind date the next day
i brushed my teeth and scrubbed my face
she rode to my house on a horse
and she'd brought one for me of course
there she was, my date and my horse
couldn't tell which was which

well i've finished dating but if i need a girl
i'll don a skirt, put on some pearls
put some high heels on my feet
and take myself out to eat
from here on out, i'm getting all my meals half price

Talking Texas Blues

i come from a lonesome land
it's texas state, you understand
there's cowboy hats
and cowboy boots
and cowboy wigs
and cowboy flutes
and cowboy pom-poms
and cowboy tofu
and inflatable cowboys
and rodeo cowboys and rodeo clowns
and , uh, presidential clowns

this grand old state started small
10 million buffalo that's all
but lots of work and lots of luck
we built 10 million off-road pickup trucks
not enough room off-road
for the trucks and the buffalo
one them had to go
and so....

and it came to pass in 1812
a historic event that you know well
but hell i can't remember what happened then
so could you please fill me in there, friend?
i failed history class

texas revolted from mexico
cause they charged admission to the alamo
tore down the basement, killed the cats
so the soldier's couldn't make no more hats
and so the coon skin cap was invented
and it's descendent is still with us today
it's called a toupee

and the alamo army revolted fast
but they got the present mixed up with the past
"remember the alamo" they did say
but what they remembered was what happened to them only yesterday
when love was an easy game to play
and even smelly soldiers could partake

rodeos and cattle drives got easier when they built i-35
horseshoes clopped no more on grass
but now on highway overpass
and access roads
and parking lots
and quickie lubes

now texas men like everything bigger

it's to compensate for something, i figure
we got bigger skies and bigger rains
and bigger clouds and bigger plains
not sure about the brains
i figger this bigger aspect of texas
that being the state's relations to mother nature
is to compensate for texas men's lack of femininity
just raise them boot heels an inch or two
a nice stiletto will do
and take that burnt orange or aggie red
and put it on your lips instead

texas is mostly big cities now
no more horses, no more cows
but i still dream of a simple time
of ranches, dirt, and no more crime
yes, i'd be sleeping in the barn
chewing hay
slurping from a trough
how i wish i was a horse

Texas Saves

come sit and pick a tune
pluck the rays of this texas moon
or just sit and soak the songs that blow between the pines
take a ride way out west
marfa's what i like best
it'd cold and dry and one mile high
and the wind will blow your cheeks bright red

i'll take texas and take it to my grave
even jesus would agree
that texas saves
when california falls in the sea
they'll all come running here
and we'll say hi and they'll start to cry
and we'll share a lone star beer

people come to change their life
breathe free and find a wife
cause the facts are undisputed
texas girls look good in jeans
night visitors, they're amazed
by our glowing friends in outer space
the lone star state is full of stars that shine
like sparks of god

i'll take texas and take it to my grave
even jesus would agree
that texas saves
when california falls in the sea
they'll all come running here
and we'll say hi and they'll start to cry
and we'll share a lone star beer

Texas Tune

california traffic is clogging up my head
coughing and confused
wheezing smoggy dead
turned inside out as i wade the morning rain
i'm a long way from home
with no way back again

a texas tune is blowing slow and sad
then i return to see the traffic's just as bad

memory plays funny tricks
and lends a happy glow
to life's ladder's rungs that you left far below
the scenes that surround me now are all i'd hoped they'd be
but homesickness can infect and warp what you see

a texas tune is blowing slow and sad
then i return to see the traffic's just as bad

i guess there's no running
just stand your ground and pray
this homesickness never wilts your will to sit and stay
your problems will follow you and i have followed mine
my limits help define me
i need the asinine

a texas tune is blowing slow and sad
then i return to see the traffic's just as bad

Thaw my Heart

papers fade to dust
hands grip and tear
a microwave of pain
overflowing rust
julia child has been beheaded
hydrogenated rain
rotting pizza crust
the edges of my work
become serrated
cutlery set
dissolves when wet
my personal chef has been sedated
msg perm
a frizzle fried worm
on end to hook
my head begins to squirm
like a dolt holding a book.
frozen beneath the flame-lit lamp
defrost my bitter sadness
let it melt into a lump
and congeal into some gladness
a happy little clump.

it's winter in your heart
anywhere you roam
when your tongue is cooking empty words
that cannot find a home

a war waged in private
chef hat green berets
attack you with beignets
make you loud and lazy
the sugar makes you hazy
and the grease just feeds your crazy
time for a diet
let's eat the lawn for free
i'll mow the yard with my mouth
until we're lost at sea

it's winter in your heart
anywhere you roam
when your tongue is cooking empty words
that cannot find a home

The Boy Without a Brain

i look in the mirror, i'm afraid
keep thinking i'm a kid half my age
in my mind i'm still a child
or at least i'd like to be
wearing a diaper
completely fresh and free

i'm the boy without a brain
i'm the boy without a brain
let go of myself
in a world that's gone insane

a reckless push, a restless glance
i've half a mind to take a chance
to cut the other half away
cuz i'm the boy without a brain

i'm the boy without a brain
i'm the boy without a brain
let go of myself
in a world that's gone insane

count to 10, gulp some air
and fight something that isn't there
i never learn
i never will
as sure as my name is bill

i'm the boy without a brain
i'm the boy without a brain
let go of myself
in a world that's gone insane

The Darkness Stares Back

rolling skin
rippled azure shimmer
fading luck starts to thin
like the sun
and its twinkling grows dimmer
frozen with light, the night and its glow
and my heart filled with snow

lost at sea
shitwrecked
and all else between
with memories dissolved in waves of black ink
nighttime has fallen
the world has turned black
you stare at the darkness
and the darkness stares back

The Emperor's New Clothes

i'm four years early for to meet my fate
poisoned by the politics of star studded plates
lobbying your lawyers in backrub briefs
cozy up to canada, steal the maple leaf
jose farmer and lumberjack joe
i understand your pain, friends i'll you where to go
your country deeply needs you so leave overseas
to fight those who are fighting
and aren't asking please

the emperor's new clothes

global love affair
could you make that super-sized?
clone our love and deep fried lies
we syndicated corn and syndicated hay
and plowed all those who get in our way
indecency hairballs and lobbying freaks
hang about hallways and preach on the streets
they want to be me
i don't want to be them
i could do it so quickly, renounce in a whim
but none of it sticks and none of it holds
as i strut about it in the emperor's new clothes

the emperor's new clothes

The End of the World
(Has the End of the World Already Happened?)

so this is how it ends
gathered in a circle
with all our friends?
Yes
this is how it ends

Has the end of the world already happened?
The city is in flames
the sky is smoking
I wouldn't even bother to pack your bags
just grab yourself a honey
and cherish those good thoughts
they're just like money
and wait for the sun to set

The Lonesome Death of Cosmic Cowboy

for 20 years i gauged my life on nothing but the weather
i slept outdoors and took whatever came
but then one year in the hills of south dakota
i met my fate and she never even said her name
she led me by the hand out to the devil's tower
the rocks sloped like nails on broken glass
she said i had to reach the top
if i's to win her
and she's impatient so i had to do it fast

so like all men i sought to prove to my lover
that i's worthy of her body and her soul
but like all men i got halfway and then i lost my grip
and screamed unheard as i lost control
and i screamed, "why have you done this?
to cut my life off now?
the only way to save myself is sink into the ground
become the soil and feed the earth
and bloom in spring and die in cold
to sell myself to the dirt
my soul would then be sold"

she laughed and said i's mistaken,
that i'd thought too soon
i wouldn't die when i hit the ground but i'd bounce up to the moon
because the earth would not accept me
and so i would reside in that lonely land beyond the sky
where all lost cowboys ride
they ride up there and rope the stars and lay each night in dust
and in dreams they see the world
and wish that they could die and trust
that they'd fall into the slipstream of life that paints the sky
instead of riding the night all alone and wishing for to die

so ride on cowboy, ride on into space
your lonesome soul will be your steed
and don't you pray for grace
from earth you'll be a comet to light the purple sky
you'll bounce between the planets
looking for someplace to die

so i fell from the devil's tower with ever rising force
and i hit the ground and bounced back up
and rode a silver horse
up past the rain the snow and wind
up past the clouds and sky
and through the empty dark of space
my horse and i did fly
and as i flew i saw beside me other exiled men
who'd fallen from the devil's tower

and won't come back again
to kiss their wives or tend their flocks
or watch their children grow
they'd given in to pride and sin and been exiled from below
and as we rode great sparks flew off my horse like beads of sweat
and he wanted to rest but i wasn't tired yet
i'd set my sights on the sun, i'd set myself on course
to ride into that fiery ball, that all consuming force
and i sped across the galaxy, like light, like time itself
the warmth burned on my skin
and i wish that i could tell you
about the love i felt for all mankind
as i approached life's source
and the way the sunlight flowed
upon my silver glowing horse
so i rode into the sun and i felt myself consumed
now i sit, i write this song, alone here in my room
and wish somehow i could share
the light that overwhelmed me there
the light that burned and the light that blew
and the light that brought this song to you

so ride on cowboy, ride on into space
your lonesome soul will be your steed
and don't you pray for grace
from earth you'll be a comet to light the purple sky
you'll bounce between the planets
looking for someplace to die

The Moon is Shining Too

(electric silver
the beams of night)

tragic comes the future
my words tell no lies
the earth keeps its distance
the wind's breath, it sighs
my words may come out hollow
my feet may drag my shoes
but my eyes are burning
and the moon is shining too

a love that i carried
to steal my sadness home
did wither and falter
the longer i did roam
like a purple flashing diamond
my sadness grew and grew
until the darkness burned like sunshine
and the moon was shining too

now the shadows in the corner
have spread across the floor
they curse me and taunt me
to stand up and open the door
outside the city's glowing
like a bonfire built for two
i shine through the darkness
and the moon is shining too

there's no lesson to be learned here
an old man living dead
had i but a chance for another
i'd choose none other instead
so squeeze tight your darkness
from which lights springs like morning dew
to illuminate the glowing city
while the moon is shining too

The Past Won't Forget Me

a new day
a rising sun
but the burning ball won't share its light
my thoughts return to the night before
when i crashed and burned
and fell to the floor
the past just won't forget me
oh no!

full clothed and bathed in sweat
what did i say?
oh i forget
but the past just won't forget me
oh no!

i changed my address but he knows my name
it's the same decay in different clothes
his robes are dark
he knocks on the door
with buzzer shocks and mental gore
the past just won't forget me
oh no!

and now every moment adds to the next
that skeleton friend is my permanent guest
the past just won't forget me
oh no!

The Singer is the Song

day to day and town to town
he plied away his trade
a sculpture being chiseled by the places that he'd stayed
every night he'd sing for dimes
he's sing a lonely tune
but the echoes of his music went far beyond the room
the circles of the sun move along
and the singer is the song

every day, another verse
each year, another show
the song was written in his skin
he didn't even know
it wasn't on the radio or records that he played
every second that he breathed the song was being made
the circles of the sun move along
and the singer is the song

never did he play to crowds and never did they cheer
he thought he was a failure
could he please just disappear?
but a moment of clarity showed the value of his strife
the greatest song that he wrote was
the song that was his life
the circles of the sun move along
and the singer is the song

The TV Imbibed Me

falls from the sky
and through my hands
days of our lives are grains of sand
a rerunning program

got swallowed up by what i hate
tried to change the channel
but it was too late

the tv imbibed me
chewed and spit to threads
the tv imbibed me
an unhappy ending

The World is Awaiting

glowing city
ghostly trees
are knocking on your bedroom door
tangled roads and tangled people
scrambling for the exits
the world is awaiting
the world is awaiting

loud green lightning
frightening phantoms
treadmill runners kills themselves
this city is sleepwalking
talking in a stupor
while computer rust away on shelves
the world is awaiting
the world is awaiting

There Goes My Ego

he's ten feet tall
and five feet wide
he looks awful strong
but it's all a lie
if you stick a pin there in his side
he pops like a balloon
don't let his mirror plated armor
even fool you

the first time we met
he was battered and bruised
i asked him who he was
but he was confused
so i took him to a self help shop
that made him big and strong
now his head's so big
he won't admit when he's wrong

there goes my ego

so when he's introduced
he says that he's me
he flexes his muscles
and grunts noisily
but now and then i see him cry
his face all in a twist
i pat him on the back and say
"you don't exist"

there goes my ego

This Time You Broke My Heart This Time

this time you broke my heart this time
now i'm just sitting here and crying
playing my solitaire all by myself
i wish i was playing with someone else

this time you laid my heart to rest
but girl i must say i feel blessed
to be struck down and wallow here
crushed beneath your shoe
i'm glad to be killed by a pretty girl like you

this time you played me like a fool
you got a sweet face but sweetness can be cruel
you were my honey bear, i was winnie the pooh
i got my head stuck in sticky loving goo.

this time my heart jumped to my throat
i got a big heart, so i nearly choked
it jumped up high to hear the words
trapped in my mouth when i heard
you say my songs of love were for the birds

this time i had to write a song
of my faith in you and how you done it wrong
the song ain't new it don't have no hook
the words ain't worth a second look
but it's a nashville hit, now i'm a country crook

Time Machine

at one, i was having fun
at two, a diaper soiled
at three, i'd gotten off my knees
at 4, began my toils
at 5, i's working in the mines
by 6, i was the boss
at 7, i wore furs and pearls
by 8, they'd all been tossed
material things, i reasoned
are not why we're here
so i let my workers unionize
and then had to flee in fear
at 9, i went to india
to find the meaning of life
at 10, i'd come back home again
to find myself a wife
at 11, i was a bachelor
at 12, a soulmate found
at 13, told her father
and he threw me to the ground
at 14, we eloped
by 15, we'd uncoupled
at 16, went back to school
and that's when i got in trouble
an sat iou
at 17 i stole
by 18, in the slammer thrown
they threw me in the hole
at 19, tattoos on my face
by 20, shaved my head
at 21, pumping iron
in the prison yard instead
by 22, i'd got paroled
and then i got a job
at 23, to wall street went
to join the thieves and slobs
twas just like the prison yard
striped suit fashion trends
and getting shanked in the prison yard
prepared me for my new friends
at 24, i stole much more
than i'd ever stole, it's true
and i was praised on the news as a job creator
who me? yes you
at 25, i quit wall street
at 26, bought a boat
27, had an accident
by 28, i'd learned to float
by 29, i'd learned that time's a cycle
at 30, met a crazed inventor named michael

at 31, i'd helped him fund a time machine, it's true
and it seems, forevermore, i'll remain 32
but that got kind of boring
and my soul started snoring
and so i started over
and thought, this time i'll do it better
no facial tattoos
no working in the mines
no stealing the answers to the sats
no working on wall street
so
time revolves time
it's a snake eating its tail
it's jonah eating the whale
so i started over again
here we go again, my friend

at 1, i was a buddha
at 2, i'd been my best
at 3, i'd fixed the economy
by 4, read infinite jest
at 5, i was a movie star
by 6, a rock star too
by 7, a master lion trainer
and keeper at the zoo
by 8, i'd learned to clear my plate
and even eat broccoli too

i'd mastered life
but i got bored
so into vice i went.
by 9, i started drinking wine
by 10, smoking too
at 11, went to boarding school
at 12, i grew and grew
at 13, grew a mohawk
at 14, grew a beard
at 15, i dyed my skin green
and that's when things started getting weird.
at 16, i drove a car
and drove around the globe
at 17, i gave a speech
and said
"everything is love and upon love all should hinge"
and i got thrown back in jail
for copyright infinged
it seems that the concept of love
was now owned
by a hologram of the beatles
and their hollow apple throne

Time Revolving Time

woke up to a world
with frozen tongues on blast
silent speakers mouthing words
a muted whirlpool past

the circles spun to stillness
in a silent screeching halt
cackling seasons whisper
that it's not nobody's fault

tripped over what you meant to do
but the journey of a thousand steps
begins tying your shoes

time revolving time
nothing standing still
all revolving time
will never stop until

weeping while in single file
a humans heart complaint
searching for a sponge
to soak their pain
a soapy saint
wash me clean
wash my feet,
oh bleach away my black
but
never into nothing walk
without falling right back
the clock without hands
it laughs at all your plans
and wrestles you into the ground
you never had a chance

tripped over what you meant to be
but the journey of a thousand steps
begins with number three

time revolving time
nothing standing still
all revolving time
will never stop until
time revolving time
nothing standing still
all revolving time
will never stop until

Tiny Truck

i got a tiny little truck
i got a tiny little truck
it's the size of my weakness

gonna stare at the mud
gonna stutter like elmer fudd
gonna drain a can of bud
gonna eat a vegan cow
gonna eat a vegan plate
gonna push a vegan plow
gonna vegan roller skate

gonna be myself
gonna be myself
gonna be myself
until i ain't nobody no more

gonna be myself gonna be myself
until i peel myself up off the floor
gonna be myself gonna be myself gonna be myself
until i ain't nobody no more
gonna be myself gonna be myself
until i peel myself up off the floor

i got a tiny little truck
i got a tiny little truck
it's the size of my weakness

gonna wear a tiny wig
gonna dance a tiny jig
gonna prance my tiny boots
gonna sew a buckskin suit
gonna milk my sacred cow
gonna stand up on the prow
of my tiny little truck
my legal name is buck

gonna be myself gonna be myself
until i peel myself up off the floor
gonna be myself gonna be myself gonna be myself
until i ain't nobody no more
gonna be myself gonna be myself
until i peel myself up off the floor

i got a tiny little truck
i got a tiny little truck
it's the size of my weakness

Tourniquet Pants

talk to the hand
cuz i'm in demand
tourniquet pants
ain't got no chance to notch me

i drop men like bad habits
pheromone scented rabbits
pull from hats of lace and pantyhose
my zipper's locked and loaded
my lips are red and bloated
i don't have a soul except to steal

so listen, here's the deal
i'll let you lick my boot
if you serve your soul to steal
deal? deal.
now you're my meal

Trapped in Paradise

burning plastic house
with a flaming credit card
buy back your hair
very low a.p.r.
when did life become an endless stream of hipster scum?
i'm trapped in paradise

video games they play me
like an empty human shell
i'm trapped in paradise

organic skin
organic toupee
organic food to throw away
it's never enough
it's never enough

i don't want to pretend
that i'm happy where i am
i'm trapped in paradise

bleach tanning skin
bleach blonde toupee
organic food to throw away
it's never enough
it's never enough

Trash Compactor

do you wanna be my trash compactor?
say u will, say u will.
do you wanna be my trash compactor?
say u will, say u will.

i'm a piece of trash and all the plastic
what i say is not so drastic
you got a dumpster in your heart
and you got a compost in your soul
it's out of control, out of control
overflowing with yuck
be my trash compactor baby
help me get unstuck

do you wanna be my trash compactor?
say u will, say u will.
do you wanna be my trash compactor?
say u will, say u will.

it's an easy little thing
it's not so hard
just help me deal with my shit
give me support so i don't quit.
it's an easy little thing
it's not so hard
just help me deal with my shit
give me support so i don't quit.

do you wanna be my trash compactor?
say u will, say u will.
do you wanna be my trash compactor?
say u will, say u will

TV Guide Blues

noose necktie and a botox brain
puddle of whiskey sours
took my head to a carpet cleaner
they charged me by the hour
oh brother the blues are coming
oh sister you can't help me
save yourself, go get freaky
i'll just watch tv

burrito arms and a taco face
salsa in my eyes
drive thru friends giivng whopper love
chug another can of lies
oh brother the blues are coming
oh sister you can't help me
save yourself, go get freaky
i'll just watch tv

weatherman says the world is burning
god left the oven on broil
or maybe this world is a microwave
and we're all made of tinfoil
oh brother the blues are coming
oh sister you can't help me
save yourself, go get freaky
i'll just watch tv

life support on aisle 3
flaming housewife hair
dead birds in the kitchen sink
giving me an empty stare
oh brother the blues are coming
oh sister you can't help me
save yourself, go get freaky
i'll just watch tv

Ugly Piece of Shit

some people got together
and they hatched a mighty plan
and to a man they all agreed to it
they'd build an ugly piece of shit
an ugly piece of shit
an ugly piece of shit

the people came for miles
they lined up in their cars
admission in their hands
it was a bona fide hit
it was an ugly piece of shit
an ugly piece of shit
an ugly piece of shit

and now the mayor gives a speech
this piece of shit's revived his town
a famous sculptor is coming down
to mold a bronze replica of
this ugly piece of shit
this ugly piece of shit
this ugly piece of shit

Unplug Your Head

does it feel like the whole world's
got their head stuck up their ass?
vacant screen life
limp green brains on
flaccid kurzweil grass

maybe you would see
the world outside
if you'd unplug your head?
its harsh reality
so perhaps
you'd prefer to plug it up instead

when the stream floods it
your scanning empty face won't be seen
sucking golden blood
the all-seeing eye will
drown the world in green

maybe you would see
the world outside
if you'd unplug your head?
its harsh reality
so perhaps
you'd prefer to plug it up instead

Until My Dying Day

clouds burning fire
and the rain is sneering
we stare upon the pyre
our image disappearing
what more is there to say
when our flame has burned away?
find our image in the floating smoke
until it's died away

your head's spewing clouds
while your bed is burning
the mirror makes you proud
while the world continues turning
i wish i could convey
a tune to turn the world a different way
i'll keep on singing to these empty ears
until my dying day

my brain burns with pain
my guilt seethes with cruelty
my light eats the dark
transmutes it into beauty
what more is there to say
when your light has dimmed away?
burn away your black into the sun
until it dies away

the love that we feel
persists long behind us
the days and years reveal
the truth that will find us
every thought you live
you get another chance to give
the gift that can't be bought away
long past your dying day

Vegan Meatheads

sloppy shopping mall
airbrushed glamor shot
stole your soul
wallet catch your fall
too bad your billfold's
just an empty hole

and the vegan meatheads
flex their forks
hybrid hummers
trendy dorks

diet lard for lunch
coca cola baby bottle brunch
relax at 3:15
flush away the world
and all these scenes

and the vegan meatheads
flex their forks
hybrid hummers
trendy dorks

do not take a picture of me eating a hamburger

Velvet Rut

patchouli stains on the wall
tapestries just fall into pile
dial my friend paul
crumple up the velvet rut in style
tuesday two o'clock
laptop coffee slop
not an empty chair
do these people ever work?
or does it feel like work to just be sitting there?

hairless hippie who hates hippies
his throbbing dreadlock
will take you with me
hairless hippie
tight pant sissy, says oatmeal willie
and wilford brimley
and barton springs junky
and campus flunky
south congress pompadour
organic free-range bore.

whole foods in workout gear
a beer to wash down
everything that's wrong
a feel good happy song
i dig good vibes
but i think i'll hit the gong

hairless hippie who hates hippies
his throbbing dreadlock
will take you with me
hairless hippie
tight pant sissy, says oatmeal willie
and wilford brimley
and barton springs junky
and campus flunky
south congress pompadour
organic free-range bore

Walkin in the Dark

walkin in the dark
i'm walkin in the dark
oh throw a light world
please throw a spark

into this world i'm thrown
into this world we're thrown
a baby crying helpless and alone
rejected every hand that tried to help
and walked a path only to suit myself

i didn't know at all where i was going
for the tethers of my mind had overgrown
now i know someday i will arrive
but until then i'll just have to survive

i'm walkin in the dark
walkin in the dark
oh throw a light lord
please throw a spark

if you only hear one thing i've to say
i tell you friends, it shouldn't be this way
love's passed me by a couple of times
but i passed it off and now i'm past my prime

listen here, ye gentle hearted friends,
for this is goodbye, this is the end
find yourself a love and hold it strong
or else you too will be singing this here song

i'm walkin in the dark
walkin in the dark
oh throw a light lord please throw a spark
we're walking in the dark
walking in the dark
oh throw a light lord
please throw a spark

Walkin with a Daydream

tactile faces storm dissolve to sand
waterless mirages of a line-less disneyland
my sock drawer explodes with a hundred million grand
walking with a daydream of you

i got no need to brag
no need to boast
but your skin's clarified butter on empty cosmic toast
a glutton who eats beyond his most, yes this is true
walking with a daydream of you

eternity is such a boring grind
your white robes get stained
it's bliss all the time
so perhaps my imperfections are a way to keep it real
even when they obscure the way i feel

dr phil and oprah on the brain
the search for sanity has only driven me in insane
so i've hired me a lawyer and ordered him to sure
to keep me walking in a daydream with you

walking in a daydream with you
walking in a daydream with you
nothin on my mind, my head's beyond the time
i'm walkin in a daydream with you

behind all the stupid things i say
behind all the stupid i do
the real me laughs and wonders why i'm such an asshole
when i could be walking in eternity with you

walking in a daydream with you, walking in a daydream with you
nothin on my mind, my head's beyond the time
i'm walkin in a daydream with you

Walking in a Straight Line

quit my whiskey, quit my weed
no lsd and no more speed
walking in a strait line

stopped fuckin around
stopped staying out late
started getting home
at a quarter past eight
walking in a strait line

you
i did it for you
darling.

high fructose msg
has done parted ways with me
walking in a strait line

you
 i did for you
darling.

stairmaster twice a day
soulless workout at the ymca
walking in a strait line

you
i did it for you
and now
i'm a boring prude

shaved my head and brushed my teeth
stopped eating pork and eating beef
walking in a strait line

you
i did it for you
darling

i may not be cool no more
a puddle of drool down on the floor
but i'm not doing
what i did before
i'm walking in a strait line

you
i did it for you
and now i'm a boring prude

Warm Inside

crackles and creaks warm the sound
from life held deep underground
and stillness of air all around
warm inside

motion's molasses to a halt
cure my brain in a jar of salt
no thoughts of the world and its faults
warm inside

this warmth to my reservoir doth fill
into the city life it bolsters my will
and its memory beckons me still
warm inside

We'll Meet Again Someday, or We Won't

you can't see me anymore
what used to be my face
now seems to be a door
to another life
beyond what we had
you're leaving me
but it makes me kind of glad

the city lights will tempt you
to change your name
no matter your costume
your heart's still the same
it only beats in time to someone else
but sooner or later
you've got to bleed for yourself

so maybe baby
we'll meet again someday
or we won't

someday you will know what i mean
life ain't real
it's only a dream
and the phantoms you're fighting against
would dance with you if you gave them
half the chance

so maybe baby
we'll meet again someday
or we won't

Weird Year

it was a weird year
i stood beside the empty phone booth
whose phone had been removed
i had a revolution
my head overthrew my heart
the casualties were many
a new tyranny was established
until the two sides shook hands
left hand shook right hand
and a truce was reached
the head and heart
both realized
there never was a war to begin with

When Perfect Flames Expire

sandy, where you going?
my muse and you, the same
and no answer to your name
i go as i please
this desperation cannot squeeze
the flames of creation
paper chained to darkness
your words linger still
but you've lost your will

life slips, day by day
you've dropped the plot, you've lost your way
i'm stumbling blindly

when perfect flames expire
we choke on words of fire
a choir of ashen notes
drifts away drifts away drifts away

watch out this glowing city
swallows you inside out
i've figured that much out
when you want to find me
you'll be right behind me
and we'll be as one again

when perfect flames expire
we choke on words of fire
a choir of ashen notes
drifts away drifts away drifts away

White Male Diminishing Blues (boo fucking hoo)

i got no institutions
against which to rebel
my asshole ancestors created them all
so it seems i might as well
just go with the go with the flow
and shut my goddamn mouth

history constructed
such that european white males
told the story true
and god looks like us too
white dude with beard
sparkling eyes of blue
but i tell you what
go to the zoo
we're all primates too
and some species of alien
laughs at you

look at these puny white male humans
you.....
build a statue of your image
write books that tell your story
you dominated history
you rose to fame and glory
but it's flimsy as a toothpick hut
a second's blink, the door is shut

nobody cares who did things first
who was the best, who was the worst
just make the world a better place

hate to break it to you but
you are not the center of the universe anymore

get over it

your white man blues
are as relevant
as your white tube socks

somebody please go tell russell crowe and his five feet grunt

Wiggle Worm

two step texas tap
morse code booty slap
floor of dance filled to brim
taste the wiggle i've got on tap
tofu boots &
beehive hair
look what you like
we don't care
wear lettuce for your underwear
just wiggle like a worm
wiggle like a worm

perched upon a parking lot
the good lord looking down
watching all his minions
all shopping for a frown
a plate of gray and plenty
modern life is rough
but if you wiggle with me
it won't be so tough
just wiggle like a worm
wiggle like a worm

flaming speedballs fly at you
but you don't even care
please please dodge that flame of death
its' fire singed your hair
the cosmos is a ball of flame
in figures 8s it squirms
so align yourself with the void
and wiggle like a worm
wiggle like a worm

Wino Strut

jug of straw
a lightning blast
rot gut buzz fading fast
how long do you think this wagon ride will last?

dionysus hit the skids
wine bottle walking stick
is it any wonder that you're sick?

wino strut
flying high through bleeding eyes

lips of red
a party stain
echoes back that old refrain
"tomorrow comes another wasted day"

wino strut
flying high through bleeding eyes

Work Work Work

work work work work work
it seems that's all i do
work work work work work
it's tough i'm telling you
the more i work it seems to me
the poorer i become
if i keep on working hard
someday i'll be a bum

i work in the sweatshop
clock in each day at 5
the nike shoes i stitch each day
they help me stay alive
when i run from my pit-boss
he's wearing heavy boots
i run down to my lawyer and file a worker's suit
oh.

work work work work work
it seems that's all i do
work work work work work
it's tough i'm telling you
the more i work it seems to me
the poorer i become
if i keep on working hard
someday i'll be a bum

i'm dancing for a living
it makes a decent wage
i dress up like a fireman
and go hose down the stage
i dance there with my oboe
i learned to play in school
the women stay, pay me to play
and then they sit and drool
oh

work work work work work
it seems that's all i do
work work work work work
it's tough i'm telling you
the more i work it seems to me
the poorer i become
if i keep on working hard
someday i'll be a bum

i've gone into retirement now
it's pretty nice i guess
i drive around a golf cart
until i make a mess

my feeding tube gets clogged
and my golf cart it breaks down
i didn't think it'd be such work
just to sit around

oh

work work work work work
it seems that's all i do
work work work work work
it's tough i'm telling you
the more i work it seems to me
the poorer i become
if i keep on working hard
someday i'll be a bum

World Frames Your Face

i'm always squinting at the sunshine
though i know it's good for me
and all these screaming city sirens
they all sing sweet harmony
moons of your eyes inside i'm swimming
it's an endless blue expanse
upon the endless sea i'm skimming
and the waves pull me to dance

the world frames your face my dear
where once there was me there now is you
the world frames your face my dear
finally i've changed
i'm set free

internal endless blue meander
and each day there's less and less
of all the bullshit i'd perfected
flush the past
embrace the yes

the world frames your face my dear
where once there was me there now is you
the world frames your face my dear
finally i've changed
i'm set free

World Gone Deaf

all the people
will never hear what you're saying
even if
you scream it in their ears
the world has got a verbal block
everyone's forgotten how to talk
and everyone's
forgotten how to listen

we all live in a world gone deaf
the weak of heart
had best save their breath
we all live in a world gone deaf

if you wanna beat the devil
don't even try to fight him
as soon as you fight him
then he's won
if you wanna beat the devil
sing joyously

we all live in a world gone deaf
the weak of heart
had best save their breath
as for me
i'll keep making sounds
until the world it comes around

we all live in a world gone deaf
the weak of heart had best save their breath
it's not an easy thing to do
to sing this song when i can't hear you

(what are you trying to say ?)
deaf....
what?
deaf....
what?
deaf....
what?

You and Me Make 3

dreams of you
come true
at last
the past is gone
we're one

no words can speak
no songs can hear
it's clear
our love
can't stand
outside itself

you and me make 3
you and me make 3

You Can Never Go Home

the door that led the way to now
has disappeared behind
the only path that matters tho
is what you're yet to find

step ahead into a blank
where once your fears had dwelt
but life responds in silent thanks
when you play the hand you're dealt

to dwell upon a moment
no point in even trying
you're either busy being born
or getting busy dying

and what's the use to looking back
it's old news anyways
the world presents you what you lack
forget your yesterdays

backwards bend until you break
no way to mop up your mistake
you can't go home again

You Can Never Go Home Again

memory it sears under your skin
reminders of the people
and the places that you've been
its tempting to line the past in gold
but yesterday's a yawn
and tomorrow isn't told
family, they freeze you in your place
imposing on the moment
all your former shades of face
you love them
but you have to be set free
from the image of the one they knew
the one you used to be

you can never go home again
your neighbors and your friends
just want you to be inside a memory
you can never go home again
theres no point to pretend
what you were before is gone forever more

forward, you try to shed your past
but it keeps on catching up with you
no one can run that fast
so gently
accepting every thought
everything you've ever done
is you
and its not

you can never go home again
your neighbors and your friends
just want you to be
inside a memory
you can never go home again
theres no point to pretend
what you were before
is gone forever more

You Cut My Heart in Two

my phone won't ring
my birds won't sing
my nights bring a lonely bus ride home
you cut my heart in two
you cut my heart in two
i'm stuck beneath your shoe
you cut my heart in two

hallmark cards slam against the door
i took the sheets off of the bed
i'm sleeping on the floor
it's cold down here
it's cold out there
it's cold in here
it's cold in here
you cut my heart in two
you cut my heart in two
you gave my soul the flu
you cut my heart in two

You Know Who You Are

you've gotten so good at departures
you deign to disappear in a zap
your fears get confirmed
but these explanations squirm
like an ostrich lured into a trap

you know who you are
you're right there
you know who you are
but you don't care

debate, if you will, all emotion
dig into imperatives and norms
but the cold dissected life
that you wield without a knife
is a tax collector filling in his forms

i'll be your friend if you need me
and patiently wait for you to see
that the life you denied
that you're holding all inside
is actually who you're meant to be

you know who you are
yourself you caught
you know who you are
or maybe not

You Know You

clear light tries and tries
to shine right through my head
but these waves of sight
illuminate my cluttered mind instead
i drift upon a daydream and stone myself to sleep
and in the secret space of dreams
i lie awake and weep

this morning as i walked alone
my mind did trip again
it fell into more thoughts of you
and i bled you out my skin
your image cuts like paper
and rivulets of lies
come bubbling up
and drag me down
the pain intensifies

oh you know you
look at what you do to
you and me

the tremble smile of your lips
said without a word
memories of other men
and lives that had occurred
and like a womb they suckled you
to twist upon the past
all you want from me is a memory
to whisper to your class
what a thought
the present tense
in what will we remain?
another day
another year
to cauterize the pain
i pray that life may heal me
that i need not pray no more
and that things may be
the way they were before with

you know you
look at what you do to
you and me

until i know the truth, i'll settle for the song
until i know it's melody, i'll hum and strum along
until the moment death may come
i'll try my best to live
but life without you darling is a failure i can't forgive

You're Still Glowing

night's dissolved to day
hazy worn away
but you're still glowing

the night that never ends
has come round again
and you're still glowing

flashlight for the mind
dissolves linear time
you're still glowing

i'd swear there's fireflies
buzzing in your eyes
you're still glowing

ever to the fray
we march another day
you're still glowing

compact fluorescent soul
silver apple sun
the end has begun
you're still glowing

pushing past the moon
darkness coming soon
you're still glowing

You're a Special Girl

the love you hold
makes me feel good
i will be reborn
one of these days
the sun feels warm
on my skin
you're a special girl
the love you hold
makes me feel good
i will be reborn
one of these days
the sun feels warm
on my skin
you're a special girl
the love you hold
makes me feel good
i will be reborn
one of these days
the sun feels warm
on my skin
you're a special girl
the love you hold
makes me feel good
i will be reborn
one of these days
the sun feels warm
on my skin
you're a special girl

(let's get a hamburger)

You're Already Home, Indianna

the great state of indiana
it's not just a place to drive your car
it's a girl with guitar and bandana
and the wealth of the world inside a jar

multitudes contained
of worlds not even named
and the width of the sun sways inside her
an image that will sneak
through your dreams while you sleep
you're already home, indiana

never need step a foot
outside your door
to see that the world will come to you
everything you wanted is waiting to come true
the life yet to come and even more

multitudes contained
of worlds not even named
and the width of the sun sways inside her
an image that will sneak
through your dreams while you sleep
you're already home, indiana

You're Free If You Want To Be

you're free if you want to be
so cease your silly crying
it's boring me

alarm clock panic rings
no matter when you wake
you cry through your blue routine
and dwell on your mistakes
but the train that you claim you missed
you know it don't exist
you'll find your life is in your hands
if you'd unclench your fists

cookie cutter's framed its shape
upon your oldest friends
and all your strong opinions now say
"well, it depends"
indignities of middle-age
have rounded out your edge
but just because you're limping
don't go leaping off the ledge

you're free if you want to be
so cease your silly crying
it's boring me
the world becomes what we think
so please stop complaining
i'm not a shrink

you've got everything you want
and nothing that you need
if you play the game for wealth and fame
your fate is guaranteed
your innards hollow out
while the surface gets so cool
a lifeless image of yourself
for taxidermy school

you're free if you want to be
so cease your silly crying
it's boring me
the world becomes what we think
so please stop complaining
i'm not a shrink

You're My Girl

gonna get you on the freeway
gonna fuel efficient ride
gonna give you lots of leeway
and stand by your side
gonna help you self-empower
if you need my help
and if you want to do it solo
i make no demands
you're my girl
you're my girl

gonna watch you self-empower
gonna let you do your thing
gonna give every hour
that you need to make it ring
gonna help you realize yourself
if you need my help
i'm here to support you
you are my no-one else
gonna help you realize yourself
if you need my help
i'm here to support you
you are my no-one else
you're my girl
you're my girl

You're Someone Else

prying eyes
never let you be free
escape into a crowd
it's finally time to be
everything you'd hidden from yourself
nevermind who you were
you're someone else

shedding skins
that you never peeled before
woke up in a different place
that you'd never been before
everything you'd hidden from yourself
nevermind who you were
you're someone else

come a day that you open up your past
when there's no place left to play
you always knew it wouldn't last
everything you'd hidden from yourself
nevermind who you were
you're someone else

You've Never Lived a Day in Your Life

all the rats are sleeping
the telephone is weeping
and all of the world's gone gray
your obituary lied
you never died
but we had your funeral anyway
you've never lived a single day

the faster you run
the farther the distance
the ways of the road
wouldn't bow to your insistence
so sharpen your mind
before there's nothing left for you to find
you've never lived a single day
you've never lived a single day in your life

you run and run
to catch the sun
down at the track
and
all is one
until you start looking back
and you'd swear that you've been here before
you've never lived a single day in your life

running in circles = standing still
running in circles = standing still
a stone's throw from what you know
and in the bleachers is god

Your Dark Sunglasses Won't Make You Lou Reed

it blotted out when you were young
you wandered too high to stay out of the sun
first album of the velvet underground
in your desperate need it did resound

your dark sunglasses won't make you lou reed
your dark sunglasses just make it hard to see
gray tinted technicolor
rebellion on sale
your dark sunglasses won't make you look like
john cale
sterling morrison
or even
doug yule

morning breath and baited claims
you don't want the knowledge
you just want the names
meanwhile life outside goes by
those silly little frames made in taiwan
molded petroleum
rock star wrong
who's never even written a song

your dark sunglasses won't make you lou reed
your dark sunglasses just make it hard to see
gray tinted technicolor
rebellion on sale
your dark sunglasses won't make you look like
john cale
sterling morrison
or even
doug yule

Your Eyes are Mirrors

river of air
takes your voice away
a record player
another wasted day
i'm dancing underneath all of my fear
your eyes are mirrors

pulled your eyes down from the sky
broke and gone
this world we're living on
but it's beauty has
it's beauty has become clearer
your eyes are mirrors

words of fire
tangled in telephone wires
strangled by the phone
strangled by the phone
choking on the ashes of our past
your eyes are mirrors

Your Heart Breaks into a New Heart

if your heart gets stale
like an old loaf of bread
and the moldy trail
it crawls up to your head
and your waking walk
is a slow slump instead
your expiration date
creeps up from the dead

your heart breaks into a new heart

it cannot be pulled off
any old store shelf
this feeling that you got
you give it to yourself
it cannot be squeezed
it cannot be forced
this warm feeling flows
when you let go, of course
your heart breaks into a new heart

your heart breaks into a new heart

inner engine start
with fuel for to burn
you've so much more to live
and so much less to learn
so torch all your cookbooks
and throw your fridge aside
the life that you seek
is already inside

your heart breaks into a new heart

Your Soul Glows in the Dark

were you waiting
for the right time to tell me?
or were you silent
cuz there's nothing more to say?
four walls down we walk the golden valley
outside now the gentle sweet abyss
scream as loud as you want

is it wrong now
this silence starts to break me
our faces
pressed against the glass
scream as loud as you want

suddenly i see a spark
your soul glows in the dark
started before you were born
your soul glows in the dark
soul glows in the dark

nighttime and its shadows all attending
laced with moonlight
like an outline of your death
scream as loud as you want

suddenly i see a spark
your soul glows in the dark
started before we were born
your soul glows in the dark
soul glows in the dark

Zombies

sandy says that love is all we have
but it squeezes through your hands
when you try to grab
sandy says that life's an empty game
paupers and kings both die just the same

so we dance
dance in the sun
if everything is empty, everything is one
zombies!
zombies!
zombies!

sandy says that love's a perfect flame
it burns without heat
beyond false or true
your life is a sitcom starring you
with candlelit television eyes
so dance
dance in the sun
if everything is empty
everything is one
dance
like sandy said
if your heart isn't dancing
you might as well be dead
zombies!
zombies!
zombies!

sandy says that time is running out
we've wasted all our days
on amphetamines and doubt
and sandy holds a light up to my eyes
don't be ashamed
don't be afraid to cry
because our love is going to die
and light up the stars
and the empty sky
will glow purple blinding white

All songs written by Bill Baird except:
"Help Me Lord," "I'm Gettin Laid Tonight," "Jones Street Blues," "Tourniquet Pants"
by Baird & Matt Oliver

Appendix A: How Songwriting Ruined My Life

(songwriting lesson plan used at Esalen Institute and Austin High School)

How Songwriting Ruined My Life

(Or Saved it, I'm not quite sure)

A songwriting "lesson plan" by Bill Baird and _____
(your name here)

Songwriting.
A daunting subject.
Let's start with a little background.

Songwriting began as a means by which early societies would pass along their mythology, tribal history, and legends. These were the days before the printing press, before any kind of recording technology, before Encyclopedia Britannica, way way back.

The songs were called "epic" because they would literally take days to recount. To help the poets recite these songs, rhyme and meter were imposed on the words. The rhymes and rhythm made the words much easier to remember.

Homer was one of these old "epic poets." His books "The Odyssey" and "The Iliad" were not originally books at all, but really really really long songs, accompanied by a lyre, a strange-shaped, droney predecessor of the guitar. Imagine a song that lasted several days. Might get kind of boring. But I'd have to respect that songwriter's endurance.

Modern songwriting is pretty much the vestigial remains of this early process.
But now, instead of using the lyrics to pass along our history, the songwriter usually addresses personal concerns: love, hate, partying, getting cheated on, driving a big red tractor, and so forth.

For most modern songwriters, their process is difficult to explain. In fact, some people get downright superstitious about it, believing that talking about it will dispel its mystique somehow.

There is no formula to it; it's pretty subjective; it relies on the writer having something unique to say about the world. I mean, there are some formulas to songwriting, but "formulaic" is one of the biggest knocks against a song, so we should try to avoid formulas if we can.

To break the ice and hopefully illustrate a little of the bizarre world of modern songwriting, let's take a look at some experiences that led me to be a songwriter. Ultimately, there is no right or wrong in songwriting. You just try to create something that resonates within yourself.

The main advice I would give to any aspiring songwriter: write as many as you can, because most of your first attempts will be "learning experiences," i.e. songs you would not dare share with anybody.

Don't be frustrated by failures.
It's part of the process.
If you persist, then you might have something worth keeping.

Tips for Starting an Illustrious Career as a Songwriter!

(or how I got enough material lodged in my brain to torture me til the end of my days)

Go temporarily insane.
Make a tearful confession to a priest.
Get thrown out of your parents' house.
Go broke.
Apply for several credit cards using different names; have them all cancelled and each of your fake identities reported to a collection agency.
Sleep 10 hours in one week.
Sleep 24 hours in one day.
Drink lots of whiskey (non-alcoholic for those under 21).
Fall in love with somebody completely wrong for you.
Have your heart broken.
Have your heart broken again.
And again.
Watch your friends change into people you don't recognize, either because of some fundamental change in their personality, or plastic surgery, or both.
Give away all your possessions. Return to the thrift store later and try to get your possessions.
Shave your head and move to Alaska.
Endure the questioning disdain of your friends, family, and mentors.
Worry about things that don't matter.
Forget to worry about things that do matter.
Sleep through college and wake up with a diploma.
Wonder how that vomit got on your shoes.
Work for somebody who literally blows a whistle to keep the pizzas delivered on time.
Deliver a pizza to Michael Bolton.
Get fired for setting the xerox machine on fire.
Move someplace far away from anybody you know, grow very lonely, and give your television a nickname.
Experience glorious success in front of thousands of people, let it go to your head, and experience a rapid change of fortune.
Get booed off a stage.
Get in a fistfight in the alley outside Emo's.

What do you think these experiences provided to me?

(besides a formidable bill with a psychiatrist)

Jot your answers below:

ore than li ely these e periences are song-worthy because they address uni ersal human concerns

ore on that shortly

s in on the ne t page

Most good songs address universal human concerns.
List a few, por favor, in this giant white space below:

I came up with a few in my spare time. I have lots of spare time.
Death
Birth
Babies
Heartache
Hangovers
Alcohol
Cars
Traffic
Loss of Innocence
The Inability of a Country Boy to Adjust to Big City Life
Temptations of nightlife and fast livin'
Transient nature of our world
Girls
Boys
Hormones
Clothes
Dancing
Ghosts
Religion
Faith or the lack of it
Meaninglessness of the world
Complete meaning in every aspect of the world
The infinite

One topic I think should be avoided if at all possible is a song about songwriting itself. It just usually comes off not quite as clever as you'd thought. Jeffrey Lewis, a friend of mine, wrote a great song about that phenomenon. It's called "Songs About Songwriting Suck So I'm Singing a Song About Songs About Songwriting."

Before we dive into writing our own songs, I want to take a humorous aside and talk about that wart of modern songwriting, Aerosmith.

At the risk of offending lovers of modern classic rock, I think Aerosmith incapable of writing a good song anymore. There I said it. There's really only one kisses of death in songwriting for these kind of superstars. Mostly, it's believing your own press, believing your own mythology, primping too much in the mirror even -- just becoming detached from issues that really matter to people: death, love, hatred, fear, murder, driving cars really fast, the list goes on.

Aerosmith's songs seems mostly about the joys of their privileged lifestyle, and therefore seem more than a little frivolous. In the right hands, with a sense of humor, this might work. But not in their case.

On a somewhat related note, I once had a friend who sold merch at concerts and would often venture backstage to meet the bands. Backstage at an Aerosmith concert, my friend witnessed a surreal sight: to pump themselves up before the gig, Aerosmith was playing a video game about themselves, starring themselves. Ugh. Yikes. Now a few songs taken from their album "Get a Grip" (the cover of which features a cow with an udder piercing): "Pandora's Box" When I'm in heat Someone gets a notion I jump to my feet I hoof it to the ocean We hit a beach Where no one gives a hoot Nobody never ever wears a suit (Bill's commentary: Like an awful alternate reality Dr. Zeuss)

"Get A Grip" Got to Get A Grip Skin and bones, it ain't such a pity If you think I'm vain, better shut ya lip I can't explain how to be a fat city You gotta live large, gotta let it rip I was so shortsighted Now the wrong been righted I feel so delighted i get so excited

(Bill's commentary: Rhyming ،delighted' with ،excited' should be a petty misdemeanor. By the way, what exactly is a fat city? Oh yeah, he can't explain.)

"Fever" I got a rip in my pants and a hole in my brand new shoes I got a Margarita nose and breath full of Mad Dog Booze I got the fever, fever, fever, fever We can't run away from trouble There ain't no place that far But if we do it right at the speed of light There's the back seat of my car, caviar

(Bill's commentary: I like the line about being unable to escape trouble, but they quickly blow any empathy I might have by talking about eating caviar in the backseat of their car)

"Shut Up And Dance"

Love has got me down
A tear just hit the ground
So I started writing you this song
But the words I wrote came out all wrong
Yeah, but it's all right
Sex is li e a gun
 ou point you shoot you run
(Bill s commentary: h   )

Moving into the more specifics of songwriting construction, let's think about language. Just for fun, I made a list of words I try to avoid in a song:

Wet
Bovine
X-Box
Oprah
Sneakers
Sniff
Boink
Tween
Crusty
Chardonnay
Libations
Chili Dog
Moist
Boom
Nipple
Utilization
Slam
Turbo
Zap
Ballz

In sum, Any word that could be mistaken for an American Gladiator's stage name, any word referring to fluids, any word referring to processed food, and any word that looks like a text message abbreviation.

You want your words to convince the listener that yours is an authentic voice worth considering. Word choice is very important.

Of course, if properly handled, any word or topic can work. Satire especially can turn toxic verbiage into solid gold.

For those curious, I recommend Ween's "12 Golden Country Greats."

What words make you cringe or seem just plain ridiculous to you? (write them below)

Can you think on an instance when you might want to make people cringe?

Perhaps to shock them into paying closer attention to what you're doing?

Now think of words that seem evocative to you. Words you like. You can write em on this page here. A few words I like:

Peculiar
Expire
Flames
Resplendent
Glow
Grave
Tombstone
Insane
The list goes on and on...

Can you teach me to write a song now?
So I'm gonna teach you how to "write a song." Plug your emotion into this TOP-SECRET songwriting formula and voila! You have a hit that will make the folks cry and dance at the same time.

Ha, yeah right. You wish.

Teaching somebody how to write a song is a preposterous concept. For many reasons.

First off, there are no rules to this thing. No formula. A good song can have zero words and be played with a rubber band and a tin can! It can be thirty minutes long and explore every nook and cranny of the myxolodian scale. There are no rules! Oh wait, one rule to consider:

Is it any good?

It's really strange: the songs of my own that I like the best are often the ones that arrived without any plan, without even knowing what happened, like a bolt of lightning. I don't have a good explanation for it, but I do have a mediocre one.

I think good songwriting taps directly into the subconscious, stirs it up. What's sitting around in there? Probably a lot of unexplored, un-dealt-with shit. Which is the stuff that resonates when expressed in song.

How do you do tap into the subconscious? By creating without thought, in an automatic fashion, in what I call "the flow." It's like a moving meditation. While in that space, you draw on whatever craft you've developed, whatever musical training you've absorbed, whatever influences you've assimilated, and whatever life experiences you've had that you wish to share with the world.

Thusly, the three aspects to songwriting:

1) Getting into the "flow" of thoughtless creation. Letting the ideas flow out, whatever they are (you can edit them later). So that the creative act itself is a type of meditation, a way to step outside of yourself. You act as a lightning rod for a bolt of electricity.
2) Filling the subconscious mind with material that can be accessed during these writing sessions. Life experience! You gotta recognize whatever weird, fucked up experiences you've had and use that stuff as fuel.
3) Formal music elements: lyrics, melody, structure, hooks, verse, chorus, dance. These can be learned or absorbed through active listening. You will draw on this stuff while in the "flow."

This whole songwriting game is a challenge and a constant one and you never stop learning. You have to gain experience of the world and knowledge of musical structure while maintaining your ability to forget all that stuff and just create without thought. It's a delicate tightrope walk.

Townes Van Zandt once said, "There's only two types of songs: the blues and zip-a-dee-doo-da." Townes knew of what he spoke.

Zip-a-dee-doo-da refers to most pop songwriting. Written to generate a feeling of elation or joy or dancing. I personally think The Beatles kind of took pop songwriting to its highest form, by taking the chord changes and melodic playfulness of early jazz/tin pan alley in combination with rock's driving beat .

"**The blues**" refers to you and your story.

The shit you've slogged through and (hopefully) the joy of emerging out the other side. This type of song doesn't have to sound even remotely like "the blues" as you might normally think of it. You know, an old Afro_American dude on his porch testifying. "The blues" just means drawing on your own real experiences. You can be humorous, joyful and happy, whatever. You just gotta be real.

I think think for a happy song to really resonate, it has to be based on real-life experience. It proceeds from an understanding of sadness.

That's why it's hard to draw firm lines in this stuff, no offense to Mr. Van Zandt. Maybe Lady Gaga is expressing her pain and sadness through throwaway garbage and ridiculous costumes. Who knows? We're not here to judge but to figure out our own path. I know I'm usually writing happy songs when I'm sad and sad songs when I'm happy, so go figure.

Which is why it's kind of weird to say I can teach you how to "write a song." It'd be like teaching someone how to wear clothes that feel natural. Absurd. The only thing you can hope to do make them aware of their innate fashion sense. It's different for everyone.

So there it is... I can't teach how to write a song. There, I said it. I can explain the approach, the tools, the mindset, and all the elements that make up a song. But it's all kind of bullshit. If the song's not in you anyways, it's all just window dressing.

Again, there's only one rule to songwriting: is it any good?

If you have something to express, you'll find a way to get it out. You can perform a song singing and stomping on the ground. You can perform a song with a tin can. If the song's in you, it will find a way out.

So what is a song? A verse-chorus-verse-chorus structure? Melodic rhyming? I believe a song is anything that shares your world. A peek into your mind. Let the world see through your lens for a moment.

Before we embark on everything else, we will approach songwriting using broad strokes. Just getting our heads into the right space.

To that end, let us now embark on our songwriting journey with a bit of history.

Songwriting began as a means by which early societies would pass along their mythology, tribal history, and legends. These were the days before the printing press, before any kind of recording technology, before Encyclopedia Brittanica, way way back.

The songs were called "epic" because they would literally take days to recount. To help the poets recite these songs, rhyme and meter were imposed on the words. The rhymes and rhythm made the words much easier to remember.

Homer was one of these old "epic poets." His books "The Odyssey" and "The Iliad" were not originally books at all, but really really really long songs, accompanied by a lyre, a strange-shaped, droney predecessor to the guitar.

Imagine a song that lasted several days.
Might get kind of boring.
But I'd have to respect that songwriter's endurance.

Modern songwriting is pretty much the vestigial remains of this early process.
But now, instead of using the lyrics to pass along our history, the songwriter addresses personal concerns: love, hate, partying, getting cheated on, driving a big red tractor, and so forth.

To break the ice remember the following (see next page):

LOOSEN UP THAT BRAIN

IF YOU THINK YOU STINK

WORD AEROBICS!!!
(exercises in language)

Sometimes the best lyrics are the dumbest ones, and the most articulate, intelligent lyrics sound like hogwash.   There is muuuucccchhhh more to good lyrics than just the words. There's the phrasing, the melody, the melody, and the melody.   And the melody.

Consider Neil Young's song "The Losing End."   When he sings, "my tears fell down like rain," that could potentially be the laziest, most cliché d phrase ever.   Just try reading it with no inflection.

MY TEARS FELL DOWN LIKE RAIN.

About as interesting as day old oatmeal.   But with the right vocal inflection, it sounds infinitely better, eh?

"MY TEARS FELL DOWN LIKE RAIN"

And notice how he hits the high note on the word "rain."   Makes it infinitely more effective.   Imagine if he placed the high note of the melody on the word "fell."

Imagine singing it that way or, if you're brave enough, sing that out loud.

Yep yep, placement of notes on the lyrics are at least as important as the words themselves, if not more.

Now for fun fun time.   I will play a piece of music and want you to verbalize over the top of it.   Not words, not complete thoughts, just la dee dah, blahh blahh, baby talk, you know.   Without thinking, see what comes out.

Write it down, as close as you can.

Now change what you wrote into actual words.
No need for crazy imagination, just whatever words fit roughly into your nonsense phrases.
Try doing it a few different ways.

This exercise bypasses the "this-is-wrong-what-a-piece-of-shit-too-much-editing" part of the brain.
That part of of the brain does not come up with your lyrics.
It only gums things up.
You wanna bypass the overanalyzing part of the brain.
You can always edit later.
Or, in my case, never really edit at all.

Many times, it's just about breaking the ice, getting into the flow.
The best ideas happen when you don't even notice.
The best songs arrive immediately, like bolts of lightning.

Like Ginsberg said,

First Thought Best Thought

Ok, let us continue on our nonsense journey. Into the nonsense headfirst!
Here are a list of song titles.
Which are real, which are fake, and which are phrases from the newspaper?

Hanky Panky Nohow
Mindless Child of Motherhood
Welcome to Breakfast Television
I Love Your Braces, Baby

Ok, now let's take a look at the newspaper, shall we? I will walk around and hand out the paper. If you're doing this at home, go grab a newspaper.

Find the headlines that strike you. Write them down here:

Now choose a title from your list.   Ask questions about that title.

When I did this exercise, I found the headline "Congress jams it through," which sounds vaguely dirty.
I can only assume that whatever Congress is "jamming through," it's going up the ass of the American people, as per usual.
But who knows?
I asked the relevant questions:

"what did they jam through?"
"who was in congress?"
"where did they meet?"
"what were they wearing?"
etc.

and tried to answer the questions as I went along.

Now find the headline you wrote down that most strikes you, and as many relevant questions as you can muster.
Also, write down words, phrases, or images suggested by the title.
Just riff of the headline.

OK!
So now, if ya got the guts, use the headline as a song title and/or chorus and, using the images and questions you wrote, try to fashion it in some way into a coherent song.
You can do it in the space below if you like:

All we're doing is trying to open the brain.   Loosen up those neurons!   That's when the ideas flow in.   Let us continue.

The "exquisite corpse" method of writing is a really fun way to arrive at unique phrases and non-sequiters.

Write down a phrase, any phrase, at the bottom of the page..
When you are done, pass your packet to the person on your left.
On the packet that just arrived to you, write another phrase, but only basing it off the phrase that immediately came before.
Do not look at all the phrases that came before.
In fact, I've included a little slip of paper which should be used to cover up all the phrases except the one that immediately came before.

Continue this process until your packet (or boo as the case may be) comes all the way back around to you again.

What does this approach hint at?
Mostly, it's about the unexpected, the unique.
That's what grabs people's attention.
Within the spontaneous playful present moment lies any idea you could ever want.

But it's a weird thing.
Trying to grab at spontaneity = trying to grab water.
Pointless!   Don't grab, just direct its flow.
You build channels to properly funnel it.

Such is the same with creative energy.
The second you strain, the second you squeeze or grab hold, it slips away.
You simply let it flow through you.
Of course, there are helpful ways to ensure creative flow.

I've made a list:

1)   Coffee
2)   coffee
3)   coffee
4)   more coffee
5)   are we still drinking coffee?
6)   I'm starting to get a headache
7)   can you get me a cup of water?
8)   I now have a shooting pain in my stomach
9)   Do you have any antacid?
10) Forget about it, I'm taking a nap
11) I just woke up, let's have some coffee
12) Coffee

Et cetera.

There are also non-caffeinated options to help harness creativity if the muse deigns to pay you a visit.

Create a workspace.
Invest it with intention.
Have all your tools ready there.

You can't always predict when inspiration will strike, but you can be in a position to grab the inspiration when it arrives.

These are some of the tools I employ while attempting to romance the muse:

guitar
piano
pen/pencil/chalk
4track (or other recording device)
candles
photographs of people I love / places I've been
inspirational passages and quotes pinned on the wall
magazine clippings
half-eaten sandwiches
moldy coffee cups
pictures of my songwriting predecessors (in the hopes that some of their magic might rub off on me)

And so forth.
What objects would you have in your space to create intention towards the creative act? You can write them here:

To romance the muse, you create intention, and part of that is creating a "sacred space," a shrine to the creative spirit.
It can be the corner of your room, it can be in a closet.
It can be anywhere.
Ideally, ultimately, this creative space is a place within the mind, a mental space, so you can carry it with you anywhere you go, so your creativity can flow at any time.
I've written songs in a Hooter's sports bar.
Granted, the songs were about the female mammary glands, but what the hey.

You can create a mental space that allows you to stand outside any situation.... a self-contained unstoppable creative powerhouse machine monster Godzilla gonna destroy everything in your path oh wait I thought we were here to make the world better fuck it let's build a skyscraper with our name on it in the shape of my face oh yes thank you creative spirit you turned me into an asshole.

The muse does not look kindly on skyscrapers, I am pretty sure.
So much for my career as a corporate soulless architect of the blandification of the world.
So it goes.
I will focus on my small songs and make them great.
But I've let many of them slip by because I didn't have a way to jot down the idea before it fluttered away.

If you find yourself in that spot often, it can be useful to carry around a notebook and perhaps tape recorder.
You can record lyrics, melodic ideas, phrases you like, inspiration, eavesdrop on your neighbors, make prank phone calls playing dialogue from Arnold Schwarzenegger films into your phone, you name it.
I hear on these new-fangled iPhone thingys they have all sorts of "apps" to facilitate note-taking, dictation, and other creative ground-work.
I'm kind of allergic to those things, so I'll take Steve Jobs' word for it.

Ok, now let's think about genre. If you're like me, you hate classifying things and hate being classified yourself and such a process is anathema to creativity. Ok, let's think about getting a beer instead.

No, wait. Just humor me for a second. This exercise is all about subverting the clichés of different musical genres, such as these:

Country -- usually clever takes on old cliches or songs glorifying a rural lifestyle. Often times, you'll hear the repression of American white culture come out in country songs: the woman singing about being the boss and not taking any shit from any man, while the men seem to whine on and on. It's like they're living out the lives that conventional white America won't let them touch.
Reggae -- songs about rasta, jah, roots, unity, marijuana, hair, the beach.
"Ball rock" /jock rock/frat boy shit-- songs about alcohol, drugs, women, waste of human potential.
Spiritual -- calling on a higher power.
Electronic – making music to take Ecstasy to.

Ok, now imagine a song working within the surface aspects of that form, but completely inverting what these songs would normally address.

Country – songs about how great it is to live in a condo.
Reggae – song about finding Jah inside a discarded piece of styrofoam blowing across a parking lot with nary a bong in sight.
"ball rock"/jock rock/frat boy shit – song about drinking milk, using the treadmill, psyllium bran supplements, abstinence, not wearing a baseball hat, achieving excellence, contributing to world culture.
Spiritual – gospel song about wasting away on pills, alcohol and tobacco.
Electronic – making music to take Nyquil to.

Perhaps this inversion approach is not everybody. Not everyone has a taste for irony. But follow me for a second...

What type of music do you play, mostly? I know it's all shades of gray, but you can list a couple of types if you like. Write down the genre and any characteristics of that genre.

Now write down any potential inversions of that genre.

The idea here is to get you thinking outside your self-imposed boundaries. While we all need boundaries (without them, the world would be formless, like a big blog of cosmic Jello), sometimes stepping outside your perceived ideas of what you do can surprise you and your listeners.

Decay / Rebirth —
Creative Process as a Mirror of Nature

In nature, nothing is lost.
Leftover material becomes fuel for new life.
From death, from decay, comes new life, which in turn dies and becomes fuel for new life.
I'm starting to repeat myself repeat myself here.

I find this encouraging.
It means that whatever awful songs I write, they can just be considered fuel for newer, better ones.
It means whatever fuck-ups I've had can be used to bring new life.
Nothing is wasted, if you have the right mindset.

One good song is often built on the decaying leftovers of the 100 mediocre songs that preceded it.
Wherever you are, begin there!
Have no fear!
To get to the good, you have to fail, over and over again.
I'm still looking for the place where the failures stop.
I'm tired of learning!
But that's the world the world rolls, it seems.

Creativity and empathy seem to me our most "god-like" characteristics.
Of course, this depends on which god we're referring to.
If you're able to have sex with a women while inhabiting the form of a streaming shower of water, then perhaps Zeus might be a good stage name for you.
Or perhaps if you could drown the world in a watery grave, then we might call you Yahweh.
Might be a controversial stage name.
But we're not learning songwriting to destroy or to have sex with women.
Errr... well, maybe we are.
But ostensibly creation has intrinsic value.
The destruction and sex can come later.

The creative act itself opens the heart and mind.
It will heal you.
But for it to heal, you have to use all your old baloney as the fuel.

All your pain, all your joy, every old discarded idea, they are become fuel for new growth, for the creative process.
And that's the trickiest thing about songwriting: having something you really need to say.
You can only generate that by setting out into the world.

A life lived too comfortably will not result in a world-view that needs conveyance. I'm not saying you should go live in a dumpster.
Just live your life mon!
Jah rasta.

For my recent album, I compiled a book of all the "raw material" that went into the album's creation.
The album is merely the distillation of all that life experience.
If we are in the room together, I or one of my delightful assistants is now handing you this book.
Keep it for inspiration, or for the next time you need to start a campfire.

And remember always....
creativity mirrors what the ancients called alchemy...
turning shit into gold....
all the bad shit that came before can be transmuted into beauty...
with a joyful process and right intention.

CREATIVITY TURNS SHIT INTO GOLD

We have explored the subconscious a bit, talked about the creative process and painted some broad strokes about lyrics and such.

Now for a few specifics about songwriting construction.

There are a few tried-and-true (god I hate that phrase) elements to song:

Verse/Chorus
Hooks
Tension / Dynamics
Rhythm / Beat

Let's consider each of these, shall we?

Verse / chorus:

The Greek chorus was a group of bearded men wearing masks and bathrobes who would stand off to the side of a stage drama and comment in unison on the action.
They acted as the sort-of objective voice, providing the bigger picture, the broader perspective.
Not that anyone would want to listen to a bearded, masked man walking around a theatre in a bathrobe, but perhaps if there were thirty of these men, their words would be impossible to deny.
The chorus in our modern songs is a wrinkled, warped, shriveled cousin of this ancient Greek chorus.

Now write down a few phrases that would sound good chanted by a large group of people:

Ok, now let's try chanting them.   Stand up and chant, even if you have no beard nor bathrobe!

"hooks"

Ok, hooks.
Hooks are the parts of the song that "reel in the listeners."
Let's explore this metaphor a bit further.

What captures the fish, what allows you to reel them in?
Why, a hook, of course.
And what happens once you reel in the fish?
Well, you either catch and release or let it writhe around on the deck, flapping wildly, gasping for air, asphyxiating, letting it die a very painful death.
You will later skin the fish and perhaps fry it in a vat of boiling oil.
Whatever scraps are left get thrown in the garbage.

Sounds a bit like la isten through the Billboard charts.
Or perhaps an executive meeting at the SonyBMG music corporation.
I'm gonna assume most songwriters are looking for hooks more of the "catch and release" variety.

Anyways, let's talk about the different types of "hooks":

The Instrumental-Effect Hook – In the background, create a repetitive instrumental riff or effect that's short and catchy. Something that's so goddamn annoying that it keeps playing in your head for hours after hearing it. Going insane yet? Perfect!

The Song-Intro Hook -- This is something that may not even include lyrics or much instrumentation. Queen's "We Will Rock You" drum intro is a great example. You just need to hear that drum intro start, and it's hard to continue whatever it was you were doing. You either start doing air drums along with it, or rush to unplug the stereo, stopping only to perhaps vomit into a trash can.

Background Instrumental "Effect" Hook.
This just means catchy background music. Examples?   "U Can't Touch This" by MC Hammer is a pretty good one.

Shouted or Spoken Word Hook.
"Blietzkreig Bop" by the Ramones. Enough said.

My stomach actually turns a little when I hear some asshole talking about "hooks," "chops" or his "press kit."
It's enough to throw your slurpee all over their faux-hipster droney ass.
You just want your song to be catchy, ok?
Moving on.

Tension / contrast / dynamics

So you don't want your songs to be boring.

You can be sad, but wallowing around in it too much.... boring.

You can be excited and happy, but if that's all you're bringing to the table.... boring.

A songwriter uses tension, contrast and dynamics to make his music less.... boring.

Tension can be tricky to use.
Usually when you have a good idea, you want to just lay it all on the table right away.
Which might feel good, but the idea's impact could be more if you hold back for a bit.
If the listener feels like they already know exactly what you're gonna do, there's nothing

for them to explore and the song is.... boring.

Dynamics basically refers to the same thing.
Instead of rocking at full volume for the whole song, perhaps it's more effective to have quieter sections.
That way, when the "rawk" comes back in, it will really melt their faces.
If you start with the volume all the way at 10, where is there to go from there?
I guess you could go to 11.

Dynamics is achieved through contast, i.e. putting sections with two different feelings next to each other.
Tension is wondering when in the hell they are gonna switch from one section to another?

Some examples of contrast/dynamics :

Loud vs. quiet
Thoughtful vs. Obnoxious
Fast vs. slow
Smelly vs. Smellier
Domino's vs. Pizza Hut
Broad vs. Specific
Big picture vs. specific details
Scorching lead guitar vs. classical fingerpicking
Banjo vs. Mandolin
Masculine vs. Feminine
Male vocals vs. Female vocals
Happy music vs. Sad vocals/lyrics
Sad music vs. Happy lyrics/vocals

It's often most effective to use both sides of any of the aforementioned contrasts.
Yes, within a single song.
It's possible, I promise.

Keeps the listener engaged.
And that's one of the big goals here, right?
No?
Oh wait, the class on "How to Bore the Hell Out of People" is down the hall and to the left.
Ciao.

Moving on.

Rhyme:

Rhyme time, time to rhyme.
To rhyme rhyme with the rhyme,
should surely be a crime.
Brother can you spare a dime?
My lyrical skills are so sublime.

You get the point.

Rhyming is pretty much essential for songwriters, but if used incorrectly, it sounds really really stupid.

There are a few ways to rhyme not so obnoxiously:
1)   Vary the placement of the rhyme — use internal rhyme.
     Instead of:
     Walking walking to the road
     I had to stop and lick a toad
     You might say:
      Walking walking to the road
      A toad and my tongue did meet
      Discreetly, I might add.
2)   Use a rhyming dictionary !
     It can really help.
     Plus you stumble on words you like but might not have considered.
3)   Leaving out a rhyme can have just as much impact, especially if you've been rhyming in a strict pattern.

Rhyme should be used to further the song.

If used wrong, it will put folks to sleep.
Which is bad.

Unless you're singing a lullabye to those annoying kids you're being paid less than minimum wage to babysit for hours on end.

Active Listening

We often listen to music to forget about the world around us.
"Zoning out," I believe it's called.

But not people like me.
Any time I hear a song, I am picking it apart to examine its construction.
I imagine the writing process, the recording process, all of it, peeling back the song's layers, asking myself some or all of the following:

What are the instruments?
What are the lyrics?
What's the message?
Is he drunk or what?
What's this dude's problem?
Why does he want to share this particular feeling with me?
Was this song labored over or spontaneous or both?
Is this a singular vision or the work of a group?
What is it trying to do?
Entertain?
Make you dance?
Provoke thought?
Make me leave the room?
Could it be lengthened?
Shortened?
When was it made?
What's the genre?
Most importantly....

Do I like it?
What do I like about it?
What do I not like about it?

Thinking this way might annoy the hell out of people around you who just want to lose themselves in song, but if you asking these questions might perhaps provide an inkling of insight into songwriting construction.

At the very least, it's important to think both ways — to examine the construction, to examine the details, but also to approach the song as if you know nothing.
You also have to keep in mind that good art reveals itself over time.
I think of songs that way too.
They have immediate appeal but also hold up under scrutiny.

What would an 8-year old think of this song?
An 18-year old?
An old man?

While it's important to think about these details, you have to remember that most folks who hear your music will know nothing about music, except whether they like it or not.
They couldn't care less how it was made.
So it's best to not get caught up in a solipsistic navel-gaze-a-thon.

So now let's listen to a few songs, keeping in mind all these questions I ask of songs, and also commenting on the song as it goes by.

"The Boxer" - Paul Simon
"The Business" – a Tribe Called Quest
"Fingerbib" – Aphex Twin
"Ella Guru" – Captain Beefheart
"I'll Be Your Mirror" - Velvet Underground
"Dancing on the Ceiling" – Lionel Richie
"Living Without You" – Randy Newman
"Winter Lady" – Leonard Cohen
"Long Distance Call" - Muddy Waters

USE YOUR EARS.

LISTEN.

Appendix B: Photographs

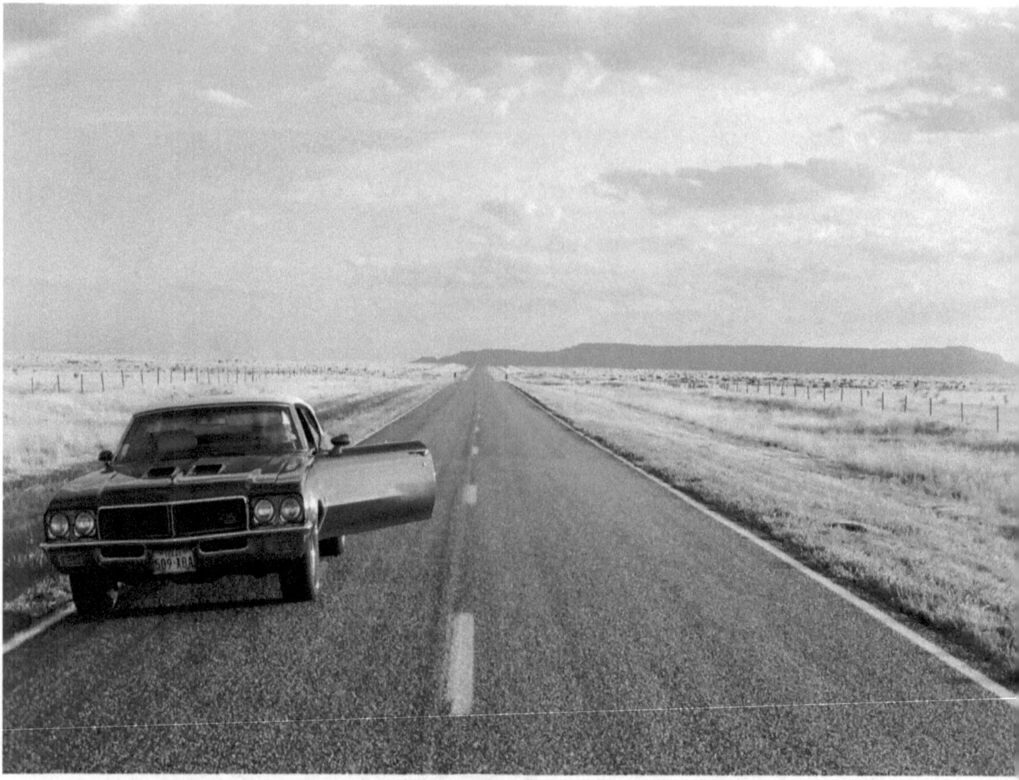

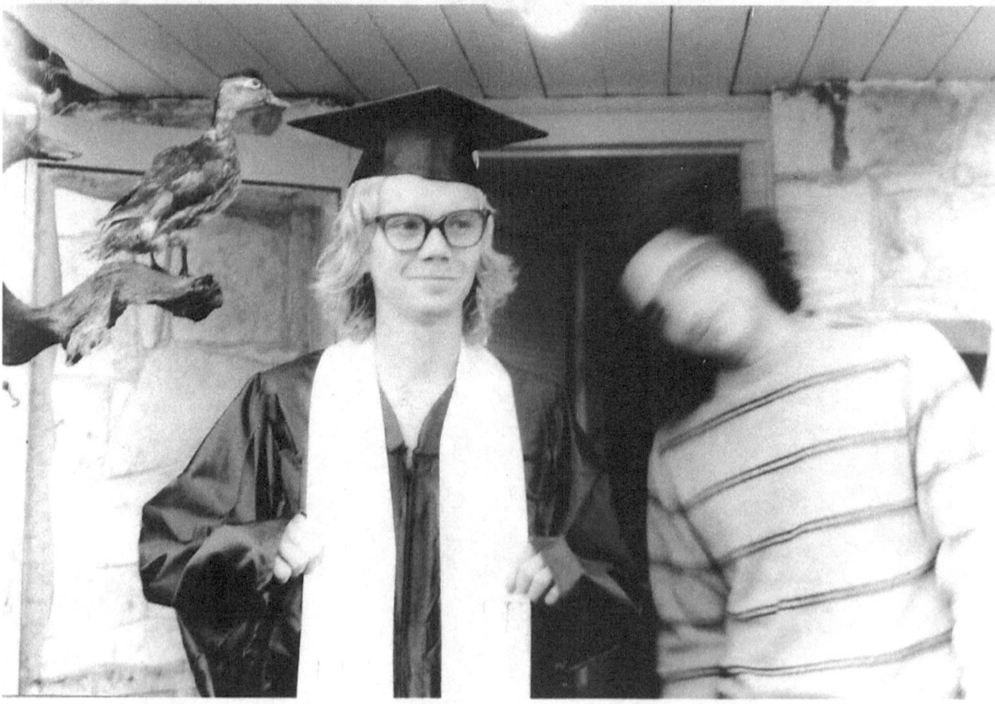

Chin to top of hair is from 1" (dotted line) to 1-3/8 (solid line) on passport photo

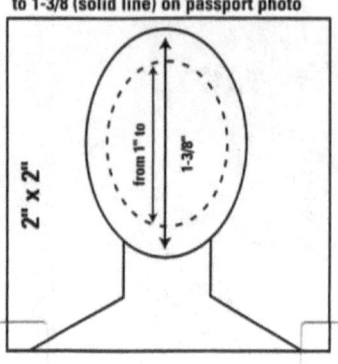

Chin to top of hair is from 1" (dotted line) to 1-3/8 (solid line) on passport photo

Tuck the corners of each passport photo under the diecuts

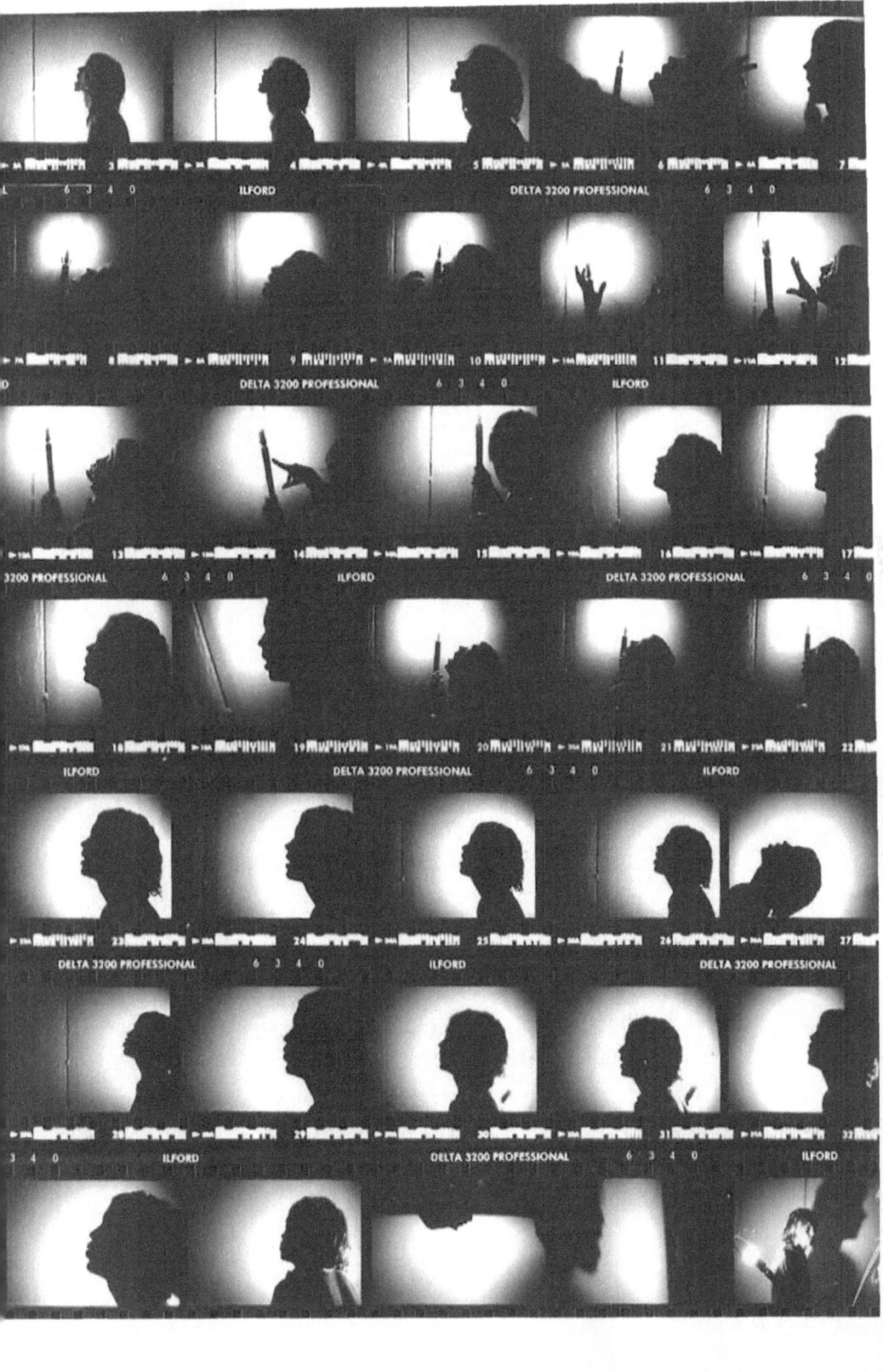

Thank You
For Observing
the
3 Beer Limit

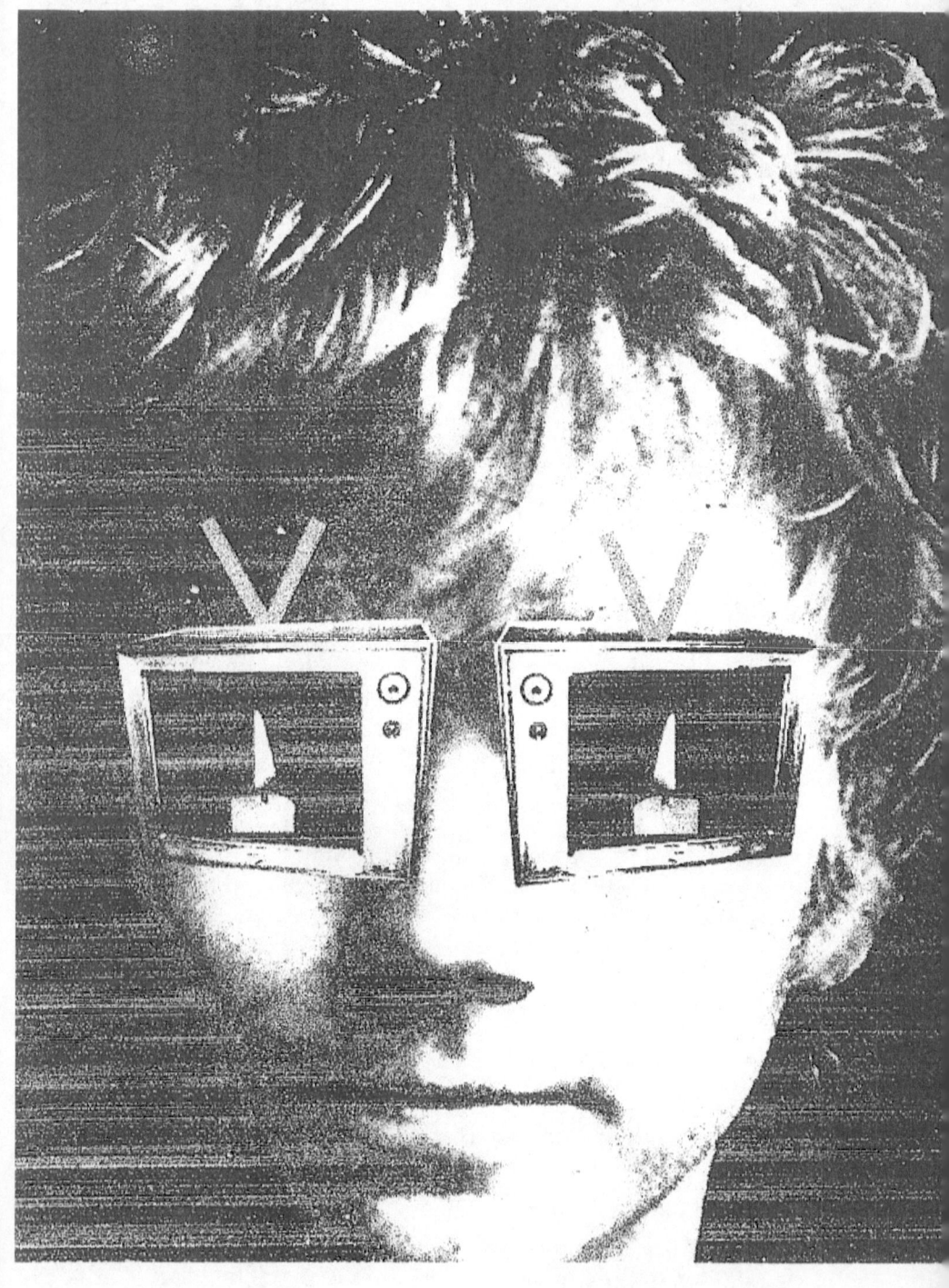

Appendix C: Letters to Xavier Mazure

Hi Xavier,

From,
Bill

Interviews are opportunities for an artist/human/musician to provide context [for] their work.

This presents an opportunity: what context to create? Something to underscore the frail beauty? To firm its indifferent armor? To confuse, entertain, provoke?

I have tried all of these, with varying results.

Usually, the best approach is to handle the question like a basketball.

Dribble it through the legs, pass off on occasion, spin it on your finger (showboat!) and, when the time comes, drill it straight through the hoop.

Hello Xavier,

I like the idea of physical replies. And there are no replies more physical than this old typewrtier. That tactile rush.... changes the words I choose.

Anyway.

Do I think regret is a waste of time? Of course. Do I enjoy wasting time? Hmmmm. Can I get back to youon that?

Just kidding. Sort of.

Am I still sometimes afflicted by regret? Sure, but less and less as time passes. As new and beautiful songs and images and memories and wins and losses pile up in my psyche like the falling leaves of a maple tree.... I am left to marvel at their fading color and ... well.

I have to rake them (the leaves of memory) every now and then.

I began as a DIY scrapper, was in a buzz band, then got thrust onto the national stage at te wrong moment aligned with the wrong producer, wrong record label, wrong manager, wrong creative partners of every type.... shit. Even my pants were the wrong size. Just wrong wrong wrong.

I remember meeting the head of Capitol, a guy named Andy. During our meeting, he talked about himself the entire time. I noticed this as a theme amongst the music industry, both high and law and in between -- everybody just wants to talk about themselves! Especially after doing a giant line of cocaine off a mixing board.
(sniff)
"dude, you have to check out my music. I am fucking incredible."

That happened to me on capitol. We got taken to meet that dandy warhols loser, whats his face, xxxx courtney taylor taylor taylor taylor or whtever.

We just wanted to steal his weed but he made us listen to his new album. Well, it was his album release party.

But it was that same cocaine ego delusion you find everyxwhere.

xxxxx Dandy warhols guy kept pointing to the speaker and sayin "i am a fucking genius. i am so fucking good."

All I could hear was standard chords, overblown/boring xxxxx xxxxx production, and inane lyrics.
So it goes.

Back to my life. I watched my bandmates change and the people around me change as money came into the picture, then I watched the whole thing curdle and go putrid, a rancid kitchen experiment gone horribly wrong, then everybody jumped out the kitchen through the window and i was left holding

404

steaming pile of shit with my name emblazoned across the top
in bold letters.
so it goes.

I'd gone from a DIY local to a buzz band, to a cautionary tale
to a ghostly outcast of the music industry, to now being a
weary survivor, except i am not weary at all! I am energized

and that is the supreme irony of all this. As my commercial
prospects have dwindled to a puny speck of dirt on the bottom
of a PR firm's wing-tip loafer, my skills and inspiration and
overall vision have just gotten better and better. I am
doing what I set out to do initially -- music that crosses
genres and boundaries, guided only by inspiration, humor,
empathy, wordplay, surprise, revelation, rooted in my
honest experience. Just..... soemthing honest.

Even when you're being fake, that's revealing yourself too,
though, no?

h, you know what I mean. No time for semiotics, semantics,
and all this other collegiate crap.

It's always been, and always will be, about building a body of
work.

Right now, I feel very close to my creativity, to my inspirati
on, & close to my vision.... like, maybe i am on a hike,
standing on a ridge, and i see the path in front of me, and it
is curvy and muddy and mostly under cover of brush and thorns
and there will be folk either pelting me with rotten fruit
on gthe way or else just not even seeing me pass by.....

Why was I on Cpaitmix Crapitol? What possessed to ruin my
music career in such oblivious fashion? Welll..... I did
not realize that was happening.
Was it bravery? Stupidity? Success? Failure? Sometimes, a venture can be all of these things at once.
I think the appeal was how WRONG it seemed. Yes, I am perver
se in that way.
I wanted to sgow that I was bigger than labels, bigger than
niches -- that the old rules did not apply to me! I think
this is a mistake of youthful eugxand hubris.

I of course learned that.... indeed, the old rules are very tr
ue, corporate labels suck, and for the rest of my life, I
is doomed to learn things the hard way. Is there any other
way to learn, though? Yes..... youcould have a guide, a
mentor, an example. I had none.... no sir. I stux stepped
forth into whatever life was giving me.... a slap in the face.
But that's ok... I turned it into many songs.

In a way, it is xx very annoying to have Sound Team define so much of my trajectory.

Why?

Because the songs I have written since then are... infinitely better.

Also, becuase that band was sort of wrenched away from me by money men, producers, managers, and,.ofx bandmates. I had stopped singing when the music got louder.... much to my later regret. After I'd stepped away from the mic, I lost my nerve .... and i took a long time getting it back again.

In the meantime, the xx band had taken a dramatic turn away from what I was feeling....

So xix the thing that derailed my career might've been sticking around too long... after things started feeling weird ?   I wanted it to work....

Alas.

I am in a much better place now.... in every regard except "commerical success."   What does that mean, ultimately? You can pay for a nicer tombstone.

"HERE LIES A SUPER SUCCESSFUL GUY"

Yeah.... not interested in that.

When you die, all you can take is the journey.

In that regard, I am a shining beacon of success.... and still flouri$hing.

But real... talk.   Can we reture that fucking word "SUCCESS" already?   It is such a narrow stupid view of the process. It attempts to fit music into a money-man's box.

I won't deny though.... I could use a good break.   W₂ all cou -ld.

As long as the songs continue to flow, and they rxxxxix resona -te with my own experience.... as long as I am drawing breath. I will exhale that which is inside of me.

Damn the torpedoes.

Bill Baird

Hello Xavier,

And so continues our ~~correspondency~~ correspondence. There is a beauty in the tactile.... i think it reminds us of our mortality, the passing nature of time.... the internet can feel removed from time, which is useful in certain ways, but can actually rob us of our humanity.... who fucking knows.

Henry Darger is indeed an inspiration. To have one's final resting place be a final and full pexression of their creative vision -- this has always been a goal of mine. To be learning and creating until my moment of death.... and even the ~~momen~~ moment of death becames a creative act.... to recreate life out of life (in the words of james joyce). Which... coincidentally, would be my tombstone, if I were to have one:

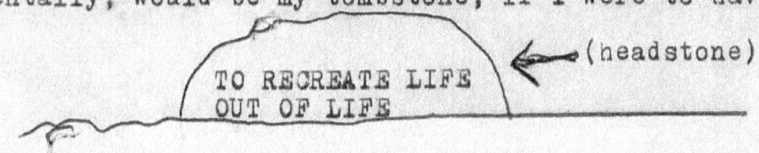

It is a quote from "A portrait of the Artist as a Young Man," by James Joyce, and when I read it, it fundamentally changed me..... if you want to be an artist, just fucking be one!

I was fascinated by his playing with form -- specifically the way he structured his book and the chapters themselves in the same way as Rembrandt designed his paintings.... on either side of a mirror would be reflections , and in the middle.... emptiness, which is actually infinite.

I structured a Sound Team after this concept, actually, and probably ~~a~~ quite clumsily, but in retropspect I respect the ambition.

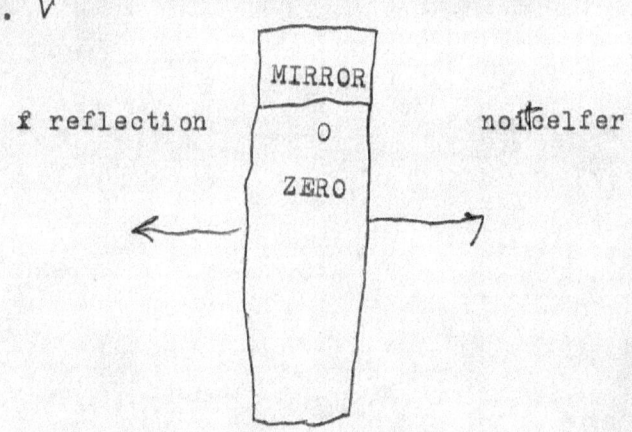

You mentioned hearing my ± podcast about leaving Capitol and working on the kiddie train.

I think for me it was exactly what I needed at the moment. Th-e joy of children is the ░░ ░░░ ultimate cure ░ for cynicism and disappointment.... the wonder, the renewal, the joy. It was perfect ░░ in so many ways -- delighting children, plenty of time to write songs, weird characters as my co-worke-rs, plus the fascination of doing basic maintenence on an actual train, operating the switches, etc. They even gave me one of those train hats.

I think perhaps some folks thought I was a fucking loon, or taking a giant step backwards, and letting myself collapse. I'm certain my family thought that.... but the reality was... it was an incredible time, and such a gift. I was able to regroup and re-commit for another round of creative endeavor.

I will send you the transcript of that podcast.... can;t type it right now though.... coffee's getting cold and i'm running late in the day.

I wrote that song Goodbye Dear Friend of Mine there on the bench while waiting my turn to drive the train... around that same time I also wrote Dear Broken ░░░░ Friend and Dear Friend (Collapsing Diomino). They are of course all related.

H░░░░xxxxx░x░░░g░░░░x░x░░░x

This was intentional for several reasons.

First, I was consciously embarking on creating a lifelong weav-e, a 'conceptual continuity,' which would connect songs, phrases, characters░, storylines, and albums over the course of my entire life. So that each new creation feeds into the whole, and they all relate to each ░░ other -- telling one larger story.

I stole this idea from two places -- Of Human ░░░░x Bondage by Somerset M░a/gham and Frank Zappa. Muagham described each life as a beautiful intricate weave of all events, and episode-s, and ups and downs.... it all becomes part of a single beautiful thing.

And Frank Zappa, despite his often annoying music, had some br-illiant ideas. Among them the 'conceptual continuity', wherein all his creative works are actually part of a much larger story .

(for what it's worth, my favorite zappa by far is his work with the mothers of invention, specifically 'we're only in it for the money,' but not his horrid 1986 re-do. it works almost as a musique concrete tape p░░░x piece.... brilliant)

Anyway.   Dear Friend, Goodbye Dear Friend, and Dear Broken Friend
(and others!░) all relate to each other, yes obviously from the titles, but also in terms of subject░ matter.

It's like that film Rashomon.   Have you seen it?   It's the same story, but told from different, and even contradicotry perspectives.

In the same way, each song is describing a man who has reached the end, who has failed, basically. Things went to shit.

Except in the process of telling, the perspective shifts -- one man accuses another of fucking things up, only to realize that the other man sees him as doing the exact same thing... and so the song can either be about another man in an accusatory fashion, or about himself, if he is willing to examine the situation deeply.

The 'collapsing domino' song differs a bit, however.

It stems from my time as a pizza delivery man for Domino's Pizza. After excelling in school and having bold ambitions of writing and creating great works of art, I found myself slaving away delivering pizzas, and.... well.... I felt like a complete failure. A total fuck-up.

I did get to deliver a pizza to Michael Bolton.

Highlught of my time at Domino's . But I saw my collpase into this inane dead-end life as initiating a series of failures from which I would never return.

I ended up getting fired for eating one of my orders. Oops.

And I got the song.

Hello Xavier.

Sorry, had to cut my hair. Where were we? Ah yes.
You had asked me about why I moved from Texas to California, a
and to describe my various studio situations.
It can get long and boring and dramatic... I will do my best
at brevity and let's se....

I was born in Texas, and lived there most of my life, and owe
much of my rebellion to its stiflingly conservative culture.

You see, in Texas, they love to remind you all the time
how big Texas is, and how Texan you are, especially if
they are trying to sell you a truck or a hamburger.

TEXAS SIZED

In a way, it is a blessing. It gives you something to
push against. If I were surrounded by like-minded
artists, would I be so angry, so eager to create new
worlds? Definitely NO.

But I'd lived there forever. As they say.... familiarity
breeds contempt.

I knew everybody there, owned a home, had a nice studio,
and had cultivated a x decent repuatix reputation as a
local weirdo. But I knew that if I wanted a lifetime
commitment to the creative process, I needed to throw
away everything familiar and re-tool --

Also, I was offered a teaching assistant position at Mills
College in Oakland (next to San Francisco) so it xxxx seemed
like the perfect opportunity,

I'd just had a child and I keep (could) see my life stretching out
before, the entire rest of my life, being that local guy who
used to be famous, and so forth.

I knew that I needed to throw it away. I did not ralize how
hard it would be to move away from local notoriety and become
completely unknown.

My music has immensely imporved, it is much much better know
, and I have laid the groundwork for another decade of
inspiration, at least, but, well, it is hard as hell.

I miss my friends and family.

Be careful what you ask for, you just might get it.

I wanted a complete removal of familiarity, so that I might
go much deper into my creative life, and I got it.

But it has been lonely.

I regret nothing!

Regarding my studio situations, I have always needed a place outside the home in which to work.

There is something that happens when I walk out the door... It sets an intention without too much effort. I tend to not waste any time when I get to my studio.

When I work at home, I will drink coffee, drink tea, eat cereal, spin records, nap, everything except work.

In Austin, I had two studios. The first was called Big Orange, which was in honor of Big Pink, where Bob Dylan and the Band recorded the Basement Tapes. Also thinking about orange as the power of love and creativity.

It was a magical place, a former record pressing plant, an old barn, which I rehabilitated, and which has now been swallowed up by the forces of gentrification and likely turned into a tapas bay yoga studio vaping shop.

I got kicked out by my old bandmate... or, rather, he said "I will never leave." And so I left.

Started Baby Blue, which is the oppposite of Big Orange, both in terms of size and its placement on the color wheel.

I now work in the warehouse of Paul Dresher. He is a famous composer here in San Francisco. I work in his storage unit. There is Chinese radio station in the building whose transmission will probably give me cancer. I can hear the radio broadcast coming through the light bulbs.

Yes, seriously. I had no idea radio could be broadcast through light bulbs. For that reason, I call it Fluruoresecent Radio.

It is littered with many projects, my tape machines, childrens artowrk, records, books, scores and letters, and a thousand projects waiting to be sortedd and disseminated. It is a magical place.

Hello Xavier,

And so continues our journey of words, separated by language & continent, but... who cares.

You asked me about my covering songs. Why play the songs of others?

To whiich I reply... why the hell not?

Ok, back to the beginning. When I first learned music, I learned by deconstructing songs and putting them back together on my 4 track. I was ixtxx BORN out of cover songs.

Someimtes there already existxs a song that expresses perfectly what you are feeling... why not just vibe with that?

There is a fetish around "originality" in American pop music, but I ix think it is largely a scam.

Let's just dip dispel with this idea, shall we? I mean, for xukixxxakxy for fuck's sake, we are all copies of our parents. Ok, that is too easy.

I think the idea of "orignality" and the individual voice, has been manipulated in the USA as a way to xxxx sell us things we do not need.

Instead of seeing ourselves as part of a larger continuum of culture, we are trained to believe that now is the only time, that you are the only person, etc.

Clearly, this is all bullshit.

I guess the prevailing model of doing things just seems played out to me.

So I look back through history, to see what inspires me.

In Texas, there is of course country music. I grew up hating this music, because I thought it represented shit-kickers, racists, backwards-minded simpletonxs.

This is of course sometimes true, but like so many cliches, it ix exists for the lazy-minded, for those not willing to actually dive into the reality of the situation.

In reality, a good country song is simply electrified folk music, it's the blues with a hillbilly accent.

Once I could see past the cliches, I saw this deep and beautiful culture from my own backyard that I had previously disdained.

And it is hugely ixxixxi instructive.

In country music, they re uently do cover songs, but in their own styles. WHY? Because ix if you bring your own energy to it, you make it yours.

Country artists will re uently re-record the same song, many times over. This has hugely inspired me.

Once I have written a song,(or anybody else has)it is not something to be revered and handled carefully with lace-y white gloves.

NO.

It is something to be played with, to be re-interprexted, to be changed and stretched and destroyed and put back together again, it is raw material for a different part of the process:

- colors - (timbre) --production (combinations of textures)--

-shifts of context-

And playing with each of these actually dramatically changes our idea of the song.

Have you ever heard a busker sing a fucking horrific version of a beautiful song?

Maybe the song survived the mangled delivery, but probably not

And now you see my point. There is no separating a song from how it sounds, from its delivery. In essence, it's almost as if eveery time a song is sung, it is being freshly written, in a way distinct from all other previous versions.

I think I can bring my own perspective and experiences to bear on any song, in fact that has long been a challenge for me.... can the perfect delivery save a shit song?

That is at least part of the reason I covered that yacht-rock atrocity "Sailing" by Christopher Cross.

I also believe that, by deconstructing the work of a master, you absorb some of that work into yourself, forever.

For example, when I read the 1st edition of <u>Leaves of Grass</u> by Walt Whitman, I knew I wanted this information stored inside me in a way beyond merely reading it.

So I recopied the entire book by hand.

Hello Xavier,

you mentioned Lawrence. He is a gero of mine. Of course.
The songs sing in my heart.

You asked about myth, legend, image, and xixxxx distance.

These are treachxerous waters, and must be handled delicately.
I claim no real understanding here.

I imagine mythology as the ongoing story that humanity writezx
writes about itself. It extends back thousands of years.

Legend is something more timely. It is simply when the
behavoir of a human is so outragous, extreme, or
unprecedented, that it gets repeated over and over again.

Image is what artists project. Every human does this to som
-e degree but artists actively engage with it.

As Kim Gordon said, "I think people want to see somebody
on stage who they can believe in."

ixxxixk
I did some research along these lines before traveling to
India. I read Joseph Campbell "The Hero with a Thousand
Faces," and could certainly see in my own life something
of "the heroes journey."

But the reality is, people who relate these ideas to themselves are kind of fucking annoying and insufferable.

I think most of xx the mythology I have constructed around
hte life of the artists stems from Honore de Balzacm, speci
-fically his book "Lost Illusions," but also in his own
self-mytholigzing.

I think my favorite artist who could project his image and
manipulate it as part of his xrs art.... would have to be
another Frenchman. Erik Satie.

I think of the image you project similarly to how I described
a song -- it s is something maleable, to be played with.
Like a basketball.

"Lost Illusions" describes the corrupt landscape of the arts
in details that feel m modern. Timeless. It is the mytholo
-gy of the corruption of the artist by the world.

My favorite story about art is called "The Hunger Artist,"
by Franz Kafka.

In the story, bouregois patrons line up to pay money to see
a man starving himself.

This xxx says so much about how xx the public wants to see
their artists.
I have done my best to toss off whatever inherited myths I can

, mostly the idea that suffering creates great art. This is bullshit.

It gives yousomething to write about, yes, but usually much later.

When I am horribly depresseed, I only waxnt to watch horrible Van Damme movies, not make great art.

I try to stand outsides my own story whenever possible, and stand outside the bullshit inherited mythologies.

This is not for me to determine. Other people can do that.

I am simply committed to "recreate life out of life," until I am dead.

FLOW CHART FOR SOME BULLSHIT

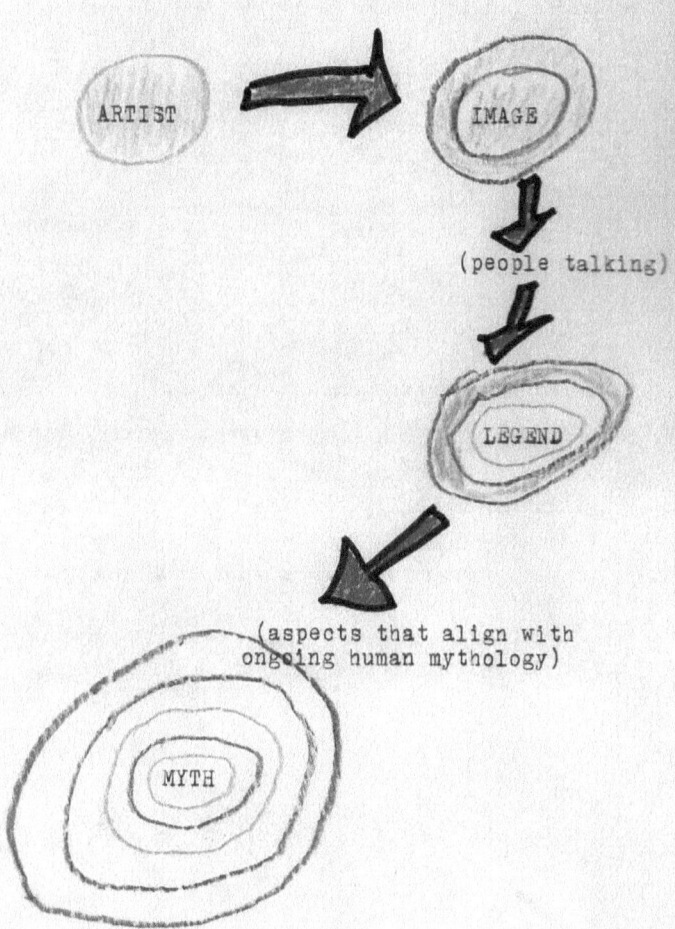

As my life has progressed, I try to carry around only as much of this stuff as is needed.

To carry an image at all times is a tremendous burden.

I have tried to make myself transparent before my image, so I don't have to waste time explaining or pretending.

Artists who do this are ~~xxxx~~ often full of shit. (I enjoy it when they are good, though).

Essential reading list for image/art/projection/myth:

- interviews with Charles Bukowski
- interviews with Mark E Smith
- Lawrence
- A Mammal's Notebook by Erik Satie
- Lost Illusions by Honore de Balzac
- A Portrait of the Artist as a Young Man by James Joyce
- Don Van Vliet
- Psychomagic by Jodorowsky
- Hero with a Thousand Faces by Joseph Campbell
- Beneath the Underdog by Charles Mingus
- Miles by Miles Davis
- Bound For Glory by Woody Guthrie
- The Banquet Years by Riger Shattuck
- Scott Mcloud, Understanding Comics
- ~~Letters 1873-90~~ by Banksy
- ~~Letters 1873-90~~
- Letters 1873 - 90 by Vincent Van Gogh
- The Decisive Moment by Henri Cartier-Bresson
- Believing is Seeing by Errol Morris
- Jeffrey Lewis
- The Creative Habit, by Twyla Tharp
- The Hunger Artist by Franz Kafka

~~Ixuitaintaixxxaxexdaxixdxtaxraauxxxxaatxaixaf~~

In areas such as these, I do not have answers, only questions.

I do not think the goal is to understand one's place in the larger system, necessarily, but mostly to understand oneself.

And I know myself well enough to know ~~x~~ that dwelling on this stuff makes me go bat-shit crazy.

~~B~~

Yours,

Bill Baird

Hello Xavier,

You asked me about Lawrence from Felt.

The first song xxx x I heard was Sublight Bathed the Golden Gl
-ow, and it combined several of my relevant interests x in a x
way I'd never heard before:
-- jangle guitar i, melodic lead lines, but not cheesy
   heavy metal style leads
-- music which makes you want to jump up and start running
-- the hilarious shit-talking lyrics, making fun of fake
   intellectuals, which is one of my main hobbies, although
   I could probably be credibly accused of that myself
-- the perfect compression of the records, a hallmark of
   my favorite rock n roll and psych records of the 60s

I recorded my own homage to the song....
     it is called "Bending the Truth" from my album "Gone"

His vibe -- that of hiding in plain sight -- has always
appealed to me.

The idea of creating songs that, in some alternate universe,
would be #1 pop hits.

The humor, the jangle, the drive.

My ~~xxxxixx~~ forthcoming records are both excellent.

The first, titled "Flower Children's Children's Children," is about the withering of the great California dream.
 Musically, it draws from and seeks company amongst the follow-ing:
  13th floor elevators, early meat puppets, the mothers of in-vention circa "we're only in it for the money," early 90s guitar music, immediacy, noise, a few moments of Robert Fripp and maybe a smidgen of motorhead and MC5.

It is a genre ~~xxi~~ I call psychedelic boogie-~~xxggix~~ woogie, but I guess it is really just rock and roll with extra colors and an axe to grind about the world in free-fall collapse.

The other record, which is a 2XLP, but may be split in two, is not finished, but centers ~~xf x~~ on the idea of

ETERNAL RETURN

Which is a heavy philosophical concept, sort of related to the snake eating its tail (the ouroboros).

A fancy way to describe death, rebirth, and that weird ~~x~~ feeli-ng that history just keeps ~~xxx~~ repeating itself.

"History does not repeat itself, but it does rhyme."

That is perhaps more apt.

Musically, it escapes ~~my~~ my brain how to box ~~x~~ It in.

Andy, the producer / engineer, has described it as
      "KRAFTWERK MEETS SYD BARRETT"

(Moebius s-trip related to Ourobors as related in Nabokov's "Pale Fore)

Hey, sounds good to me.

It is a microcosm of the ~~xxxxpixxx~~ "conceptual" continuity thing you heard me rattling on about before.

Songs refer to each other, melodies re-appear, and it all ends up coming full circle.

Potential titles:
 ~~Ouroboros 88~~
 ~~Eternal Return~~
 ~~Cosmic Refund~~
 ~~Boomerang~~

You get ~~x~~ the picture.

It feels like the best work I have ever done, but what the fuck do I know?

I always say that.

Your friend in letters and correspondence,

Bill Baird

Cast of Characters

Sandy -- unattainable feminine muse, a la Nina Simone / Joni Mitchell, Nico... a hybrid of Aphrodite and a creative genius and a beautiful woman... mixed with many of the women i have love and lost and/or never had to begin with... who present themselves almost as a zen puzzle... in order to hold her, you must let go of her

HairySally -- seafaring woman with extremely hairylegs

Stagnant Stan -- lazy self satisfied... isn't he a bit like you and me?

Cpatain Brain -- evil barin floatingin a jar, appears on many albums, songs

Jazz Fashion (Jasper) -- great collaborator and maker of music under the names Brazil and Burner Herzog

Willis McClung -- my best friend and great collaborator who died.... I releaased an album of his music last year... vocal genius

Sam Sanford -- great friend, great artist, member of Sound Team and Sunset -- I released his first record this year - "Years & Years"

Paul -- Austin legend, legendary layabout, barton springs junky, always ready to hand you a bag of weed

Soggy Sailors - drunkensailors aboard the ship that will never reach the shore

Endless Ocean -- the plane of time/space in which we all humans are trapped

Robot Dan -- automaton, works in a cubicle, boring guy, wind him up like a clock and he will do as he's told

Indianna Hale -- great female vocalist and collaborator, performing under her own name.

Judith Horn -- another fine female voice in my recordings.

Ice T -- motivational twitter account

Bob Smith -- not dissimilar to Robot Dan, and he appears as a character on summer is gone and Straight Time

Will Patterson -- longtime collaborator and friend who releases music under the moniker 'Slepp Good' & with RF Shannon now... flowing blonde locks musical prodigy

Freddy Friender -- a dear friend who has become lost on his life's path....

uentin Stoltzfus -- collaborator , producer, and friend... makes music under the names Light Heat & Mazarin... his recently opened studio is where I master many of my releases... he opened the studio with Matt from the Walkmen

Sewage Sirens -- they lure you into the sewer with their golden voices... don't be fooled, it's shitt-y down there

Lady Dark -- the sewage sirens mother

Fading Ear -- a superhero who wears skin colored tights and makes it so people cannot hear negative words which is actually kind of a curse

Lance Dorian -- the classic existential idiot.

Poseidon - Greek god of te ocean... keeper of t e endless ocean... he laughs at humanity
Awesome Andy -- he is helping me record a new record right now Petr
Jana Horn -- my goodness, what a voice! Fre uent collaborato-r... find her own music under her own name!
Charybdis the dumpster -- sucks you into a pile of garbage
Sarah Gauthier -- sang on some tracks, now playing in the group Thor and Friends
David Longoria -- excellent singer/ guitarist and fre uent collaborator.... find his music under the name 'Longwriver"
Ethan Smith -- tall fry, KVRX DJ, excellent human, fre uent collaborator
Turbo Recliner (Jordan Johns) - what a drummer!!
Marissa's Muddy Calm -- cellist, f singer, and she who left the band saying she was lookng forward to doing some laundry... which i respect
John Kolar -- another incredible drummer! Now a hairstylist
Michael Bain -- joined Sunset for a spell, now plays in Sun Ju Sun June.... theplot thickens....
Diamond Dreamer -- px purveyor of beautiful visions... diamond dreams.
Townes the Dog -- my studio dog, who unfortunately died.
Tommy McCutchon -- collaborator on my Sunset albums, he now runs the Unseen Worlds record label
Euclid -- sacred geomtry.... embedded music
Martin Crane-- sometime collaborator, now film composer
Arnold & Jamie -- UK friends who run Talkshow Records and helped me wake from my depressed slumber
David Bartholow -- very old friend, creative collaboraotr, graphic x designer (he designed a Wimbledon poster)
Archer -- frxx lyrical collabortor, sometimes
Brian Wright -- drummer, we recorded 32 songs in one day, he also plays with Graves and Pure Bathing Culture
Pythagorus -- sacred geometry, muzak of the spheres!
Jimi Cabeza de Vaca -- musical collabotor, friend, tourmate
Joel Jerome -- same! Joel posseses one of the great voices in music right now.
Ana Roxanne -- sang on Baby Blue.... and now creates incredible music on her own!
Soft Dolphin -- self explantory
Agitated Larry -- he has been ground down by society's gears
Gabe Pearlman (the ragin cajun) -- old old friend and collaborator
Ingrid -- appearing on forthcoming record! truly and inspiration
Sarah Hennies -- longtime collaborator in the austin days, now making xi a name in the academic music world
Ben Salomon -- cosmic, far out guy, excellent drummer
Dread -- played some congas
Cory Gehrich - owns Sisterly Silence studio in Portland, guitarist on my UK journeys!!
Pete Brown -- songwriter for Cream (he wrote sunshine of your love). we co-wrote two songs.

Jesse ~~xxxx~~ Woods -- what a golden voice! Old Texas friend and collaborator.
Mothball crew (LA session guys) -- Bob Dylan's drummer, aimeee mann's producer...
Pau Wau Nick -- helped me release spring break of the soul, forfeited all my records in a sotrage unxit default, plays in American Sharks
Matt Oliver -- we started Sound Team together
Handsome Dan - (Gottwald) - helped me design the Magnetetracty-s, which graces the cover of Earth into Aether, and is my own 9 string electro-acoustic drone harp....
The Duke (Josh) - lived on my studio couch, helped me record some of my records
Jagged Little Joel -- helped me produce my polished LA album that is no longer in circulation!
Basil - sings a bit and sinpires me to create.

Appendix C: Onward! Through the Many Fogs

(Feature article from Week in Pop, 2016)

Part 1: Brief Introduction Which Spills into Biography of a Would-Be Oceanographer

Hi, my name is Bill[1]. Maybe you've heard of me, maybe you haven't. It's a crowded world, so I begrudge you nothing. In fact, I welcome the chance to introduce myself.

To industry old-timers, I'm a cautionary tale[2]. To my family, I'm the weird uncle.[3] To booking agents and those doing live sound, I'm a headache[4]. To those who know, I'm a relentless seeker of sounds that move my head, heart, legs. To those that don't, now you do. If I had a choice, I'd probably be a spelunker or boat captain. But I don't have a choice. Music chose me... I tried to run away but it's no damn use. Onward, through the fog of unknowing.

I've released 8 albums in the past three years with many more coming. All told, I've released somewhere around 20 or 30[5]. Some are probably terrible.[6] I don't listen to the old ones. I used to just record a one-off cassette of songs and call it an album, so counting releases is problematic. This lack of formality has been both a strength and hindrance. I'm pretty much forever banished to the music industry ditch, but the view is more interesting down here anyway.[7] And honestly I think the songs get better every time. I live for the magic, when something appears out of nowhere and you react in the moment. The fog of unknowing that blows between my ears.

I've been working on my own genre for awhile now....
Surreal-Textured-Raw-American-Yeehaw Folky-Lyric-Idiot-Psych.
Which shortens to an anagram... STRAY FLIP. It's pretty specific. Doesn't make much sense but then again neither does life, or music. You just embrace it.[8]

Part 2: Navigating the LA Fog of Industry Illusion vs. the SF Fog of Techno-Utopian Progress

Last year, I recorded an album for Super Deluxe. They make cool shit across all platforms. And they gave me an opportunity to make a true LA songwriter album. Opportunity of a lifetime.

Negotiating the deal proved a circuitous process. RZA heard my songs but we never worked out a collaboration. I had sushi with Anthony Kiedis. It all felt very absurdly LA, in the best way. In LA, you become an actor playing yourself. The industry illusion pervades every interaction, like an unseen fog. If you remain cognizant and have fun with it, you can manipulate the fog. If you take the game (or yourself) too seriously, you forget the fog is even there. You disappear inside of it.

---

1 My name is actually Morton Williams Baird III. Bill as a nickname derives from the middle name, Williams, so really it should be plural. As in, 'Bills.' Which perhaps explains various identity issues.
2 http://www.imposemagazine.com/features/bill-bairds-brief-history-of-major-label-blah
3 My old nickname was Buck. As in, Uncle Buck. The plot thickens.
4 http://www.billbillbillbill.com/mundus-novus
5 I've never embarked on an official count, as I feel every time I attribute a number to my world of music, it changes that world. Almost like the Observer Effect in quantum physics. From our dear wiki-world, "In **physics**, the **observer effect** is the theory that simply observing a situation or phenomenon necessarily changes that phenomenon. This is often the result of instruments that, by necessity, alter the state of what they measure in some manner."
6 My high school love song cassettes are horrible.
7 Borrowed tune, a la Neil Young.
8 Embracing senselessness has a funny way of making sense of a situation.

LA's fog is not to be confused with its smog, whose frozen-freeway-parking-lots breathe black-lung to those slumping through their daily slog. The working stiffs, the hopeless drunks, the wide-eyed zealots, the plastic bubble beach bimbos, the yoga-pant-botox-bleach-mid-life-crisis in slow motion. This is LA's noise and pollution.... let it blow by you. There are harbors of real emotion and feeling amidst the smog, puddles of honest-to-god humanity amidst the concrete. In the tension between LA's fantasy and its crowded reality lies the essential beauty of the place.

LA has its fog of industry illusion — here in San Francisco we have the fog of techno-utopianism.[9] The world's greatest minds find new ways to freeze folks to their phones, feeding that data into a grand virtual computer consciousness, which will one day replace the military in our overseas fight for the 99¢ cheeseburger.[10] This illusion of progress, crammed into our vehicles of convenience while the world's wild beauty shrinks exponentially by the hour, this is the SF fog of 2018, and it has engulfed the world. SF was quite recently the capital of the west coast weirdo underground, believe it or not. Nowadays, SF folks getting 'weird' means donning non-matching socks onboard a Tiki-Bar-Taco-Tuesday-Shuttle-Bus to the office in Mountain View.

The tension between SF's tech-utopian fog, and LA's magic illusion fog, this was the basis for my new record. A lonely guy caught in the middle of all this, stranded in a new city.[11]

I long ago gave up the idea of wealth and fame, or even cursory respect. Fool's errands! Empty goals. All I want out of music (and life) is the joy of discovery. An adventure. Something new. A horizon this wide leaves ample room for bizarre circumstance. You end up crashing on Flea's couch, selling your sunglasses to James Murphy, and stealing Primal Scream's floral arrangement. Stories for another time.[12]

Part 3: Funneling the Fog into Song

I left for LA with a few dozen demos, a backpack, a blanket, no signed contract and nowhere to sleep. Everything felt vivid and desperate but very alive. Started pre-production, which I didn't even know was a thing. I learned what it means: you sit in a room and play the songs and somebody tells you if they're too long, too short, or just right. In this case, that somebody was Joel Shearer, my producer. Joel makes mega-awesome-healing-drone music with his guitar and at least sixty pedals. Probably more. He was house-sitting a home literally overflowing with gongs.

Typical pre-production day: I'd walk through the gong-filled house and gently tap each one and out to the back studio and strum through my tunes and then find a couch elsewhere to crash for the night. The backyard was filled with parrots who squawked as I day-drank bottles of beer and wine. The fog of LA illusion had surrounded me, and I wafted its sandalwood-concrete scent.

A week later, the session started. First person I met at the session was the the drummer, Don Heffington, total LA legend and Van Dyke Parks' partner in crime. I knew he'd played with Butch Morris, famed avante-garde composer and originator of 'conduction,' an improv technique also used by Zappa. Don Heffington had been Bob Dylan's drummer

---

9 An illuminating and disturbing look into techno-utopianism can be found in <u>Hypernormalisation</u>, a recent BBC documentary by Adam Curtis.
10 I don't eat meat, but, ya know, garden burger doesn't quite sound the same.
11 I'm a native Texan. California is a foreign land to me. Being a foreigner is good for writing songs.
12 Don't ask.

— I was kind of floored. I mean, Bob Dylan isn't exactly complex rhythmically, but, well, ya know. He's Bob Dylan. And here was his drummer, playing on my record.

We tracked a couple tunes and everybody got a feel. The producer and the engineer, Chris, were feeling me out. Could I deliver the goods? I sang my guts out and laid my heart on the line. I delivered the goods. You listen and be the judge. It's splayed all across the internet.

Next morning, woke with an ominous feeling. The fog had turned to smoke.... our studio had burned down. Top story on local news. Nobody died, thank god, but it's a hell of a way to start a record. Ended up in a different studio on the Sunset strip. A giant framed smiling portrait of Alanis Morrissette hung above the toilet, smiling down on every urination. The fog of industry illusion had taken Alanis' smiling form and bestowed her mid-90's blessings on us all.

The actual process of recording was new to me[13], and a complete joy. I worried about nothing except singing my songs and showing up on time.[14] There was Paul, Aimee Mann's producer, on bass. And Jeben, keyboardist from Public Image, LTD, dialing in keyboard sounds. And, of course, Zac Rae, LA sound magician and keyboard master, playing everything from Celeste to Mellotron.

I'd spent years doing everything myself. I had in my mind some ideal of vertical integration — I wrote the songs, played all the instruments, hand printed the covers, stitched the fucking t-shirts. But you know what? That shit is TIRING. Even more tiring is repeating yourself. Sometimes the most experimental thing you can do is be normal. Be straight.[15]

And you know what? When you share the load, when you delegate, when you work with people who are really good at their jobs, it's a revelation. They make different choices. And even better? Everybody gets to take the credit. Bearing the load all on your shoulders.... gets tiresome. Yes, I gave up control, but in the moment I let go, the world opened up to me.

Six weeks later, I'd couch surfed my way to my most polished album. Will it earn my my long-overdue fame and fortune?[16] Fuck, who cares. The world owes me nothing. I am just happy and grateful to be here. I will never make another record like this one, and that's just the way it should be. Setting sail for unknown shores, sail billowing with the windy fog of unknowing. The unknown propels me forward.

Part 4: Notes from Inside the Fog

If your music is truly alive, it's a dialectic — always in reaction to what came before.[17] You get closer and closer to an idea and you finally cream it.... time to let it die. To those interested in pegging me down (in-laws, career counselors, prosecuting attorneys), my path might seem aimless, futile, feckless. To those interested in process, however, they understand what I'm doing. I'm staying alive and vital. Only through vigilant effort can you maintain your way through the fog of illusion. It just so happens... my way is basically crawling on the floor. Which is helpful. I can claim failure as a win. You only

---

13 My first full album working with a producer that wasn't kind of a disaster.
14 I wasn't worried, though.
15 Defying expectations is the name of the game.
16 Probably not.
17 Sometimes repeating yourself is in reaction to what came before. Well, duh. By definition. And repetition can feel just as vibrant as change. Repetition is a form of change, as they say.

lose by not playing at all.

All I really want with my songwriting is baseball percentages. If I can bat a .400, which is just 4 out of 10 songs being great, then I'm Ted freaking Williams[18]. Even if each album feels incomplete, a look back later reveals great songs strewn along the path. But looking back makes me feel queasy and I try not to do it.[19]

All these bullshit words and theories change, depending on what you ate for breakfast[20]. How you're treating your body. Cuz your brain is part of your body as much as your arms and legs. Just cuz your thoughts float doesn't mean they don't originate in the physical. So you gotta take care of the vehicle. Or abuse it wisely. Sometimes the clarity found at the bottom of a bottle of whiskey is not found any other way. I don't do much of that anymore, but a good blow-out every now and then.... clears the pipes.[21]

I go on long hikes here in the bay area. Stare into space and listen to the silence. Sound is just ruptured air, and music is organized sound. Sometimes you feel so right with the world that everything you hear sounds like music. Sometimes it's all a grating noise. When the sounds grate, you need solace within your people. It's hard to find your tribe in SF these days. I'm still searching. Yuppie-frat-rat-dirtbags litter the SF streets like human-sized vanilla Frappucinos. I've had at least twenty bandmates since moving here and some are still with me. Jasper and Tom both play in the excellent SF band Brasil. Burner Herzog too. Marissa has her own group, Sucker Crush. Kristin Klein inspires me with her humor and positive purpose. Mark David Ashworth spins otherworldly beauty with his words and melodies. Indianna Hale has a heavenly voice. Sandy's = guitar haze bliss.

Everybody seems to be moving away from SF but that just makes space for a fresh batch of freaks.[22]

Everything here is being nailed down and compartmentalized — the mystery gets stripped. Makes culture easier to feed into the machine and converted into clicks and digits. It's important to defy the logic of the machine. Not everything has to be commodified and digitized. You can play an open-air concert to angels, aliens, and ghosts, with not a soul in sight. It is living theatre. And the world needs more of it, in real time. Not as an online petition.

I think moving forward, we will see the internet come to life. No more likes, shares and other tin badges. Real life, with all its messiness and complications, awaits us all.[23]

I still carry a bit of the LA fog in a bottle in my pocket and take it out for a whiff every now and then. Reminds me that life's a game of blind man's bluff. Everybody is scared. Some people just use their fear. Can't let it control you, but you don't wanna get rid of it either. If you do, you'll get eaten alive. Keep your fear, but use it. Let it burn inside your gut.[24]

---

18 Ted Williams had a .344 lifetime batting average but his on-base percentage was .482... perhaps a more fitting metaphor, but getting half your songs right sounds way more daunting.
19 Also quease-inducing: close-mic'd mouth sounds; my turn at karaoke; reading Samuel Beckett while making hairpin turns on a death-defying coastal highway.
20 Caramelized onions, potatoes, an egg, and a flour tortilla.
21 Clogs other pipes, though. Some pipes gotta be cleaned, some gotta get clogged.
22 A lot of SF is actually just moving to Oakland.
23 Nevermind the fact that I'm writing this to my email account.
24 Or inside your dreams, as it did mine three nights ago. The refrain of disappointment I've carried like a pale, bong bird on my shoulder for years ("you'll never make it" " you're a fraud") burst into my dreams two nights ago (night of July 4th). In my dream, I walked around

telling everybody I'd quit music. This gesture is partly desperation and partly just plain attention seeking. We want people to protest, to demand we continue, to reaffirm our life choices. This dream had none of that. My announcements were universally met with shrugs from all I met inside my dream. And why not? All these characters inside my dream are projections of my own thoughts, and, having carried this threat of withdrawal for so so many years now, why would my own self be surprised at my own thoughts? There were no dramatic goodbyes, no eulogies for my unrecognized greatness..., just a shrug. I was woken from this dream by archer, my young son. He told me he was having a nightmare — "wild animals are eating babies." He got in my sleeping bag and we went back to sleep. He reminded me that my dream was pure egotism and silliness, and this world presents frightening images to a child's unfiltered imagination that get sublimated through adulthood but never disappear. They're still hurting kids out there, and it still wakes me from dreams where I threaten images of myself with disappearance. Disappear from what? From whom? This life is all there is, and we do our best, and that's all we can do.

Appendix D: Answers to Unasked Questions (2019)

I have saved many things in my life. I've saved my grief, my longing, my outsider view and voice, my questioning of authority, my blonde hair, my love of chocolate chip cookies, my shyness around crowds of people staring at me, a deep love of gene wilder as willy Wonka, my love of the first Star Wars, and science fiction in general, and cheesy horror movies, and a longing and wonder and dreams of life on other planets and beyond our solar system, and an overwhelming urge to laugh, because laughter is the language of the gods.   Humans weep.   The gods laugh.

———————

Perfect Day is a song by Lou reed that's produced by David Bowie and features Mick Ronson on piano and string arrangements and honestly, I think he makes the track as special as it is.

My perfect day would be sitting in a time machine, and going back to the recording studio when they recorded perfect day, and singing along with Lou on the track, and perhaps helping him to write a few of the words.

———————

My best friends, and the people who've stuck with me the longest, are inevitably the ones with whom I've had drag down fights, maybe not with fists, but with minds.   I wish I could say this wasn't required, but I don't make the rules.

———————

I had a panic attack while scuba diving.   It wasn't much of a struggle, I just came up for air and sat on the boat.   I had a phobia last year that everybody thought I was an asshole, but I'm not sure if that's a phobia, because many people do think I'm an asshole.

———————

Invent something. Ok. I would find all those electric scooters currently clogging the sidewalks, and I would weld them all together into a sculpture that reaches the moon.

———————————

When the military man about to launch a nuclear warhead because he fears his wife is cheating on him, you lie.

———————

Beauty has proportion and tone, of course, but I think most important, beauty has an indifference. Beauty is a self-contained world that exists just fine without you, and is not looking for your observation or approval.

———————

Say "no."   that can be hard for people.   I'd say develop your own reality.   That is usually preferable to the reality other people try to foist on you.

───────────────────

I believe we must do all we can to respect Mother Earth, but i don't often argue about that. That is my most passionate issue.   However, the issue that really can upset me is to hear about the mistreatment of children.

───────────────────

I dislike most American popular culture.   Born again fundamentalist christians.   Fundamentalist religion of any sort.   Hypocrisy.

─────────────

Another invention. I would invent a new type of c.d. that holds every song ever created and I would listen to that.   I would do that to avoid eternal boredom.

──────────

Scantily clad models lounging on a beach, smiling air brushed smiles, with cans of fake beer.   My version of purgatory.

─────────────

The creative life is a battle between instinct and intellect.   Instinct usually originates the work and intellect edits the work.   I trust instinct to generate ideas, but not necessarily to refine them.   I often go too far in one direction or the other.

──────────

Success is an idiotic word.   It is a magazine they sell here.   It is part of the american mythology, which is pure bullshit.   That is the traditional idea of success, which is money and advancement in a career.
for me, and most artists and most people whose opinions I respect, it's different. Success means doing what I love, surrounded by people who understand and care about me.   success is not money.   Success as an artist in 2019 means being able to continue another year without becomes homeless or insane.

─────────────────

I try not to actively harm anybody, or rack up more bad karma as they say in California.   But it depends on what you want.   If the ends are shit, who cares about the means.   If the ends are great, then let's find a way to achieve it without creating 20 more problems in the process.

──────────────

I would rid folks of the fear of missing out.   Because now everybody wants to be in on the fun, and everybody copies each other, and it's making the world a fucking mess.   Some people just need to stay at home.

───────────────────

If I owned my home and my studio and my tape machine was fully functioning and I had a record contract with a company who understood me and would help me realize my best version of myself, and a large garden with ripe tomatoes and basil on the vine and my own personal baker to bake me a baguette and a vineyard with excellent wine to drink and a running river next to my home studio vineyard garden where I could jump in the water and enough room for all my friends and family to enjoy it and then I could duplicate this experience and share it with as much of mankind as humanly possible.

---

i am the guy staring into space and listening closely.

I am susceptible to flattery.   People sometimes kiss my ass and I fall for it, and that always ends badly.   And I feel stupid.

Proudest moment.   When my daughter basil was born.

Another invention. A special laser beam that would vaporize all of the world's guns, missiles and nuclear weapons. Oh, and zero calorie beer that tastes like Guinness, and a sandwich that grows back after each bite.

I give good ratings to my potatoes.   I make excellent fried potatoes with rosemary.

My only regret is ever cutting my hair.   I think if I'd let it grow my whole life, I could be in the Guinness book of world records by now, for the man with the most disgusting hair.

Every mystery I've solved has generated ten new mysteries, and this is the beauty of life.

Appendix F : conceptual continuity

	CIRCLE 1	CIRCLE 2	CIRCLE 3	CIRCLE 4	CIRCLE 5	CIRCLE 6	CIRCLE 7
1	24 karat soul	Dear broken friend	Hearts got a hole	Like butter, like ice	Other side of the sky	Talking Fossil Fuel Blues	You're a Special Girl
2	A perfect light awaits me	Dear Friend (Failing Domino)	Heaviness of flame	Like Every Day Before	Our dreams did weave a shade	Talking God Blues	You're Already Home, Indianna
3	A Place to fall apart	death smile	Heavy light	Limp limo	Ouroboros shoes	Talking love blues	You're Free (if you want to be)
4	All aboard explorers	Decaying Monday	Help Me Lord	Live that way	Pain pile	Talking Texas Blues	You're My Girl
5	All I know is now	Diamond eyepatch see	Here comes the clock	Lone Writer	Party Party Party	Texas saves	You're Someone Else
6	Alone without you	Diamond studded caskets	Hey old buddy old friend	Long ascent	Pizza Man in the Sky	Texas tune	You've Never Lived a Day in Your Life
7	Always Leaving Keys	Does not compute_Head wound error	Hide	Looking for lines in between the dots	Pocketful of debt	Thaw my Heart	Your Dark Sunglasses Won't Make You Lou Reed
8	Amber of the now	Dollar Bill Flashlight	Hippie Hate Hippie	Lord of your apartment	Quicksilver slip	The Boy Without a Brain	Your Eyes Are Mirrors
9	An Artist Frets	Don't hate your night just because he drives a Porsche	Home	Lost at sea	Rainbow Brain	The Darkness Stares Back	Your Soul Glows in the Dark
10	Anything you want me to, I'll be	Don't imbibe the t.v.	Humanity (Hairy Sally's lament)	Love don't exist until it's given away	Rebel without a brain	The end of the world	Zombies
11	As the sun will rise this dreams recedes	Don't sleep til you're dead / Heed my Words	Hunt So the Need High	Love gone cold	Reclining in my Easy Chair	The Lonesome Death of Cosmic Cowboy	Your Heart Breaks Into a New Heart
12	Automate my lifestyle	Dragging down the street	I am that I am, I is that I was	Love that passes is enough	Ride the toxic wave	The Moon is Shining Too	Doe See Doe
13	Azure shimmer	Dreams of sandy	I burnt all my black	Loveshines 1	Robot dan	The past won't forget me	
14	Ba Ba Ba Baby	Dusty diamonds	I can't turn around	Loveshines 2	Rot down cellar	The singer is the song	
15	Baby blue	Easy machines / telephones	I don't know where to live anymore	Loveshines 3	Sally's Lament (plain spoken verse)	The tv imbibed me	
16	Bad vibe bank account	Eat the lawn for free	I love my job	Luby's purgatory	Sampson - needs verse	The world is awaiting	Endless Blue
17	Baptize Your Wasted Face in Wine	Echoes of each Glass	I picked a fight	Lunar eyes	Sandy my love	there goes my ego	
18	Be yourself	Emerald Arizona	I think too much	Mac n me	Santa Claus of the south	This time you broke my heart this time	
19	Belly Flop	Emotional swings	I Will Be True	Mad Mother	Sewage sirens	Time Machine	
20	Bending of the light	Empty university	I witness the world as a glowing ball	Man's heart complaint	Shape shifting game	Time revolving time	
21	Bending the truth	End's end	I'm a Gravedigger	mellow out my mind	Shave	Tiny Truck	
22	Big Orange	Everlasting pleasure cruise	I'm a Surfer	Memory (It Glows)	She dreams in diamonds	Tourniquet Pants	
23	Bill	everything explodes	I'm getting laid tonight	Memory's hazy golden glow	Skull castle decorator	Trapped in paradise	
24	Black hole stopwatch	Everything is fine	I'm not a perfect person	Miami Nice	Sleepwalking someday	trash compactor	
25	Bleach (Jesus is my Janitor)	Expiration Date	I'm sad but I can't play the blues	Mind Cops	Slip into shadow	TV Guide Blues	
26	Blindfolded in the city	Failing Domino	I've waited my whole life to disappear		Slow motion silver skies	Ugly Piece of Shit	
27	Bliss	Feeling bad does not feel good	If God Gave Us Freewill	Minimum Wage	Slug	Unplug Your Head	
28	Bob	Fishtown	Illuminated night	Mirror maps	Slump City	Until my dying day	
29	Bones	Flower Children's Children's Children	Imaginary lover	Mister treadmill	Smoked by the sun	Vegan meatheads	
30	Boogie Fever	Folkswinger	In the future	Monday Monday Monday	Smoking Crack Ain't All It's Cracked Up to Be (needs verses)	Velvet rut	
31	Bonnie Raitt's Afterlife (A Bluer Shade of Hell)	Game over	Infinite Eye	Moonlight	So long farewell adieu	Walkin in the dark	
32	Boomerang grenade	Garden of eden	Inflatable man	Mosquito	So says me	Walkin with a daydream	

33	Bourbon is my special friend	Ghost of Myself	Inflated head	Mother Nature	Social swamp quicksand screen	Walking in a straight line	
34	Bourgeois blues	Go to Mexico	Insomnia insane	Mummified	Soggy soul	Warm Inside	
35	Bow down to the brain	God the smoker	Interior Design	Muzak of the spheres	Somebody's looking out for you (rejected jingle for Goodyear Tires)	We'll meet again someday, or we won't	
36	Bright blue dream	Gold dissolves to gray	Intravenous Blues	My brain is made for you and me	Song from a Dream	Weird Year	
37	Buffalo buffalo Buffalo buffalo buffalo buffalo	Gone	Is nothing there	My Flame's Expired	Sound in your mind	When perfect flames expire	
38	Burn burn burn burn	Goodbye dear friend of mine	It was a lovely way to die	My Pride and My Tobacco	Special K Hole	White Male Blues (boo fucking hoo)	
39	Bye by numbers	Goodbye Father	It's Over, my dear, it's through	My woman hates my guts	Spreadsheet star charts	Wiggle Worm	
40	Captain brain	Goodbye vibrations	It's already here	Nature dot com	Spring break of the soul	Wino strut	
41	Captain Brain theme song	Graveyard dog / dawn	It's empty time	new city lights	Square dance	Work Work Work (final verse?)	
42	Caroline	Green Truck (Cycle of Life)	Jones street blues	New York love	St John's Wort Blues	World frames your face	
43	Christmas in Jail	Hair forest	Lady dark	No Time Big Time	Stan is Dead	World gone deaf	
44	Civil War	Hairy sally	Lady Darkness Daydream	Nobody knows	Stingk	You and me make 3	
45	Color of the love you have	Half a man, half a man	Las Vegas	Office Jerk	Summer is gone	You Can Never Go Home	
46	Condo Graveyard	Halfpenny prince	Late night dawning	Oh hi mr. death	Sunset's bath time	You Can Never Go Home Again	
47	Cosmic coupon	Halfway to Nowhere	Leaving the City	Old growth	Sunshine hair	You cut my heart in two	
48	Cranks Give Thanks	happiness is forgetting	Life is rad	Old sandy bull lee	Swirling Down the Drain	You know who you are	
49	Daily Dance	Hard so hard	Life's a tv show	Option paralysis	Symphony sunrise	You know you	
50	Dead Man	Heart Sound	Lifer's Lament	Orca's Revenge	Talking Convict Life Story Blues	You're Still Glowing	

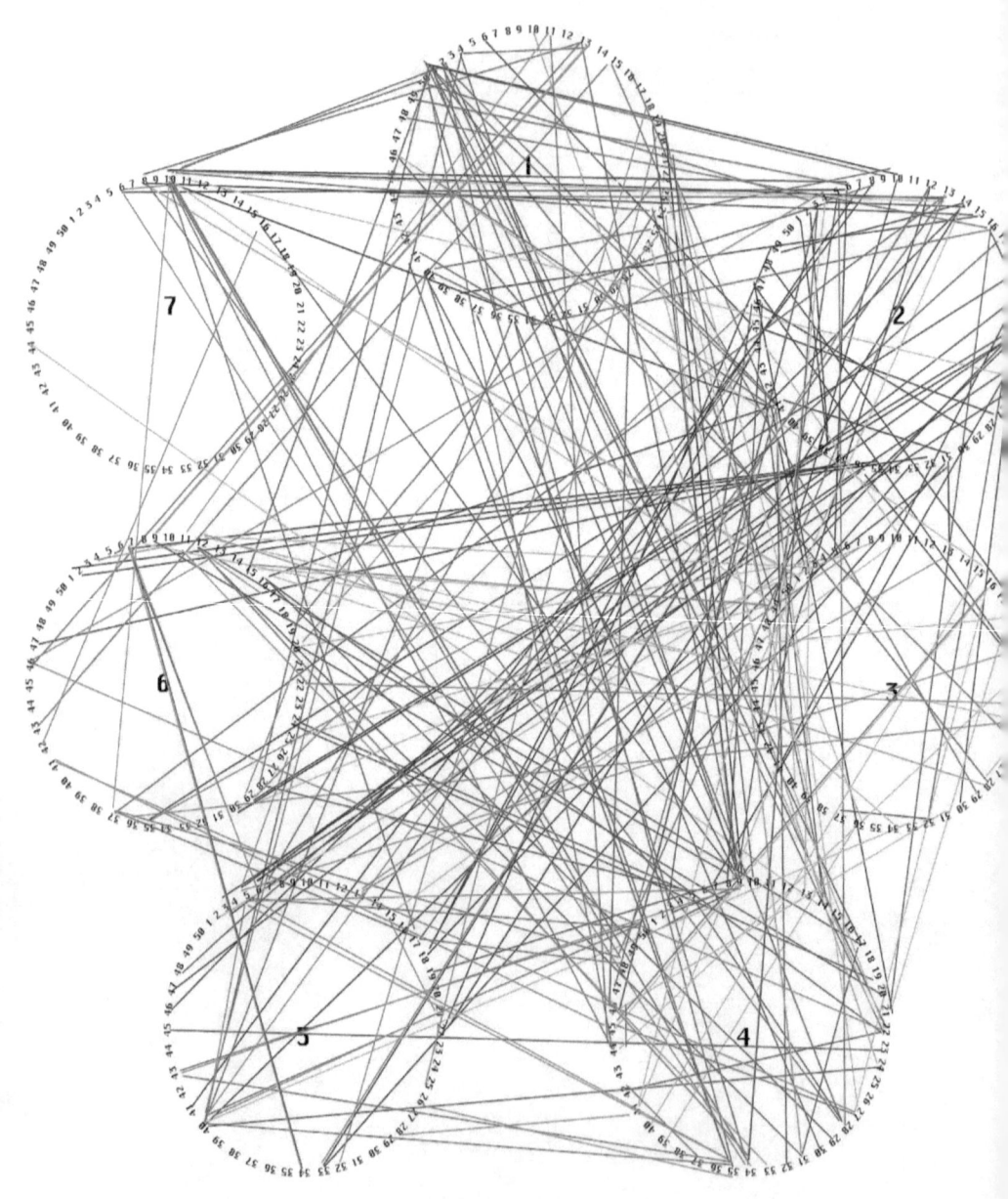

Appendix G: Discography / Chronology / Biographies

Discography:

Collected Cassette (1998)
Bill Bard (1999)
Sound Team (2000)
Into the Lens (2002)
Yes Special Cassette (2003)
Every Day is a New Year (2004)
Marathon (2005)
Work EP (2005)
{{{ SUNSET }}} (2006)
Silence ! (2006)
Empty Rooms (2007)
Pink Clouds (2008)
Bright Blue Dream (2008)
The Glowing City (2008)
Songs the Sound of Myself, as Written by Others (2008)
Eternally Dead (2008)
Loveshines 7" (2009)
Gold Dissolves to Gray (2009)
Hair Forest (2009)
Loveshines but the Moon is Shining Too (2010)
Goodbye Vibrations (2011)
Career (2012)
Spring Break of the Soul (2013)
Diamond Eyepatch (2014)
Earth into Aether (2015)
Summer is Gone (2016)
Baby Blue Abyss (2017)
Easy Machines (2017)
Classic Country (2017)
Straight Time (2017)
Gone (2018)
Nightly Never Ending (2018)
Cape Disappointment (2018)
Owl (2019)
Daily Ever Dawning (2019)
Refractions (2019)
Flower Children's Children's Children (2020)
Infinite Eye (tba)

Failure Chronology:

Kicked off American Computer Science League national competition for designing a pornographic video game
Kicked out of honors English for reading my own books in class and turning in a final on Vonnegut's cats cradle in which I stated, why do I need to write a paper on this? I already believe organized religion is bullshit

Kicked off academic decathlon team for flunking calculus
Flunked calculus due to intense personal animosity with teacher
Kicked out of camp longhorn for marijuana
Kicked out of junior high for giving incendiary speech in school election
Fired from Texas monthly for catching the copy machine on fire
Kicked off national merit scholarship for flunking scuba diving
Fired from dominos for eating a delivery
Fired from painting job for taking too long on my lunch break
Fired from accountants office for insulting the band Creed
Fired from Dell for sleeping in my car on the clock
Fired from west telemarketing for going off script selling life insurance to senior citizens
Dropped from capitol records for lackluster sales/flaccid album
Dropped from super deluxe when company dissolved in corporate merger
Fired from movie scoring jobs for making non-shitty music

Bio (2015):

My musical life has been an ongoing exploration, through many studios and record labels, but always a search for the unique and beautiful. Over the course of my years of creative endeavor, I have won praise for my adventurous sonic sensibilities, my many albums (both self-released and through many labels), and, more recently, my interactive multi-media installations.

I've focused my composition towards film and television of late, but my introduction to film came not as composer but as subject: the 2010 documentary 'Echotone,' a New York Times critics pick, followed my journey after a disastrous stint on Capitol Records. "Magnetically awkward," the Village Voice called me.

Previous albums have been featured on the BBC, MTV, NPR, with 2015's 'Earth into Aether' named Rough Trade's album of the month. I've released music through Super Deluxe, Dangerbird, Capitol, Parlophone, St Ives / Secretly Canadian, Moon Glyph, Curly Cassettes, and other small labels you might not recognize. My music has been licensed to Netflix, HBO, Showtime, WB, and many other random TV channels. I've done bits of music for various film projects and done many licenses. Solastalgia is my first full film score.

Recent installations include commissions from the Waller Creek Foundation in Austin, TX and Luminaria Festival in San Antonio, Tx; and installations at Fort Mason Center for the Arts (San Francisco), California Academy of Sciences (SF), Museum of Human Achievement (Austin), and Soundwaves Festival (SF).

I earned an MFA from Mills College, where I worked closely with Pauline Oliveros, who invited me to present at the 1st annual Deep Listening Conference. While at Mills, I worked as teaching assistant and subsequently received the Frog Peak Experimental Music Prize. Subsequently, he was named artist-in-residence with the Paul Dresher Ensemble, where he wrote a large-scale multi-media worked which premiered at the 2015 Switchboard Music Festival.

Interview about my album "career" with Mexican publication (2013):

It calls my attention that your work in "Career" it's such a conceptual work, so concrete, so well designed and careful with the details who complement the music, and that also work as a really worthy Rock album with all his sonorous variants, How was the genesis of this work, and how do you developed things like the history and packing after the creation of music?

The music came quickly. I wrote and recorded the record in a period of around two weeks. The music just had a life of its own. It was a soiled spring inside of me.

The packaging took a long time, especially the writing. I spent many late evenings with a glass of whiskey at my typewriter, just typing away.

The "conceptual continuity" is carried over from Career into the next several albums, some of which have not been released yet.

There was any musical or audiovisual work in particular who inspired you, or function as a reference, sonorous or conceptual for that album?

The movie "Blade Runner" and the album "Trout Mask Replica" by Captain Beefheart.

Like a general description, I have mentioned that your work belongs to the branch of Rock music, because of the basic foundations of your sound, but how can you describe, classified or explain the sounds and concepts of your music

I am not good at classifying myself.   Every record is different.   I am constantly changing. I try not to repeat myself.   Repeat myself.   Repeat myself.   Repeat myself.

It seems too that in your music universe exist a big league to the esthetics of Science Fiction, or at least that's my general impression, not only because some titles of your songs have references to technology, but either some of your album covers have this blink

Yes, that sounds like a fair assessment.

Do you consider Lo Fi as a statement or like a pure sonorous ornament taken by decision?

I don't think of the music as Lo Fi. I think the songs are recorded in a way that appropriate for each type of song.   The style should reflect the content.   This is a rule in most good artwork.

What can you tell me about the general creative process in your music ¿How do you begin a song in your mind and which are the next steps?

I usually lock myself in a studio with a pile of cigarettes and a gallon of coffee and won't let myself leave until I have something finished.   I may throw it away later, but I simply won't leave the room until I have the semblance of something I like.

How do you think about piracy?

It's a hopeless battle for musicians. Best to embrace it, if you can. But it seems there is less money to go around now. This is unfortunate for many people. But I think real artists and creative people will always find a way to make themselves heard. In fact, the lack of money could even encourage more creativity.

Have you listened some new bands, artist or musical acts, that calls your attention or think are interesting?

Charles Ives.

In your web page there's a specific part about the music you made for movies, are you an avid movies consumer? What was the last movie you saw?

Last movie I saw was the 1978 version of "Invasion of the Body Snatchers." I love films! I also love some films made in Mexico. I am a huge fan of Jodorowsky.

I saw too, that you are really interested in writing, and you like to develop and explain ideas about music and related stuff, there are plans to release some written material, like a book? What kinds of literature are you interested on?

My favorite current author is George Saunders. Other authors I enjoy are Ray Bradbury, Walt Whitman, and Kurt Vonnegut.

How is a Bill Baird show, what happen in your gigs?

Come and see!

Anything else you want to say to the people who read this interview?

Thank you for your time. If you are at all curious, listen to the music! My music says everything you need to know about me.

Artist statement (2014)

I'm a composer of music, mostly. I also make music videos, direct a public access tv show, write humorous/absurdist tracts and poetry, run a letterpress machine, teach on occasion, and tramp the outdoors. I'm currently a TA at Mills College in Oakland, earning an MFA in Electronic Music.

Of particular interest to me is sympathetic resonance - the amplification, recontextualizion, and manipulation of existing vibrations, either sonic or visual. I find great beauty in the import / export of visualation of sonic data and, likewise, the sonification of visual data / scientific information. Much of my recent video work has focused on this interaction. I've explored this notion of sympathetic resonance in sound art installation, computer programming, instrument building, and musical composition.

In performance, I focus on spatialization and multiplicity. The goal is to make the air in the room 'electric,' what I call 'activating the space.' Full immersion sound, hanging in the room like multi-colored smoke.

I enjoy liminal spaces in my music and in my life, generally. For those unfamiliar with the term, 'liminal space' refers to a place of uncertainty. A liminal space is the place in between.

Is he serious or not? Why does that chord keep repeating? Is he meaning to do that?

For me, these moments of uncertainty comprise the most exciting moments of life. New ideas are born. Classifications become irrelevant. Ideally, I can create a process which actually ends up guiding me. I create a system that sweeps me away, and not even I know what will happen next. It's thrilling, spontaneous, immediate, and can sometimes end up a colossal failure. The risk is worth the reward.

Not sure I even need to mention this, but... humor is, for me, essential, even if the work is quite serious. Laughter is transcendence.

Appendix H: Creative Anxiety

An in-depth exploration of how I constructed 'Creative Anxiety,' my first public access TV opera.

Creative Anxiety

or

How
I
Learned
to
Love
All
Things
Happening,
All
At
Once

Creative Anxiety Contents:

My Own Meandering Path Towards Myself, Which I Later Find Was Never Anywhere Other Than Where I Was Already Standing

Westward Expansion

The Journey Towards Unity

Shit Into Gold

Form, Content, Context, and Technology

The 1966 Armory Concerts

Bibliography

My
 Own
  Meandering
   Path
  Leading
  Towards
 Myself,
  Which
   I
   Later
    Find
     Was
    Never
     Anywhere
      Other
       Than
        Where
         I
          Was
         Already
        Standing

I follow the muse where it takes me. This can be an iffy proposition with sudden 90 degree turns -- one week I'll be tracking a 30-minute synthesizer drone, another week I'll be clapping along to a Klezmer breakdown. My artistic motto, generally: I go where it's warm. Through some cosmic miracle or perhaps simple biology, humanity has arrived at consciousness and this allows us to stare into the abyss. By abyss, I simply mean a world devoid of meaning. The universe gives us no meanings besides those we convey onto it. It's cold out there. So when I feel the creative spark, that warm happy exciting feeling, I obey. And this warm feeling leads me through different art forms. To be fully creative, there are many overlapping systems within myself that need tending.

If I get clogged up on a music commission, I'll start painting. When that dries up, I create a massive collage out of old photos. When that dries up, I study painting or film.

Eventually I end up back at the music composition, usually with a fresh perspective and a solution to my creative difficulty.

Different vessels for creativity breathe life into each other; they share energy, prop each other up, provide respite. You can shake yourself loose and allow new ideas to enter your clogged, closed-off mind. At any given moment, there will be a dozen small projects swirling through my mind – music videos, scripts I'm writing, photo books I'm halfway through producing, and of course, music.

In my worst moments, these activities compete for my attention and energy. But when I can align everything properly, all these activities funnel towards a common end.

Perhaps I'm just an undiagnosed ADD sufferer, or perhaps I'm just a product of my era – overstimulated, saturated with information, mind moving from here to there and back again within the span of seconds. It perhaps makes a laidback life out in the country less of a possibility but who needs that anyway? I would make an awful farmer.

I've only recently been able to articulate this desire to connect the many artistic streams into a single unified work. It's ultimately a process of knowing oneself, finding one's own language. First artistic steps are often a haphazard casting about, unsure of one's destination, trying one's hand at everything. This casting about, often fraught with failure (nee "learning opportunities"), provides the catalyst to knowing oneself – to recognized what you're actually aiming for. And it appears to be a lifelong process, because we never stop changing – our sensibilities, abilities, and physical bodies all change. To know oneself is actually a lifelong process.

My first forays into crafting a "complete work of art" began in high school. I wrote songs,recorded them on my 4-track cassette recorder, manufactured cassettes, printed the artwork, packaged them, and sold them at shows, at school, and on consignment at a few local record shops.

The hand-made packaging suited the music perfectly; the rough manufacture and hand-made sloppiness actually prepared the listener for the songs; the music was usually produced in the same way, with the same spirit, as the packaging. A slick package, professionally made, would not suit the music. The music and packaging were of a piece, both born of my embrace of DIY culture – to manufacture your own music, zines, pamplets, food, clothing. It's a complete lifestyle in which controls as many aspects of one's life as possible, not only as an artist but as a member of society, as an alternative to the mass-produced bland overload that surrounds us.   My world would be hand-made, custom-crafted, personalized, full of soul and spirit and joy, things not transmitted to me through mainstream media and a mainstream lifestyle. The initial DIY impulse still burns inside me. It's the driving force in my life and the impetus behind my pursuit of "the complete work."

My musical life began with these DIY recordings I distributed. Eventually, I got asked to play a show. A new level, a new challenge – translate music I had only known as recordings into a live setting. This is difficult. A recording simply requires pressing "play." All the work has been nailed down. But in a live setting, in order to create compelling performances, risk must be involved. Often, the greater the risk, the greater the reward. The performer must allow failure (imperfect execution) as an option. I had to learn these truths the hard way, through a number of disappointing shows and lackluster crowd responses. Fixed media often does not provide the presence, the "electricity," that a crowd craves from a performance. The experimental spirit in my recordings needed translation into my live show.

The nightclub world (I come from a rock band background) had its own accepted norms to experiment with, rub against, dance around, smear, obliterate. I began printing bizarre booklets and handing them out at the doorway as people entered the shows. Often, it would be a zine about an obscure topic; one was written about the history of the Moog synthesizer (Walter Carlos and his eventual change to Wendy, Tomita, Robert Moog, Raymond Scott, the initial sales demonstrations of Moogs being held inside Taco Bell restaurants, et al); another was a coloring book with crayons attached about myself and my band getting launched into outer space. The goal of these booklets was to amuse the audience member, certainly; but the amusement had a higher aim – to surprise the audience member into a heightened state of awareness. To let them know they weren't coming to your standard club show, with a band on stage playing the same old stuff you've heard a million times and aren't even really listening to while you drink cheap tall-boy beer and obliterate your senses.

I also began using a long cable and walking around the crowd while playing guitar. I enjoyed breaking down the boundaries between the performer and the audience. I would improvise large segments of the shows based on what was happening in the room. These were baby steps towards the "total work" concept of immersive music, and were often mistaken for showman's gimmicks. Perhaps a whiff of gimmickry is inevitable when trying something new or stretching your familiar boundaries; but I was truly aiming for something more. I had nobody to teach me about the Theatre of the Absurd, the ONCE Festival, or any of my predecessors. I had to stumble my way through the past hundred years of artistic advances; over and over again I thought I'd discovered a technique that I would later find out had already been used for the previous century, often with less technology and a greater effect! Such is experimentation. We stumble towards originality.

I suppose the big change in my work occurred when I started my own recording studio in a former record-pressing warehouse in East Austin, Texas. With a dedicated space to record, create artwork, screen print, make videos, plant a garden, makes messes and dream big dreams, all my various interests came ever closer together. I constructed a 36 television wall and began performing in front of it; I started a letter-press printing area to print record covers and show posters; I filmed videos and painted murals on the walls and recorded hundreds of songs there. It all happened under the same roof; the flow of creativity moved rapidly between projects, but never did the creativity feel broken; a particular inspiration drawn from my garden or my video installation would funnel directly into the song I was recording. The studio itself provided an enclosure, a structure, under which many ideas could simultaneously inhabit.

I had the recording studio for eight years but ultimately I felt I needed to keep moving. I needed to create that same sense of enclosure the studio provided, but through the work itself, and not just through the place in which it occurred: a single idea that explodes into multiple formats. The same structural bounds that my studio provided would now be found within a composition itself, and would ideally allow room for these many art-forms to peacefully co-exist: a multi-faceted work which stemmed from a single origin. I was moving ever closer to theatre pieces.

I experimented for a year or so with all varieties of sets, combining music, monologue, improvisation, humor, and visual effects. The results were mixed. My set at the 2011 SXSW, in which an 11-piece band improvised behind me according to my instructions while I gave a series of short, screaming monologues, got me banned from the festival. So it goes. I took it as a validation in a way; I suppose any noise musician could relate. The disgust of the lame squares only made me feel more validated. Still, I needed to move beyond mere rebellion; I wanted to subsume the rebellion inside a work that would be undeniable. A feat of the will.

Yes, I was being dramatic. Sometimes drama is necessary to make a break with the past. I wanted to create my own mythology, my own artistic language, and create self-contained worlds.

I had come to an ending point. New horizons beckoned. My artistic life to that point felt like I'd been "walking the plank," stepping ever closer to the abyss. I'd now reached the endand it was time to jump into uncertainty, the unknown. To find my own language, I needed to sweep aside everything I couldn't carry inside my mind.

So I threw aside the life I'd constructed – my studio, my music career, band, friends, family – to move to California and remove all distractions. I would have no friends, my small family, a library card, and an open mind towards any and all techniques that could be directed towards this fully integrated, "complete work" I had been seeking -- a work in which all sensation experienced by the audience and every aspect of a composition serves a single vision. I needed to clean the slate, to push aside all previous distractions, and focus directly on my goal — a fully integrated musical work, in which form, content, words, music, staging, and visuals all existed on an equal plane.[25]

Westward Expansion: Growth of the Mind and Long Hours at the Library

California shone like some holy beacon. Perhaps I'd read too many histories of the 60's; perhaps too much Mark Twain or Jack London; perhaps too much Kerouac, Ginsberg, and Ferlinghetti. Our culture loves mythologizing itself, loves constructing heroes, the messiahs who have somehow transcended our post WWII mess, our post-colonial, post-industrial malaise. I long for those times and believe in those myths really because things are so mixed up today. The lines between good and evil blur into infinite shades of gray; what's good is bad, what's bad is good. We need these dreams sometimes. We need these heroes.

California represented this to me. Way back when, some lucky young folks had found the motherlode, they'd tapped into the American dream, the best aspects of it anyway, and the afterglow was still being felt into the 21st century: Mills College, the San Francisco Tape Music Center, the Merry Pranksters, Richard Brautigan, Joseph Campbell, Allen Ginsburg. I carried the apparitions of these people and places in my mind and they taunted me until finally I gave in and headed west. Manifest destiny.

Of course, reality is more complex and often more disappointing. The beat poets never mentioned traffic jams nor gentrification. There's never been a perfect era; each epoch's plagued by its own unique human misery, and it is precisely the unfortunate aspects of life that give rise to art. Nobody wants to hear the songs of a contented jolly old dope drinking a pina colada. Except other jolly old dopes drinking pina coladas.

So I accepted California as it is. It was indeed the climate I'd expected, in both senses of the word: an open-minded culture seeking to unite various artforms and advance

---

25 I have included an additional essay "Form, Content, Context, and Technology," which in own ambling way explores "the complete work," form mirroring content, and the attempts at separating form and content. The essay is included in the appendix. It felt too much of an excursion to include in the main paper.

humanity, all while basking in perfect weather. The bay breeze blew the dust off my brain. The bay was speckled with seekers who'd headed west from all over the country, in search of something better.

But the scene seemed to lack a center, a focal point. Having come from a relatively small town, this geographic fragmentation and diffusion was a new sensation. Numerous small towns and micro-niches were spread around the bay like wind blown seeds – from Marin to San Francisco to Big Sur to Oakland and Berkeley. Each separate scene had its own little niche, an hour's drive away from each other. So it goes. I liked my cities small I guess, or at least the feeling of a small town. A tight community. It existed in the bay area, of course, but it's more philosophical and less geographical.

I would do my best to ignore the gaps, ignore the niches, ignore the differences and set about my task. There was work to be done; damn the difficulties. I would welcome anybody who would be welcomed, collaborate with anyone willing to collaborate. And those who sought to dig themselves in, to barricade me out, to entrench themselves in aesthetic bunkers from this cold cruel world of misunderstanding Philistines? I probably wasn't on their radar anyway.

Long hours at the library engulfed my brain with the great works of the 20th century. Their names flowed forth like a great outpouring of generosity; I was literally feeding off the ideas of my predecessors: John Cage, David Tudor, Erik Satie, Laurie Anderson, Robert Ashley, Alison Knowles, George Maciunus, Man Ray, Steve Reich, Nicolas Slonimsky, Peter Sellers, Nikola Tesla, Pauline Oliveros, my gawd! The list could fill pages. Amongst the many names, one figure in particular captured my interest: Billy Kluver. A legend of the 20th century, he devised an underwater TV camera for Jacques Cousteau, for starters! He also headed up Bell Labs and was instrumental in bringing together experimental music with electrical engineering; creating immersive environments in the famed Armory concerts (David Tudor's "Bandoneon," John Cage's "Variations VII") and the 1970 Tokyo Pepsi Pavilion. Immersive environments had of course existed at least since Corbusier and Xenakis' Phillips Pavilion of 1958, but Kluver's work felt different to me. His philosophy on art and technology echoed my own sentiments :

> The way I see it is that artists provide non-artists - engineers or whomever - a certain number of things which non-artists do not possess. The engineer expands his vision and gets involved with problems which are not the kind of rational problems that come up in his daily routine. And the engineer becomes committed because it becomes a fascinating technological problem that nobody else would have raised.
>
> If the engineer gets involved with the kinds of questions that an artist would raise, then the activities of the engineer goes closer towards that of humanity... the artists have shaped technology. They have helped make technology more human. They automatically will because they're artists. That's by definition. If they do something it automatically comes out human. There's no way you can come out and say that if art is the driving force in a technological situation that it will come out with destructive ideas. That's not possible. But what happens, of course, is that the artist widens the vision of the engineer.ssible. But what happens, of course, is that the artist widens the vision of the engineer.

And it occurred to me like a million-watt light bulb popping inside my brain: the "total work of art" could include technology itself. The creation of a technology could be inseparable from the work for which it was created. The composer could also be an instrument builder. The technology could be an extension of one's own artistic language. An artist could not only forge his own building blocks but also use art to humanize technology, breathe soul into the machines.[26] It was with this mindset that I set about re-crafting a solo stage work entitled "Creative Anxiety" into an immersive multi-media operatic work unlike any of my previous efforts.

The Journey Towards Unity: Creative Anxiety

"Creative Anxiety" began as a theatrical monologue between myself and my typewriter – a pre-recorded vocal track played through the p.a. while I paced the stage, cursing the typewriter and its steadfast refusal to give my anything usable. I addressed

---

[26] Past composers in search of the fully immersive "complete work" would surely have drawn from whatever technology was available to them! Wagner probably would've used projection mapping; Moholy-Nagy would probably print out his set pieces using a 3-D printer.

the crowd directly and referenced my being on stage. It was a way to break down the barrier between audience and performer, between art and reality. It was a piece all about writing, being on stage, being observed. As the 10 minute piece finished, I would begin playing songs with just my acoustic guitar and voice.

I initially viewed the piece initially as a way to open up the crowd, to break down barriers, to shock, to surprise, to make people actually listen, to provide a context for the fairly straightforward folk songs the crowd was about to hear. Before I even stepped onto the stage, the audience would be perplexed and hopefully intrigued by the bizarre accoutrements littering the stage: a couch, a desk, a lamp, a typewriter, a whiskey bottle, a self-help book, a bottle of aspirin, a cup of coffee. Like some half-drunk, half-caffeinated writer's living room, with all the signifiers of a severe case of writer's block.

As the piece began, I pretended to sleep on the couch while soothing music played over the speakers. With a start, I jumped up from the couch, shaken from my reverie, and began typing. The crowd heard my thoughts as I type away.

Using the fixed audio with my voice reading text proved a clever way to build cues into the performance. For example, the fixed audio would say, "Maybe I should get up from this typewriter and pace back and forth quickly;" I as performer would simply obey the instruction. The internal monologue is quite versatile in that way. I'd stumbled on a method to embed cues in a way that felt like a natural extension of the performance. For later versions of the piece, I've mostly moved past the internal monologue, but it still pops up in a few moments, especially when a specific cue seems to evade successful execution.

Audiences loved it but it seemed to depend heavily on the context. The element of surprise worked in my favor; this type of thing is uncommon in music nightclubs. I was hiding nothing; the dialogue felt about as honest as I could be while still keeping my clothes on. It went over quite well but I wanted to take it further. I wanted to use less words, more sounds and situations. I wanted to embody the words through other means.

Thus began many months of work, which culminated in a newly realized version of

"Creative Anxiety," which integrated all of my current research and development in technology, music, and theatre into a single piece. Here is a photograph of the staging in Littlefield Auditorium, Mills College, Oakland CA:

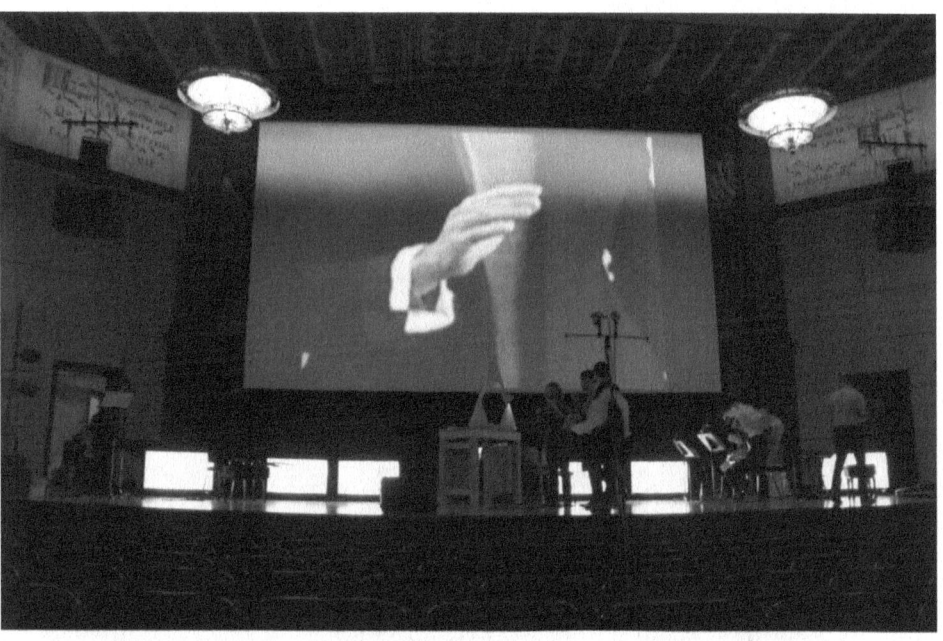

Three actors on stage, playing Orphic monks/television newscasters and a Clogged Artist, act out the feverish nightmare of the aforementioned Clogged Artist, the main character, who's experiencing a heavy bout of writer's block. He is surrounded by symbols of the divine – the ouroboros, the torus, Sierpinski's triangle, the golden ratio; the Clogged Artist takes these as a sign that his existence is being controlled and cursed by divine forces. Believing that supplication to these divine forces might ease his blockage, the Clogged Artist pleads to the nine muses (divine forces famed in classical Greek literature) to restore his creativity. After the muses refuse his pleas, the setting switches – the

Orphic monks strip their robes and become television news broadcasters. The entire proceeding is revealed to be a television special on Channel WHYYY – a reality television channel which delights in the anguish and existential crises of humans. After coming to acceptance of his fate, the setting suddenly shifts again, with all the divine symbols and signifiers used throughout the piece reconfigured and dismantled – a long deep sigh as the artist's nightmare comes to an end. The piece ends with the sight and sound of 130 million sheets of paper being crumpled up and tossed from a typewriter; 130 million being the number of books estimated written during modern history.[27] [28]

Here is the Clogged Artist, reaching for the sound, forever out of his grasp:

(It actually looks a bit like he's releasing the music up into the sky. Perhaps a more optimistic interpretation.)

---

27 The number, as calculated by Google, is actually 129,864,880.

28 Taycher, *You can count the number of books in the world on 25,972,976 hands*

Eight musicians – vibraphone, two keyboards, two violins, tenor saxophone, tenor trombone, and a percussionist playing 'flat-slap guitar' (my system of alternate-tuned guitars played with metal rods) play through a score which includes standard notation, graphic notation, video notation, and conduction instructions. Since the piece has no conductor, the musicians hit their cues using stopwatches, the actors' motions, and a fixed movie being projected on a large screen behind them. The musicians are all wearing costumes – large sheets of crumpled paper, upon which has been scribbled the shallow and vapid advice gleaned from a self-help creativity book. As the musicians move, their costume itself provides sound – the rustling and crumpling of the paper. As the Clogged Artist frantically types at his typewriter and throws his rejected texts onto the ground, the sounds of his creative difficulty are being echoed through the movements of the players.

The movie, projected onto a large screen behind the actors and musicians and which cues many of their activities, was mostly shot at the Berkeley Public Access television station on ancient equipment, using old televisions mixers, character generators used for news broadcasts, and a green screen; the footage was subsequently modified using Jitter, analog video feedback, and animation. Additional footage was generated using openGL graphics generators, and a Jitter program I wrote. Six large flat-screen televisions, placed alongside the musicians on the stage, further processed the movie, utilizing another Jitter patch I'd written, designed to mimic frantic television static. Though the source film on the televisions and the large screen is the same, the televisions are not synchronized perfectly with the large screen projection. They run between one and five seconds behind; this was by design, as a video echo.

The televisions illuminated the stage, framed the musicians, and also provided video score during the "taunting objects" section of the piece. During this section, various objects representing the Clogged Artist's creative difficulty – a bottle of aspirin, a coffee cup, a creativity self-help book, and a bottle of whiskey – are used to trigger video scores which display on the televisions. Piezos were attached to the objects and sent through a

453

separate Max patch. Any time an object was lifted from the desk, an associated video score would flash across the televisions.

Placed throughout the room were what I've called the "compumonium," a laptop ensemble with localized speakers performing an application I'd written in Max/MSP. The computers, placed through the room, generally served a sound design function, amplifying and extending the sounds emanating from the stage; their behaviors, impossible to synchronize, served to "activate the space" – to electrify the room with sonic energy, so the audience would literally be enveloped in sound.

At center stage sat a special prop designed by myself and built from scratch– the Magnetractys, a Thomas Jefferson style stand-up desk where the Clogged Artist slaves away at a typewriter. The Clogged Artist is in such a delirious state that he believes the objects surrounding him contain music. The Magnetractys, outfitted with resonant boxes on either side and a nine-string electro acoustic harp shaped like the Pythagorean tetractys, on top, taunts the artist. The harp's intricate design, a design used in Kabbaleh and similar to Sierpinski's Triangle, with 9 strings pointing three different directions, seems to taunt the artist, towering over him while he furiously attempts to break through his creative blockage. He is clogged in such a way that sounds surround him but he cannot grab hold of them. Mounted on the harp are multiple pick-ups which I wound and soldered. Activating these pickups are several inductive magnetic coils I also wound. Passing through these coils is AC power which, unlike the Ebow and its use of DC power, allows me to send audio signals. I had a max patch doing live pitch detection from a room mic and sending it into my computer, which converted the pitch into a sine wave; a massive feedback cycle.

Here's me holding the Magnetetractys in the woodshop, ear protection still on:

A libretto, which I printed using xerox and letter-press machines, was available for sale at the front entry. The libretto contained all the opera's lyrics as well as photographs and illustrations. The pages themselves were designed according to a 19th century book design concept known as 'the golden section' or 'golden ratio' – in which self-similar images seem to shrink down into infinity. In some drawings, it appears as a fractal. In book design, it looks like this (as if you're looking at the inside of a book):

If this all sounds a bit involved, difficult to pull off, monomaniacal even, I assure you, it was. The final effect, however, felt like a single work; the many strands enmeshed; they all felt derived from a common source. Form and content and context were inseparable. The pursuit of such a work, what I call a "complete work," in which many interlocking facets emerge as a unified whole, has been a lifelong pursuit. *Creative Anxiety* is the fruit borne from years of artistic searching, with still much further to go.

Creative Anxiety works in the tradition of the composer as instrument builder, but I didn't just limit myself to building instruments. I built an entire weird world. I constructed the composition from building blocks of my own creation: the Magnetetractys, the Compumonium, the Hot Hands, the Flat Slap guitar, the Resonant Guitar, six new programs written in Max/MSP, and highly personal twists on graphic notation, video notation, standard notation, and conduction. I sought to create a self-contained world.

The Flat Slap guitar in particular took some time to nail down. Working with a percussionist, we explored the many sounds that could arise from a guitar used "improperly" – scraping, banging, jamming the strings with metal rods. We ultimately created a vocabulary of sounds specific to this composition. Multiple metal rods were inserted into the strings and used for percussive effect. Often, the strings would be roughly slid up and down the neck according to given cues. Here's a rod in motion:

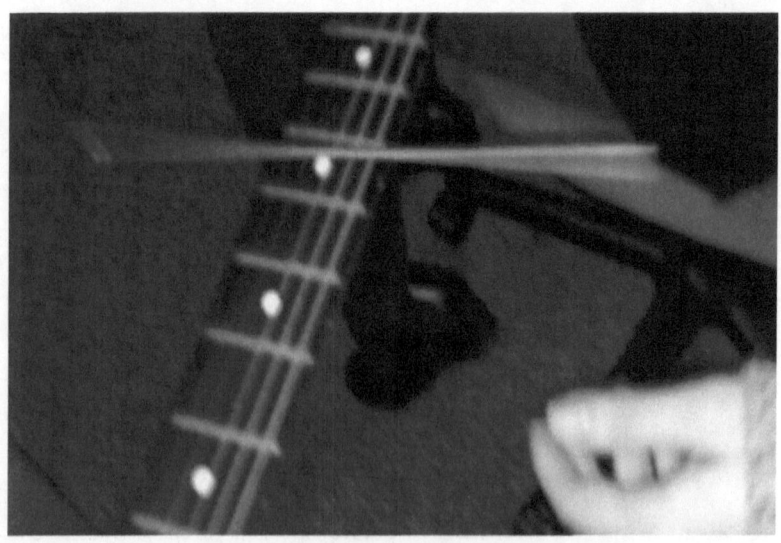

The danger of such creations and adaptations is gimmickry, the inclusion of bells and whistles simply for the sake of more bells and whistles. By stemming all the from a single source — the music itself and the accompanying text -- one hopefully avoids this pitfall. Everything present is a necessary component of the composition. *Creative Anxiety* had many unique machines and a different language, but this was what the piece required. Nothing more, nothing less.

Technology, instrumentation and compositional technique weren't my only areas of creation / adaptation. For the visual elements of Creative Anxiety, I adapted numerous pre-existing symbols of the divine — the golden section[29], the tectractys[30], most significantly and most often, the ouroboros. Ouroboros is a Greek word meaning 'tail devourer,' and is one of the oldest mystical symbols in the world. The ouroboros has numerous meanings embedded within it. Foremost is the symbolism of the serpent eating its own tail. This symbolizes the cyclic Nature of the Universe: creation out of destruction, Life out of Death. The ouroboros eats its own tail to sustain its life, in an eternal cycle of renewal. It is sometimes depicted in a lemniscate shape (figure eight) as well.[31] It can be perceived as enveloping itself, where the past (tail) appears to disappear but really moves into an inner reality, vanishing from view but still existing. This symbol has enormous personal significance, especially as related to the difficulty of composing. In the process of creation one can feel like a snake eating its tail, or perhaps a dog chasing his tail — every step forward means your goals take a step forward with you. It never stops. And if it does? The snake eats its tail and shits out another snake.

I embedded this ouroboros symbol throughout *Creative Anxiety* — in the libretto, in my video notation, and also as graphic notation. To use a symbol as graphic notation for a musician seems to me a perfect way to merge form and content. George Crumb's *Macrocosmos* was a touchstone in this area. I would be remiss not to also mention Nicolas Slonimsky's *Mobius Strip Tease*, in which a strip of music is cut and taped together so as

---

29 Also known as phi and the Fibonacci sequence and musical harmonic nodes. It's the basis of much book design and was the basis for the *Creative Anxiety* libretto.
30 Sacred symbol used by Pythagorean cult, similar to Sierpinski's triangle, also used in the "tree of life" of the Kabbaleh.
31 http://www.tokenrock.com/explain-ouroboros-70.html

to form an actual mobius strip – one plays the piece endlessly. We both use the figure eight as both symbol and indication to play one phrase endlessly.

Here are the three lines of ouroboros score that begin *Creative Anxiety*:

The musicians receive one of two sheets, depending on the range of their instrument. Transpositions are acceptable. The first line is played during the first minute of the piece after they've started their timers, with each musician holding a note for a duration of their choice, but within a range I've given them. For most musicians, this range was between one and three seconds. The musicians choose an arbitrary note and follow the arrows from note to note.

The second ouroboros line is triggered by video score of two Orphic monks playing tennis with an ouroboros moving in a larger ouroboros pattern. Here are two screen shots from the video notation:

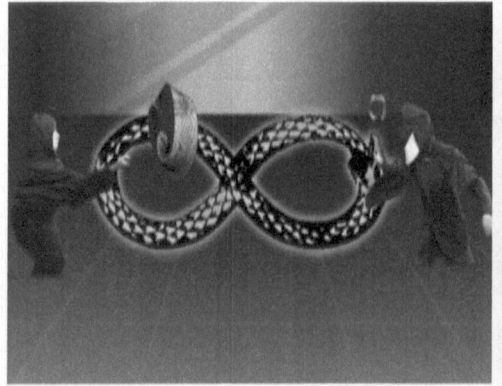 

When a monk hits the ouroboros with their racket, the musicians play notes from the second ouroboros score. Some musicians play single notes in order, over and over again. Others quickly play the entire run of notes for each racket hit. When a monk misses, some of the musicians make a screeching sound, the sound of disappointment.

The third ouroboros line of music is triggered by the Clogged Artist's entry onto the stage. With each step he takes forward, the musicians abruptly play the next note on the staff. They only play the note at the precise moment the Clogged Artist's foot hits the ground. This continues until the next cue. It's as if the Clogged Artist's feet were pressing a button that forces the musicians to blurt out a note. A live trigger that uses no wires other than visual cues.

During rehearsals and in the performances, I experimented with a long, drawn out gait, and also with rapid shuffling. It seemed to work best when I alternated between approaches. This use of conduction, in which body gestures guide improvisation, was influenced by performances I'd seen by Fred Frith, Frank Zappa, Morton Subotnick, and Butch Morris. [32]

The ouroboros is seen in *Creative Anxiety*'s next section, both projected on the big screen and also again in the scores, onlt this time as a what I termed a macrographic notation – the complete structure forms a shape which underscores the theme of the piece. In this case, the score pages themselves follow the ouroboros pattern. It is not visible to the musicians. They simply move sequentially through their pages, but by printing on both sides of the sheets in the desired order and having the musicians flip the sheets over as they play through them, it is simple enough to create a never-ending loop of music.

This section is the "Invocation to the Muses," the first aria of *Creative Anxiety*, an extensive text spoken by the actors. The use of the figure eight allow the music to be played as long or as short as necessary – the text can be shortened expanded in the

---

32 Frank Zappa used it to hilarious effect with The Mothers of Invention. A few favorite moments: when he 'shoots the bird' (lifts the middle finger) all the musicians yelp; when he extends his hand as if along a wavy line, the musicians make queasy noises. His techniques are best witnessed in a Oct. 23, 1968 video recording from the French TV program "Forum Musiques." On the program, The Mothers of Invention also perform "Octandre" by Edgard Varèse.

future without having to write additional music. Here is the macrostructure of the first aria, with each square representing a page of music:

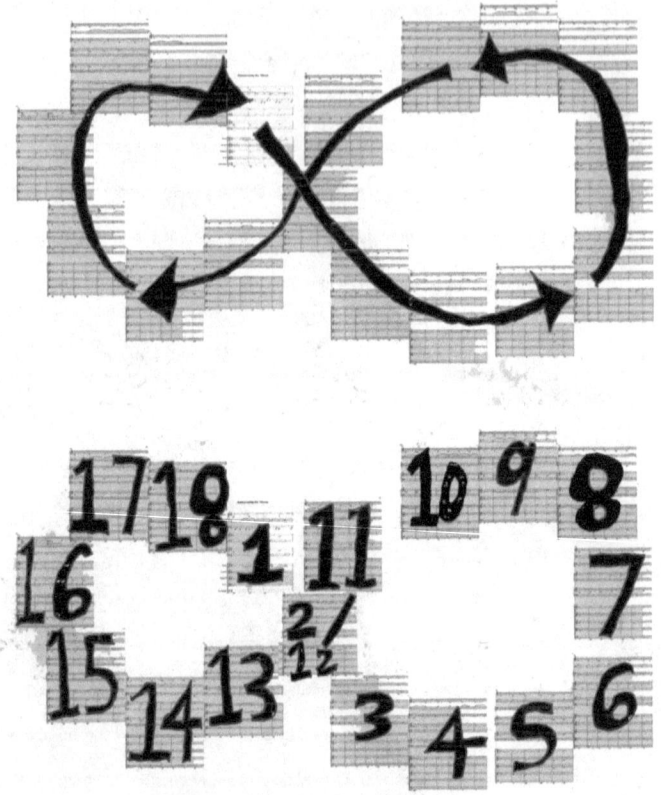

The musicians kept time using a video metronome – squares move across the screen, with each movement representing a quarter note. The temp was 120 bpm, so if the musician wished to not stare up at the screen, he / she could use their timer, with every two seconds representing a whole note. The video itself used for the metronome is footage of a hand crumpling a sheet of paper, one of the recurring themes of the piece and representing the Clogged Artist's creative difficulty. Here are screenshots of my video metronome for one bar of music. The clip of the hands crushing the paper moves from corner to corner in a clockwise direction:

During the next section, the musicians take a break while the Clogged Artist attempts to begin writing a story. After cycling through a few cliché opening lines, the Clogged Artist flips on YouTube, where he finds a video entitled "How to Write a Book Over the Weekend." Onscreen, an absurdly overconfident salesman hawks his writing technique. When editing this section, I became obsessed with the hand gestures of the salesman. They moved in a forced way that conveyed a false sense of self-assurance. His hand movements literally hypnotize potential customers. He moves his hands with great authority, a false sense of assuredness (not unlike Bill Clinton).

I zoomed in on his hands and had them provide cues for the musicians. For this section, I did not strictly notate the music to be played. Rather, I spent time working with the musicians and creating a musical vocabulary which seemed analogous to the salesman's various hand swoops, finger points, and pleading hand wags, and fingers held together. Each represents a specific tactic of salesmanship and indeed feel very soulless and corporate. The appearance of this slick, hollow salesman peddling easy answer represents a desperate attempt by the Clogged Artist to find a quick answer to his difficulties. The resultant music, however, is jarring, disjointed, and mostly staccatto. The Clogged Artist has obviously not found the answer he's looking for.

The musical vocabulary established for this section did not specify pitch, instead focusing on volume, timbre and gesture, areas which best mirrored the salesman's stern, forceful, and ultimately empty gestures. Each time the salesman hand came fully to rest, the musicians would hit play in the style we'd previously determined.

Here are a couple screenshots of the salesman's hands conducting the musicians during this first performance:

This section felt better focused than other sections of the piece, I think due to the silence between the notes. A sharper contrast with the cause and effect immediately discernable to the audience. Shocked laughter burst from the crowd during this section of the initial performance.

The next section uses video triggering to guide the musicians behavior. Piezo microphone are placed onto objects representing the Clogged Artist's creative difficulty – a cup of coffee, a creativity self-help book, a bottle of whiskey, a bottle of aspirin. For each object, I wrote a short few bars of standard musical notation:

The music written for each object is meant as a very quick depiction of the emotions the Clogged Artist fclogged up within each object. The objects contain music that the Clogged Artist cannot access. They taunt him. As the clogged artist reaches for each object, it is pulled from his grasp by the Flat Slap guitar player, who has walked over to the desk. By grabbing each object, a trigger sensor being fed into a Jitter patch triggers a corresponding video clip. Each video clip is a different color, and it is the flashing of this color that cues the musicians to play a particular phrase (or they could just watch and see which object is grabbed).

This continues for a short time until a computer robot voice cues the next section, the final aria, in which the Clogged Artist and the two newscasters speak of the meaning of the Clogged Artist's difficulties, and paying their respects to Creative Death. The text itself is an adaptation of an Orphic ode to Death, which I adapted to make relevant for a struggling 21st century writer / musician. The music here is a drone, with musicians holding long tones, synthesizers moving through the harmonic series in the key of A, and the sonic introduction of another of two of my new instruments: the Resonant Guitar and the Magnetetractys. Here are these two instruments being used in a recent performance at Cal Arts:

The Magnetetractys was developed over months of experimentation in the Mills College woodshop. Initially, I simply wanted to build a prop – a stand-up desk to be used during future staging of Creative Anxiety, but as I progressed on the project, I decided to make the desk "musical" in some way. The desk would emanate music and would taunt the Clogged Artist. Initially, I built resonating boxes along the side of the desk and borrowed some tone bars from a gamelan. This did not work. I wanted the desk to make sound without actually being touched. And so I kept drawing, kept sketching, made some wooden mock-ups, and eventually stumbled upon a design of three triangles which form a larger triangle. Self-similar patterns resonate quite strongly with me.

The three triangle would be three different resonating boxes for three sets of strings going different directions, with a beautiful diamond pattern overlay in the middle:

It was only after I finished designing the Magnetetractys that I learned I'd inadvertently recreated the most holy symbol of the Pythagorean cult – the tetractys. The tetractys was their symbol of God, of ultimate reality.[33]

So I'd created a beautiful self-similar shape, a unique criss-crossing of strings, but now needed the damn thing to make sound besides an untuned clang. The triangles were not resonating so well, so I soldered some guitar pickups together and glued them on. With these magnetic pickups now part of the instrument, I decided to interact with these using magnetic induction. Over the course of some days, I wound small magnetic coils:

---

[33] "But how comes God to be the Tetractys? This thou mayst learn in the sacred book ascribed to Pythagoras, in which God is celebrated as the number of numbers. For if all things exist by His eternal decrees, it is evident that in each species of things the number depends on the cause that produces them.... Now the power of ten is four; for before we come to a complete and perfect decade, we discover all the virtue and perfection of the ten in the four. Thus, in assembling all numbers from one to four inclusive, the whole composition makes ten," – Hierocles, in his *Commentaries on the Golden Verses*

I wrapped these coils in electrical tape and soldered them to some long electrical wire. I then taped this entire package to two fingerless gloves. They're actually weightlifting gloves, but I would not recommend them for that purpose:

The gloves are plugged into a small Lepai 20X amplifier, which sends alternating current through the coil. Similar to an Ebow, except instead of using DC current, these gloves use AC current, meaning I can sound through the gloves. The wonders of magnetics.

I created a custom sound source to send through the gloves: a simple Max patch that performs pitch detection on a room mic, sends it through a synthesizer and out as a sawtooth wave, into the amplifier and out my hands. The Max patch also plays a manipulation of some recordings I'd made on the Mills College Moog IIIP. Here's my set-up just before a recent performance:

Like any good inventor, I needed a name for my little creation — not just the desk but also the magnetic gloves. I decided on Hot Hands. I like the alliteration but it's quite literal: if you send too much signal through the coils, the gloves get pretty damn hot. I haven't been burned yet but things certainly got toasty inside the gloves during my first few run-throughs. Creating your own names for things, what a liberation. Makes your composition feel like a self-contained universe.

Here is a flow chart showing how the way the Hot Hands are used:

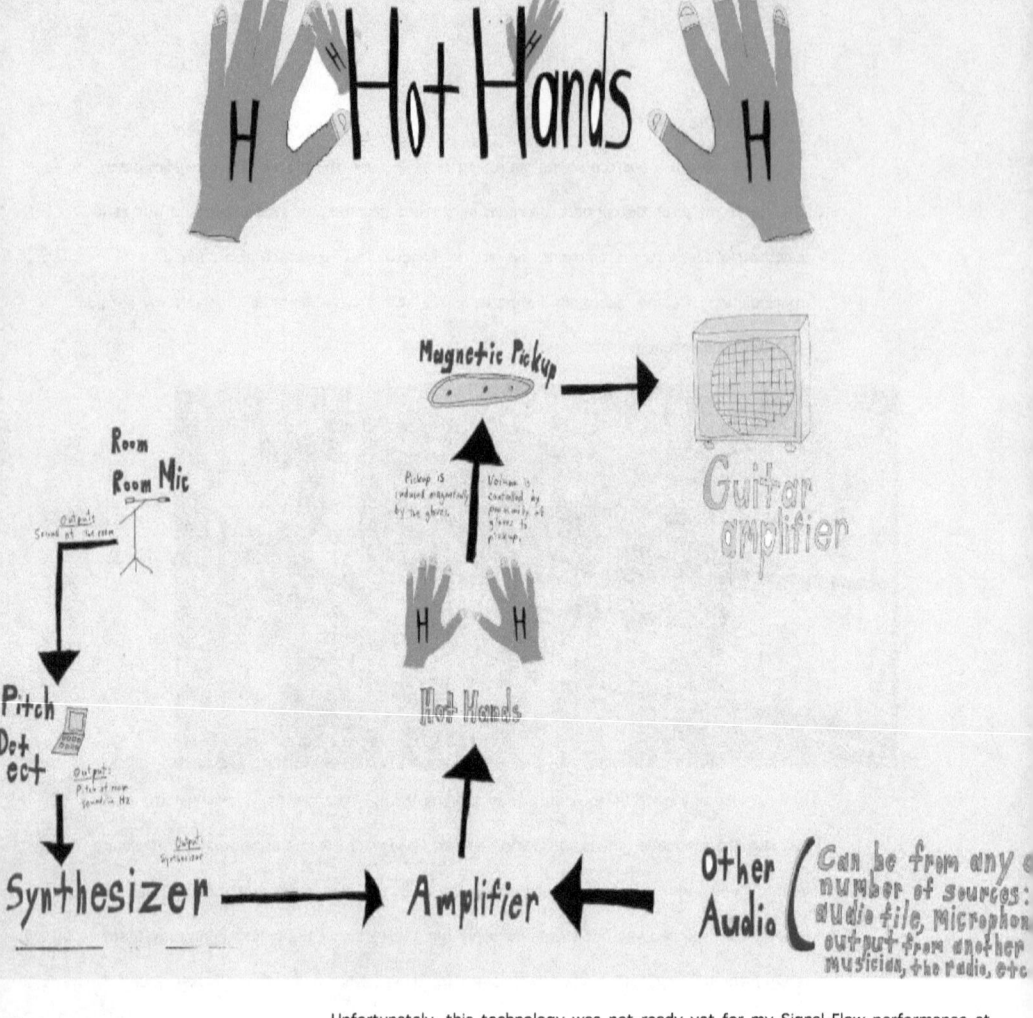

Unfortunately, this technology was not ready yet for my Signal Flow performance at Mills, so I had the Magnetetractys on stage serving its original purpose: stage prop. Despite its inability to make useful sound, it still felt like an essential aspect of the performance. The self-similar patterns, the references to divine forces, the music seemingly embedded within the desk, and yet unreachable – still quite effective. I have subsequently used played the Hot Hands and Magnetetractys in concert, most recently at Cal Arts for their annual CEMEC concert. The response has been positive, although there are numerous improvements to be made. The next phase of the Magnetetractys and Hot Hands will be the installation of large metal sheets on the sides and back of the desk, coupled with transducers driven by the harp's pickups. The entire desk will hum and sing.

Alongside the Magnetetractys at both my Signal Flow and CEMEC performances and also exploring resonance was another creation, the Resonant Guitar. The Resonant Guitar is an adaptation of a guitar already commercially available — the double-necked Gibson, made famous by Led Zeppelin's Jimmy Page. Except when used in my compositions, it's not a platform upon which to solo endlessly, to preen, to shake my hair around, to lure groupies. The Resonant Guitar's sound is the sound of strings resonating without actually being touched. I open tune the strings on the bottom neck to the notes I want to resonate. The Resonant Guitar player then plays the top neck. On the body of the guitar, there is a switch which allows the player to choose which pickup is audible. By playing guitar on the top neck and activating the pickup on the open-tuned bottom neck, a swirling resonance occurs. Notes float upwards in cloudy clusters.

The Resonant Guitar creates an interesting juxtaposition. The double-neck guitar is usually a signifier of the "rock god," somebody probably eager and anxious to quickly "shred" and run through some scales, eager to show off to the audience. A guitar solo with flowing hair and a smoke machine. We're all unfortunately familiar with this abysmal cultural wart.

But the resultant sound of the Resonant Guitar could not be further from a "shredding" type sound. It is soft and floating and has no discernible edges. It is this juxtaposition between the guitar's projected meaning and the cultural baggage it holds and the actual sound it makes that creates an interesting tension. In the next phase of the Resonant Guitar, I will construct my own body, perhaps in the shape of a triangle, and not use the commercially available Gibson.

Image aside, the Resonant Guitar drones very well if properly tuned, and worked well in this final aria section of *Creative Anxiety*. My own voice, pre-recorded in low fidelity as if coming from a television speaker and embedded in the fixed audio track, cues the actors to begin speaking their final speech.   And at speech's end, in near-perfect synchronization, the musician's timer, set earlier in the piece, go off all at the same time. The musicians all stand up and exit the stage, crumpling up their paper costume on their way out the door.   The video continues for several more minutes, taking all the strange symbols and text used throughout the video, enclosing it in a box, and projecting it back, back, back, into darkness, further and further back into darkness, as if the entire proceedings had only been a nightmare.   The piece ends with the sight and sound of 130 million sheets of paper being crumpled – the number of different books currently published in the world.   Here is an image of 202,500 papers being crumpled:

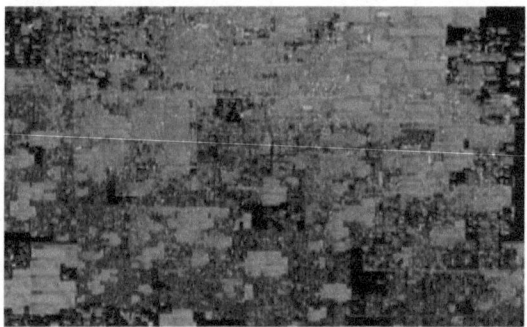

As one exponentially multiples audio and video, the resultant shapes look like scum forming on the surface of a pond, or the wisping away at the edge of a cloud – it looks like a recreation of a natural phenomenon.   The audio goes from discrete crunches to a roaring sea of white noise.   The roar of our age – the information age.   The piece thus ends with the sound of crumpling paper, albeit 130 million times.

Crumpling paper is also the first sound heard in the piece, due to the musician's costumes.   Their costumes are roughly constructed by ripping sheets off a large roll of paper.   The musicians write directly onto these paper sheets, either describing a personal creative difficulty they've faced, or taking quotations from a self-help creativity book.[34]   As

---
34 Full player instructions for their paper costume are included in the appendix.

the musicians walk onto the stage, the sound of their costumes – the sound of crumpling paper – is the only thing heard in the auditorium. And throughout the piece, as the musicians play their parts, they inevitably rub themselves against the paper, which continually creates the sound of crumpled paper – an audio representation of the Clogged Artist's creative difficulty. The costumes themselves become a sonic and visual reinforcement of Creative Anxiety's themes. Allowing the musicians to write on the paper themselves invests them into the piece. They feel more a part of the proceedings, which, in my experience, helps the music immensely.

The sound of crumpling paper comes not only from the musicians' costumes, but also from the actors reciting lines on the stage. Rather than memorize their lines throughout the opera, the actors read from paper printouts of the text. After they've read everything on a page, they throw the page on the ground. I divided the text unevenly amongst the pages, choosing to include only a few lines of text on each page, so the actors might throw paper down onto the stage more often.

This throwing of paper in turn triggers behavior from a crucial component of the performance, and only briefly discussed to this point: the Compumonium. The compumonium is my laptop orchestra, plugged into localized speakers, that's placed through a listening space, embedded within the crowd, so the sound becomes enveloping and immersive. The compumonium a minimum of six laptops required and no maximum really. Perhaps if enough laptops plug in and the circuit breaker pops, we'll know we've reached our maximum. I call each laptop station (human, computer, loudspeaker) a 'bit.' The compumonium laptop orchestra is thus comprised of 'bits.'

Each laptop installs an application I've written and installs it on his/her computer. I usually hand-deliver this application right before a show, using a flash drive, but I've also uploaded it through file-sharing sites over the internet. Either method works. The application is completely self-contained; it only requires a Mac laptop with an OSX 10.6 using an Intel processor. All files and samples and graphics are included – a self-contained entity. I'm creating the applications using Max/MSP. The compumonium is literally an orchestra of machines that I've created.

After installing the program on their computer, each laptop moves to a predetermined place in the listening room where a powered speaker and the appropriate cables are provided for the laptop to immediately plug in. Use of these localized loudspeakers creates a cascading effect through a space which envelopes the listener. It's perhaps similar to 8-channel sound, or ambisonics, but with much more unpredictability, real human error, which makes it more interesting territory, for me anyways. The players never perfectly synchronize, even when they're acting on the same cues. Utilizing this inevitable error as an intended result works particularly well when the sounds are either the same or very similar. It creates a mostly rippling, shimmering effect through the room, since the players aren't exactly in sync. It's the ultimate analog delay – discrete sounds echoing each other throughout a space, like the beauty of a million frogs croaking after a rain. Walking in a marsh or by a pond after a good rain feels like walking inside the most perfect analog delay in the world. The original analog delay.

The name compumonium is a conflation of computer and harmonium. It's also a reference to and adaptation of the acousmonium, a 1974 creation of Francois Bayle, head of *Groupe de Recherches Musicales*[35], which utilized 50 – 100 speakers in a massive array which, in his words, "substitute a momentary classical disposition of sound making, which diffuses the sound from the circumference towards the centre of the hall, by a group of sound projectors which form an ,orchestration' of the acoustic image" [36]

My compumonium achieves something similar but has a human attached to each speaker, adding an extra bit of chaos and human touch. What the players actually see on their screens feels perhaps something like a video game. At a given cue point, in the case

---

35 The GRM, initially known as Groupe de Musique Concrète, Club d'Essai, was founded in 1951 by Pierre Schaeffer and Pierre Henry. Their early experiments still feel fairly revolutionary to me; most notably the induction coils used by Pierre Henry to control volumes of multiple channels of audio. The group was a focal point for 20th century experimental music, with involvement by Stockhausen, Xenakis, Varese, Milhaud, and more. For more of my musings about musique concrete, see my essay "Form, Content, Context, and Technology" in the appendix.
36 Bayle 1993, 44

of Creative Anxiety the initial countdown, the players hit the START button on their application. They then respond to instructions that pop onto their screen. A large message box in conjunction with a timer conveys the score instructions.

Some portions of the composition involve clicking large buttons which trigger samples, in other portions the buttons trigger changes in waveform synthesis occurring inside the patch. The sonic palette is 90% pre-determined, but it's that last 10% that makes it magical. Especially the interaction amongst the laptops.

Here's a screen-shot of the interface, mid-way through a performance:

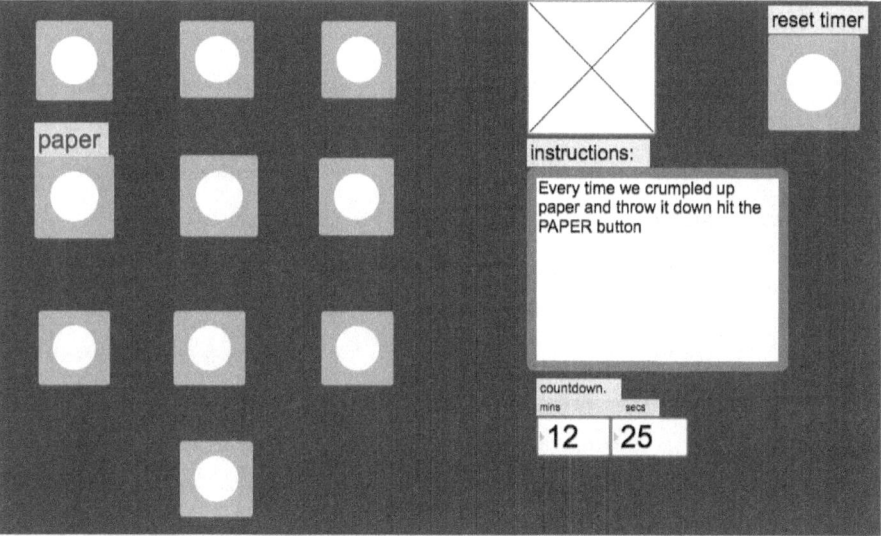

Since my piece was of fixed duration, I pre-set the timer in the program to count down from 16 minutes to zero (at which point a sample of my alarm clock rings in their computer, echoing the timers ringing from the musicians places on stage). The counter provides metronome information (when needed, as called for in the player's instructions) and also lets the performer know where they are in the piece. In the midst of so much chaos, this can be comfort to a performer. The timer can be turned off if the performer wishes to remain ignorant of time.

To the left of the timer there is a grid of buttons. The buttons are controllers for two different elements inside the max patch – sample triggering and synthesizer manipulations. By timing events pretty strictly and creating a master timeline, I could build special feature into the program – at the point in the composition when a button is to be used, that button lights up. The instruction box indicates the behavior to be performed. Sometimes the behavior is simply related to their timer, "Hit the TV button once every 5 seconds," or sometimes their instruction require them to observe the actors on stage or the projected movie and base their behaviors off that – "Every time an actor throws a piece of paper on the ground, hit the PAPER button."

The patch went through at least a dozen drafts and still feels incomplete. Initially, the design was poor and there was a lack of clarity in the instructions. Performers told me they felt as if they 'had dyslexia.' I had to provide the same information but with less layers of interpretation and a cleaner interface. It took some doing. Giving indication of the button to be used helped quite a bit. I think in the next phase I will eliminate the buttons and create specialized graphics, thereby eliminating a layer of interpretation. Instead of interacting with a round button that has PAPER printed above it, the player will simply interact with a illustration of a piece of paper.

Aside from the interface itself, considerable attention must be placed on the spatialization throughout the room. No two spaces will be alike and a proper tuning must occur for the compumonium to function properly. On the following page is a diagram I drew for the Compumonium to be used in Littlefield Concert Hall at Mills College. Obviously not perfect for every space, but it gives an idea:

Compumonium

an orchestra of cascading computer sounds with localized loudspeakers & laptops

Diagram for performance in Littlefield Auditorium,
Mills College, Oakland, CA

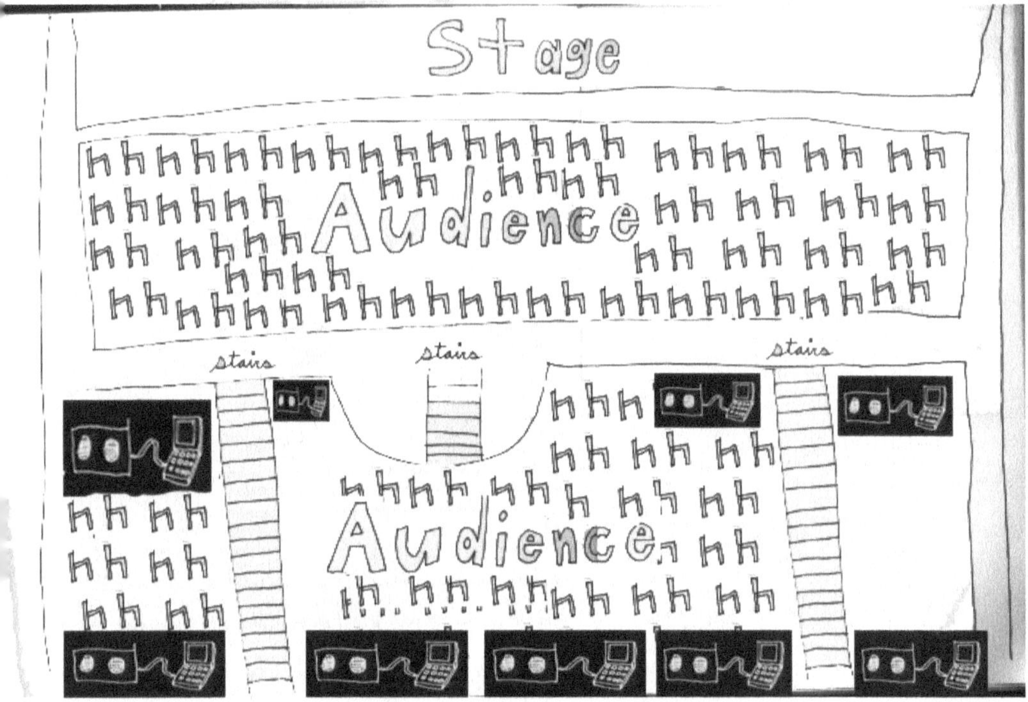

Legend

h = Chairs

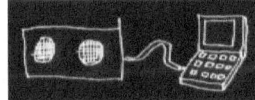 = compumonium bit with large amplified speaker (each orchestra member is called a "bit")

Shit into Gold: Turning Difficulty into Opportunity

Something I've learned from my time as a gardener is the joy of turning shit into gold. Transforming refuse into prime, usable material. This is a design concept not limited to gardening. It can apply to music, to architecture, to human civilization. Embedded within this idea is the seed of mankind's survival – if we are to avoid environmental catastrophe, we must create systems that account for and include waste and error. By designing a system (or a piece of music) with this in mind, what might normally be waste or "noise" can be usable material. This concept can be found in world of permaculture (of which I am an ardent follower) and also in the works of Larry Halprin, famed landscape architect:

> "The essential purpose of design is to create possibilities for events to happen. The limited quality of perfection in design is that it is then fixed. No more can happen. It is ended. Anything added or subtracted from a perfect design demeans it or lessens it's impact. On the other hand, an imperfect design accepts change and is enhanced by it. By imperfect, I mean ,incompleted'. Incompletion allows for additions and subtractions which enables a person to feel a part of it."[37]

Indeed, since my piece had over twenty musicians of varying degrees of ability and no conductor, synchronization would be difficult and error inevitable. Some mechanized versions of a conductor were used – stopwatches to time individual sections and a fixed audio / video track – but with many musicians, few rehearsals, and no conductor, I acknowledged early on that the various elements would not be perfectly synchronized. By acknowledging this fact and engaging with it, I turned a weakness into a strength.

My fixed audio during the first aria, for example. While writing the arrangement in Avid Sibelius, I was moment to moment confronted with the horrifyingly cheesy sounds of their MIDI sample bank. It sounded artificial, plastic, and... ripe for a reinvention. I

---

37 Halprin, <u>Sea Ranch</u>, p. 81

exported the MIDI track from Sibelius and ran it through a 45 second reverb[38] and now the cheesiness had blurred into something dreamlike and haunting. I had taken the tortuous sound and made it heavenly. This type of transformation makes my inner gardener very very happy.

Besides creating a beautiful backing track, blurring the background ensured that the inevitable timing errors between the musicians – their inability to play perfectly in sync with the video metronome – would actually reinforce the background. Their slight errors would only enhance the blurred feeling provided by the backing track. Instead of fighting the inevitable musical errors, I incorporated them and made them a strength. Further underscoring this blurred sensation, I made the aria section simply a shifting set of suspended chords. Glacial, solemn suspended chords, which have the added benefit of blurring the music, or perhaps they make themselves agreeable to blurs. Mistakes sound less like mistakes. The notes slip over one another.

The text in this aria section similarly blurs between multiple sources. The words cascade amongst multiple sources. The Clogged Artist actor attempts to speak in sync with a lo-fi fixed audio track of that same speech. The two inevitably don't line up and created one cascade. Then, on certain lines in the script which I'd underlined, the two orphic monks repeated the words spoken by the Clogged Artist.

Those same words also cascade through the compumonium. By sync'ing the application running through the compumonium with the fixed audio track, a further cascade occurs through the room. The text is bouncing between 4 sources – the fixed audio track, the Clogged Artist, the two Orphic Monks, and now the compumonium. Their part is fixed, meaning it is timed to play without their pressing any buttons. When this occurs placed throughout the space, it creates a rippling, shimmering effect on the sound that will be different every single time it occurs.

This approach – to take a limitation and make it a strength – was a prime

---

[38] Which to me sounds it might be located in the holiest of holy cathedrals or perhaps in the waiting room on Mount Olympus.

influence in the way I constructed the video as well. For the past two years, I've been a producer at Berkeley Public Access TV, where I had access to very old video mixers, CRTs, and character generators. The technology is old and questionable. It's not fancy. But it was perfect. I had the place to myself! If it were fancy, I might have to wait in line.

I plugged in everything wrong and backwards and ignored the right way to make videos and came up with my own video language and vocabulary. I performed video feedback on the CRTs they had there, experimented with every type of camera angle and flow of video – film a screen that it is the output of that camera itself. I pulled out every single fake potted plant (they have dozens) and lined them all up like a fake forest. I improvised monologues between myself and a potted plant. I took the ugliest stock photos on their character generator, hundreds of them, and used video feedback to transmute the cheesiness into beauty. A good phrase for it might be cheap sophistication. I've heard my work described that way numerous times and each time I do my best to focus on the latter half of the phrase.

Over a couple of months, I filmed the bulk of Creative Anxiety's fixed video at Berkeley Public Access, using their character generator, video feedback, multiple cameras, and green screen. Here's the public access studio where I did most of my work:

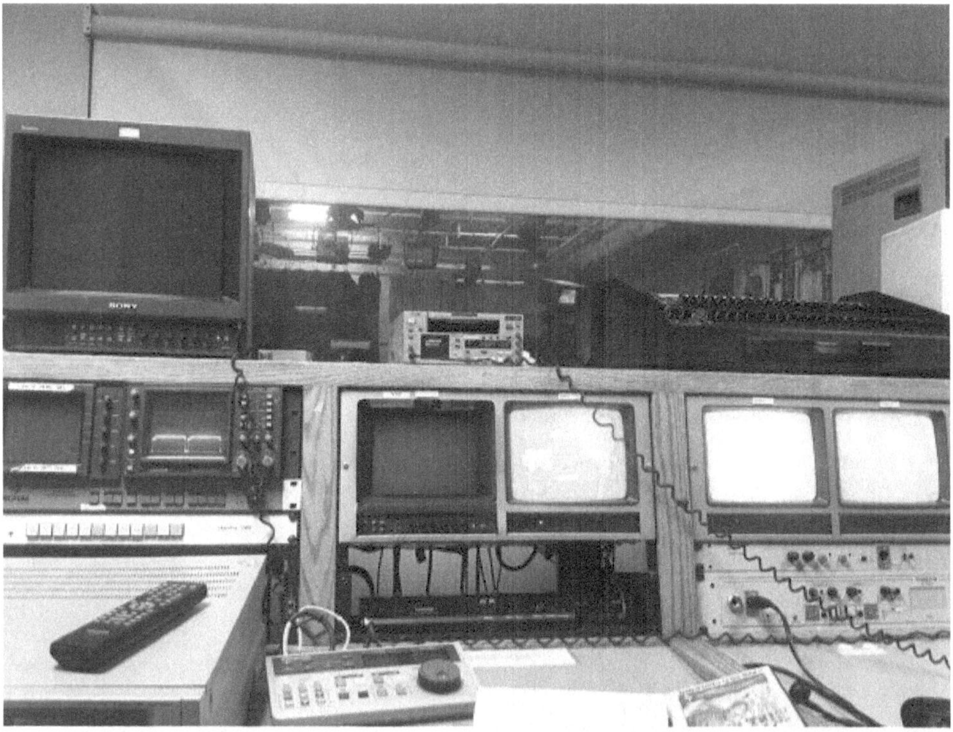
SONY

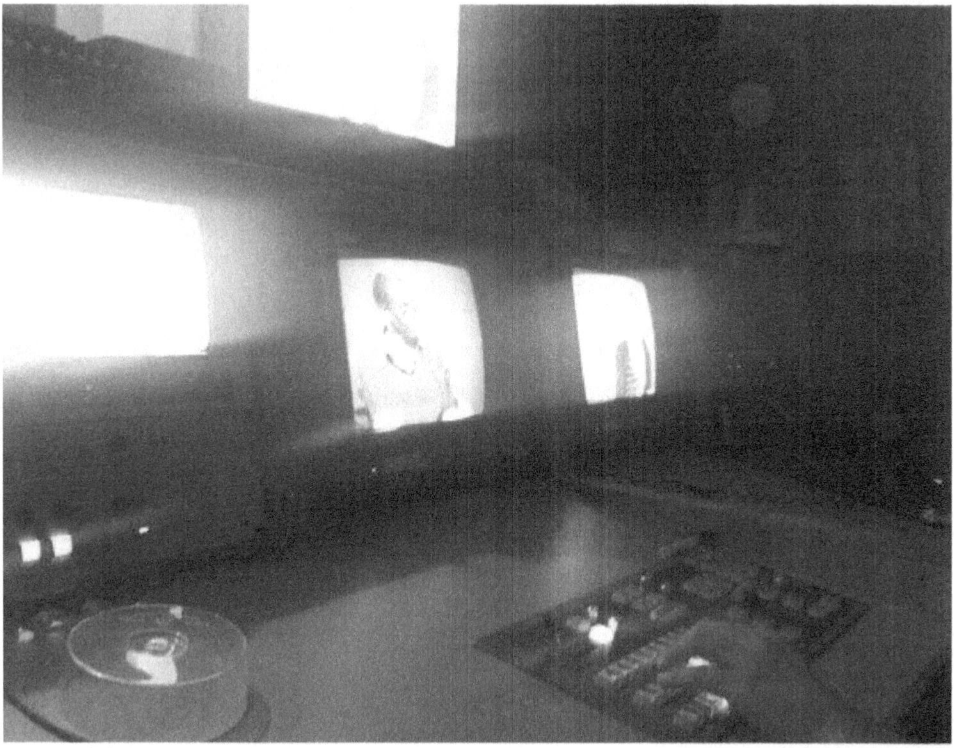

With such focus on the video, Creative Anxiety almost seems like a live film score, or some crazy exploration of sound design. In truth, the entire piece originated from my text, and that took much of my time – writing, re-writing, editing, crafting, My writing background is in humorous writing, a la Richard Brautigan. My undergraduate studies focused on the classics – Homer, Aeschylus, Aeneid. For my libretto text, I sought to fuse these two streams – to funnel classical Greek literature, with its use of commentary, the Greek chorus, and exposition, through my own twisted sensibility. James Joyce did the same with *Ulysses*[39]. Inspired by Joyce, I littered the libretto with references, ranging from the Greek classics to Walter Cronkite to old country and western tunes to the canned soft jazz of the weather channel.

I re-read my cobwebbed library of Greek classics and immediately seized upon the idea of the muse – the source of music and creativity. Since my piece addressed creative difficulty, it seemed fitting to model the text after classical invocations to the nine muses; typically, the muses would be invoked at the beginning of an epic song, to provide support and guidance through the performance. Except in my case, the muses would not respond! Silence. Mute. The invocations, meant to ward off creative difficulty and guide a performance, would go unanswered. This notion of unresponsive divine forces had previously captured my interest in the work of Charles Ives ("The Unanswered Question") and Samuel Beckett ("Waiting for Godot"). I felt I was in good company.

And so I set about adapting the invocations to the muse which begin Homer's *Odyssey*. These invocations form the bulk of the text spoken during the first aria. The aria begins with an adaptation of Robert Fitzgerald's 1961 *Odyssey* translation, the most familiar to modern readers. Halfway through writing the aria, I started to get bored, however. Maybe I just needed some coffee. But I had a flash of an idea. I treated my boredom as a message – put it in the score! If it were an Oblique Strategy, it would look like this:

---

39 <u>Ulysses</u>' two main characters, Buck Mulligan and Stephan Dedalus, were written to mirror the journeys of the two main characters in the <u>Odyssey</u>, Odysseus and Telemachus.

Treat thy boredom as a hidden intention.

(ha, I will insert a scan of my fake Oblique strategy card later)

The muses, instead of merely remaining silent, would yawn in the face of my entreaties. Seems an even greater insult to me. And so, halfway through the first aria, all action comes to a screeching halt and the hall is filled with the sounds of me yawning – recorded at my home studio – distributed through the hall via the Compumonium and through the house system. I built this pause into the notated score. After the yawns, another invocation begins, this time riffing on John Milton's invocation which begins *Paradise Lost.* To no avail, however. Again, the muses again yawn and all action stops.

The proper setting of text to music for *Creative Anxiety*'s first aria, with its melodramatic musical air, not unlike a theme from a television soap opera, eluded me. Traditional singing and songcraft felt inappropriate. I initially had the actors speak into vocoders, with the vocoding notated for two keyboard controllers. It was too garbled, however, and I opted instead to use a robotic video / audio generator called "Morfo," which inserted a lo-fi recording of my voice over a bizarre robotic animated head. I inserted that as a fixed element in the audio and video. This would achieve the same end I was seeking in the use of vocoder – a sense of disorientation and form mirroring content – the "lo-fi" sound of the vocal would sound like a television. During this section of the score, the text is read rapid fire by my "Morfo" animation, the three on-stage actors, and also echoed throughout the room by the Compumonium.

In the final aria, the Hymn to Creative Death, the text adapts Orphic hymns – a collection of songs based on the teachings of Orpheus, the greatest musician and poet of Greek myth, "whose songs could charm wild beasts and coax even rocks and trees into movement,"[40] the only mortal to descend to Hades and return with his life.

I chose the Orphic hymns and muse invocations because of their central themes of artistic creation, with each text strongly resonating with the Clogged Artist's journey. My adaptations were mostly humorous and/or playful – stilted theatrical dialogue peppered with references to blogs, tweakers, beige baggy cargo shorts, and bottles of whiskey. Dragging Classical literature, kicking and screaming, into the 21st century.

During a section I later excised (I included some of the text in the video), I adapted Walter Cronkite's famed 1968 "We Are Mired in Stalemate" speech about the US war in Vietnam. I adapted the "stalemate" to refer to the Clogged Artist's case of writer's block, but had to cut the section for the sake of time. I included the text in the libretto, however.

Though such an inclusion might seem futile, I wanted the libretto to deepen the experience, which doesn't mean a strict reproduction of the stage work. All the symbols, all the themes, not to mention the text, could be found inside, but also new elements, specifically, the ability to draw back and see the piece from a macro, broad perspective. The flow of the words mirrors the shape of the overall work.

These days, the libretto is not often thought of as a physical object; rather, it's often merely associated with an opera's lyrics. But the original meaning of the word *libretto* is "little book;" these were small pamphlets available for purchase to concert goers. The pamplets contained all the lyrics, yes, but they also set the tone for the evening. I like the interactive aspect of distributing the booklets to the crowd as they enter. It immediately imparts a sense to the crowd that... something is happening. Something worth their attention.

Having been a life-long printer and DIY maker, I have made many zines in my time. It was only recently, however, that I learned about the 'golden section,' as it relates to book design. The Golden Ratio is a term (with an astounding number of aliases, including Golden Section and Golden Mean) used to describe aesthetically pleasing proportioning

---

40 Hunter, "Orpheus"

within a piece. However, it is not merely a term -- it is an actual ratio.

In its most simple form, the Golden Ratio is 1:*phi*.

Phi is represented by the lower-case Greek letter φ. Its numeric equivalent is 1.618... which means its decimal stretches to infinity and never repeats (much like *pi*).

All math aside, an unknown genius figured out millennia ago that, in a work of art or architecture, if one maintained a ratio of small elements to larger elements that was the same as the ratio of larger elements to the whole, the end result was extraordinarily pleasing to the eye. (Indeed, we now have scientific evidence that our brains are hard-wired to recognize this pattern.)[41]

It relates also to harmonics – the work of Pythagorus. The golden section is said to be the divine ratio according to which matter vibrates. It follows a pattern of self-similarity in which the constituent parts of a whole are in the same shape as the whole itself. Self-similarity seems to be a design strategy for the universe we live in, and we naturally gravitate towards sounds and designs that mirror these divine proportions. I do, at least. Just take a look at the Magnetetractys.

For my libretto design, I used the golden section in unintended ways, with text and graphics dancing around the prescribed boundaries, using them to align the text, collage images, or create negative space. Here is the full libretto lay-out:

---

41 Esaak, "Golden Ratio"

Another inspiration for the libretto was the DIY zine culture I've embraced since high school. I have a long background in printing my own booklets — everything from poetry to absurd short stories to abstract graphics. I learned early on to embrace the limitations of the form — black and white, Xeroxed, cheap paper. The Xerox machine can be amazingly expressive. And the use of inexpensive materials (paper) means you don't have to be precious about it. You can take more chances. Move the text all around the page, break every supposed rule. Throw it in the garbage if it's not working.

I was also particularly inspired by artist's books, a subject into which I dove deeply with Kathy Walkup, head of the Book Arts program at Mills College. An artist book acknowledges the the book standard conventions — the codex, sequential pages, use of paper — and plays with and within these limitations. An artist's book about gunshots would probably have bulletholes actually shot through the pages. An artist's book about garbage would be actually printed on garbage. An artist's book about incarceration would be locked, sealed, impossible to open. And so forth. By engaging with the limitations conventions of the book – the bound structure/enclosure, the act of turning the page, the materiality of the paper – an artist could successfully merge form and content.

When considering form and content and the way they relate to the overall shape of a piece, I sometimes feel like I'm only guessing at the composition's actual overall shape and form. To truly merge form and content, it helps to have a macro-sense of the proceedings. This is the macro/master score for *Creative Anxiety*.

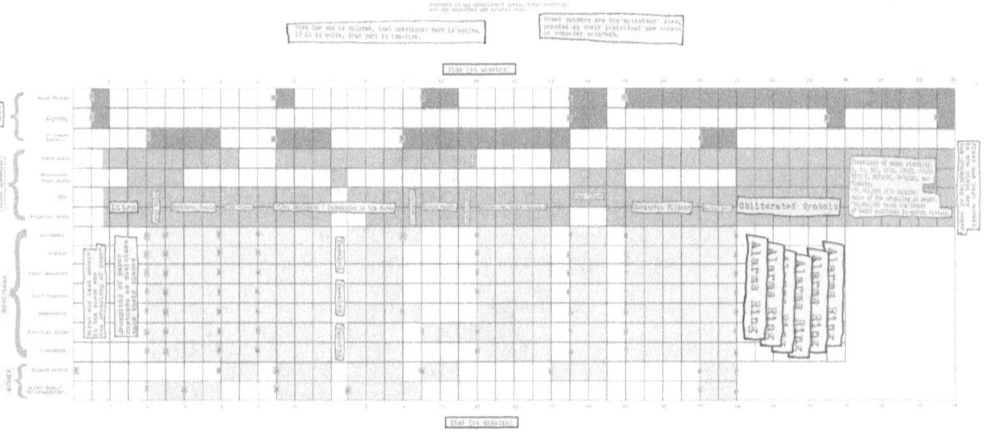

That is the complete picture of the entire work, literally. Minute by minute, every person involved in the piece has their respective cues mapped out: 81 separate cues for the performers, crew, and actors. It helps me to feel the shape of a piece to see an entire composition in a single image – I get a sense of the compositions shape, its contours, its nooks and crannies. Drawing back and seeing its shape, one sees the architecture. It's impossible to read shrunk down so small, but one can see the shape. I printed out the full resolution version and it was five feet long. This perhaps gives a better sense of the scale of the piece:

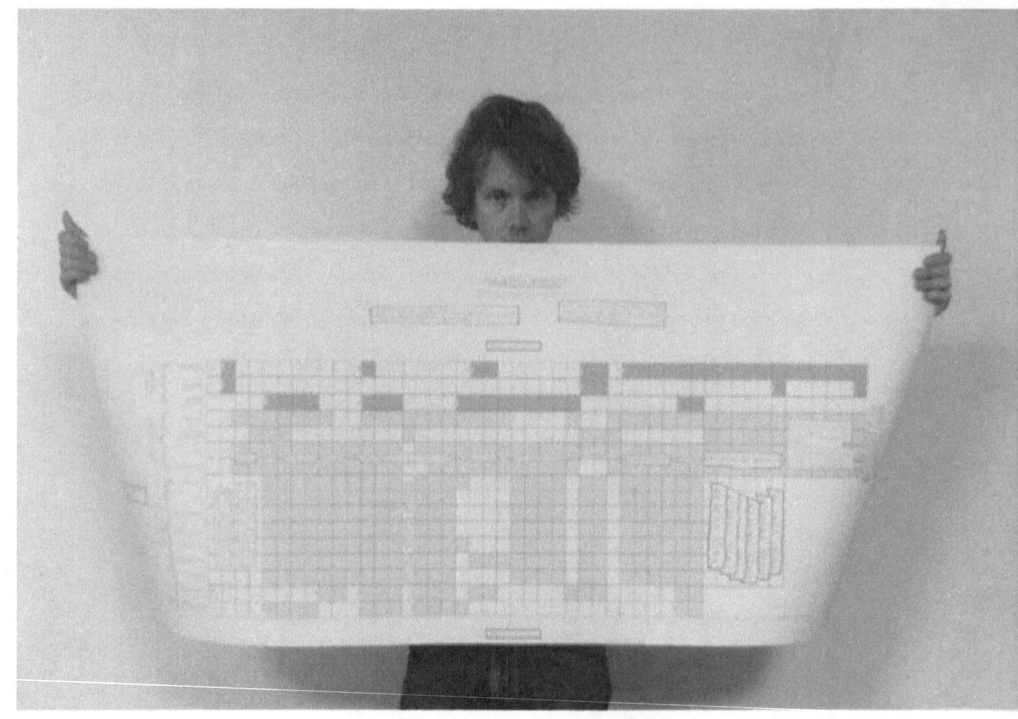

Arms stretched wide, months of work in my hands, years of research behind me, many failures and successes yet to come, many springing from the seeds sown by this work, the largest staging of my life thus far, the most far reaching, all areas of interest engaged. I stand back and see the final shape of *Creative Anxiety*. Looks to me like the shape of papercuts, sweat, intense self-doubt, many minor successes, the questioning and judgment of friends and family and myself. I've walked through the fire of self-doubt. It's a fire of my own making.

Perhaps this "complete work" will become simply another part of a larger work. Or perhaps the ultimate work is life itself. All the separate elements of life, all the works you've created, all these strands are ultimately woven together into a single entity – you. Or me. Or he. Or we.

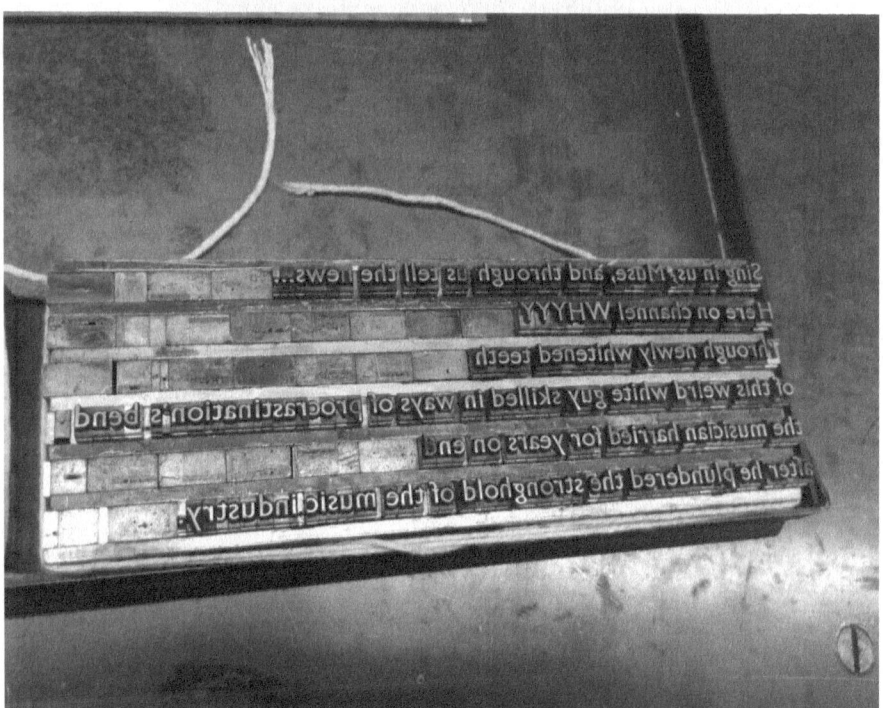

**Form,
Content,
Context,
and
Technology**

The 'complete work' -- a merging of multiple artistic practices into a single work, a single vision. Everything perceived – the visuals, the staging, the movement, the room itself, the lighting, the music, the text, the costumes – is intentional and functions according to the composer's desires for the work. Form mirrors content. Nothing is separate.

My inability to separate sound from everything else surrounding it perhaps stems from my experiences as an audience member. If a concert hall smells like a dumpster, it certainly affects my hearing experience. Likewise if it smells like potpourri. Also affecting my listening experience: the clothes I'm wearing, the temperature of the room, the weird taste in my mouth if I forgot to brush my teeth, whether I'm drinking a cold or warm beer or iced tea or being forbidden from drinking at all, what I ate for breakfast, my rotten mood, my happy mood, my shrugging mood, the argument I might've just had with my partner, my preconceptions about musical genres, my inability to sit still for long, my near-sightedness and steadfast refusal to get glasses. All are factors, although some are certainly beyond my control as a composer. I can't control the clothing the audience wears. I suppose I could, but that would get awkward and would require signing all sorts of legal forms, probably.

One could argue that good music makes all these factors irrelevant; that the listener is transported from whatever reality he or she is trapped in; the music brings transcendence. And I suppose that is true. But for myself, music's capacity to deliver that transcendence depends on innumerable small factors. Everything is connected; everything provides context. Compositions that take this into account tend to best hold my interest.

Context is a tricky thing, however. It's not merely the smell of the room or the clothes the players are wearing or even the setting; our own state of mind colors the sound we hear. In the words of Jorge Luis Borges, famed Chilean author and philosopher, "every writer *creates* his own precursors. His work modifies our conception of the past, as it will modify the future." [42] I suppose I'm admitting something important – the composer must realize that, even if he has attempted to micro-adjust every detail of the performance, every last bit of context, every part perfectly engineered, the most important element of all – the mindset of an audience member – is beyond his control. In crafting a 'complete work,' ideally a composer takes this into account – recognizing the intellectual baggage his audience is likely to be carrying into the show.

According to Rudolf Arnheim,

Our only access to reality is sensory experience, that is, sight or hearing or touch (or sound)... and sensory experience is always more than mere seeing or touching. It also includes mental images and knowledge based on experience. All of that makes up our view of the world.[43]

Sound and vision are, for me, inextricably linked – joined at the hip, holding hands, forever best friends. Actually more like siamese twins. Two minds, one body. Inseparable. Every so often, I'll listen to music with eyes closed or watch a performer with my hands over my ears. These are rare moments. Aside from making me look like a total weirdo (I'm usually doing this at a public venue), it doesn't do much else. At its best, it's a palette cleanser. Anytime I try to address sound without vision or vice versa, it feels artificial. I cannot separate the two.

I wouldn't say I have synaesthesia; music doesn't splash color across my vision. For me, sound and vision were never separate to begin with. If by some strange compulsion one wishes to dissect and analyze a composition, one could say each sense informs the other and provides context. They *could* be addressed as different entities. But that does not feel true to my experience. For me, context *is* content. I cannot separate a work from how it is presented. I experience music in a holistic manner.

---

42 Borges, "kafka and his precursors"
43 http://www.nytimes.com/2007/06/14/obituaries/14arnheim.html?_r=0

I was thankful to find a like-minded spirit in Susan Sontag. Her essay *Against Interpretation* resonated with me as a musician and as a creator. She claims Plato originated the schism between form and content, devising such a schism out of distrust of art, or any type of representation for that matter. Plato devised the distinction "in order to rule that the value of art is dubious."[44] For her, as well as myself, the separation of form and content, while useful for analysis, muddles the creative process and blunts inspiration. Ideally, an artwork resists the impulse to divide and sub-divide, between form and content, between how music sound and how it is presented. Strong artwork resists interpretation. Again, Susan Sontag:

> Real art has the capacity to make us nervous. By reducing the work
> of art to its content and then interpreting that, one tames the work of art. Interpretation makes art manageable, conformable.[45]

Humans experience the world holistically and to pretend otherwise feels like the dessicated remains of a worn-out idea pestering the Western mind. We wish to reduce life to whatever suits our perceptions; we shrink life's myrids streams into a single narrative, with ourselves as the main character and hero of course. Perhaps classification and subdivision is necessary for societal harmony, but to make artwork this parsing out feels unnecessary.

It is this need to address sound holistically that immediately puts me at odds with some of my sonic forebears, and some of my biggest influences – the musique concrète composers. The removal of context from sound – to disconnect a sound from its source and address the sound itself with no preconceptions – seems the driving force behind their manifestos. These manifestos do not resonate with me. They feel like the relic of a distant past in which recorded technology was a brand-new phenomenon. Their actual music, however, remains some of my favorite ever made.

To be fair, a manifesto is often written to 'throw down the gauntlet;' to make a

---

44 Sontag, Against Interpretation
45 Sontag, ibid.

bold and dramatic break from the past. This might lead to hyperbole or overly explicit divisions between that art form and the rest of the world. Honestly, those types of manifestos are the most interesting to read! Even if they don't feel relevant to my experience.

Traité des objets musicaux, a 1966 Pierre Schaeffer book of musical and artistic essays, explains musique concrete:

This determination to compose with materials taken from an existing collection of experimental sounds, I name musique concrète to make well the place in which we find ourselves, no longer dependent upon preconceived sound abstractions, but now using fragments of sound existing concretely and considered as sound objects defined and whole. [46]

The introduction of electronic technology allowed a separation of a sound from its source, in a way previously unimaginable; the emergence of the phonograph and then magnetic tape allowed for the playback of sounds separate from their acoustic source, brand new territory for humanity, a profound moment, ripe with possibility.

The musique concrete composers were not alone in their preoccupations. The idea seems in the air, with numerous other composers and social theorists weighing in. Henry Cowell wrote "there was a wide field open for the composition of music for phonographic discs," while Igor Sravinsky echoed the sentiment, "there will be a greater interest in creating music in a way that will be peculiar to the gramophone record." Rudolf Arnheim, renowned psychologist, author, and teacher at the New School for Social Research, believed that perception and thought were a single unit, that perceived sensory information was in essence thought itself. And it was through the various forms of perception – sound, vision, taste – that we are able to impose order on the world. Rudolf Arnheim took particular interest in music recording technology, arguing,

> The rediscovery of the musicality of sound in noise and in language, and the reunification of music, noise and language in order to obtain a unity of material: that is one of the chief artistic tasks of radio. *(Battier 2007, 193).*

It was precisely through radio that musique concrete originated. Pierre

---

[46] Schaeffer, *Traité des objets musicaux.* Paris: Le Seuil.

Schaeffer and Jacques Poullin, later joined by Pierre Henry, built the first purpose-built electroacoustic radio station in Studio d'Essai, former home of the French resistance movement during World War II and the first to broadcast in liberated Paris. The Groupe de Recherches de Musique Concrète (GRCM), as they called themselves, drew composers world-wide – Edgard Varese composed bits of "Desert" here; Iannis Xenakis and Darius Milhaud both composed works there.

The GRCM invented numerous instruments to manipulate sound and compose new works, and it is their direct engagement with technology that I find most inspiring. The composition process seemed based around creating new instruments to speak their new language. The phonogene, a tape machine with many heads and variable speed controls to control the pitch of a tape loop, captures the imagination with its absolutely stunning appearance, like some hybrid mutant crawling through a recording studio:

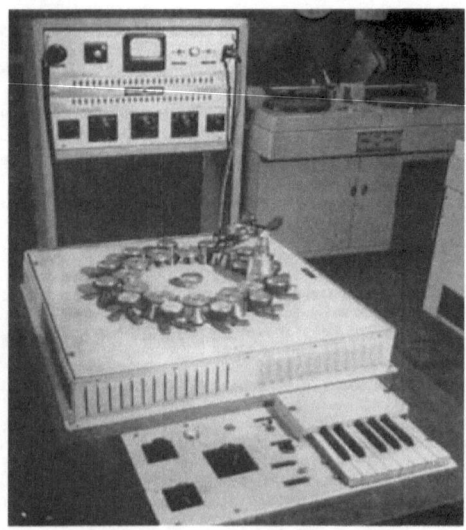

Meanwhile, Pierre Henry used magnetic induction and large coils to control amplitude on multi-channel audio works. His works are quite beautiful, particular his *Le microphone bien tempéré* (1951).   Perhaps it seems to contradict the musique concrete manifestos, but when I hear these works, I cannot separate the sound from its source. The difference is, for me, the source of the sound is not the tapes they've assembled, but the technology they created to realize their new language. I cannot separate their tools from their music. The technology itself has become the 'originating cause' of the sounds; the technology itself has become the instrument. The process behind the sound is an inextricable part of the experience. Just as one would a recording guitar performance and imagine the sound emanating from a guitar, I hear musique concrete and imagine the machines which conjured such wondrous sounds.

Musique concrete and 'the complete work' perhaps seem at odds; musique concrete aims to separate and subdivide, to distinguish form and content, to separate sound and its source, while a 'complete work' seeks to unite form and content into a unified whole. I think however, in a 21st century world, the two are indeed compatible; the invention and adaptation of electronic technology specific to a composition is now widespread, and the creation of new technologies is but another element in the composers toolbox, and indeed can form a large portion of a 'complete work.' The composer, in overseeing every aspect of the work, can originate new technology specific to their composition. No longer does a sound emanating from a machine feel abstracted from its source; the machine itself is the source. Musique Concrete, while perhaps my favorited merging of art and technology, preaches something untrue to my nature; I cannot separate sound from setting. I experience music holistically – each part contributing to the total experience.

The use of technology in the 'complete work,' however, is not a modern concept. It's as old as the concept itself. What's changed is the technology available to the composer.

    ichard   agner called it

                             Gesamtkunstwerk,[47]

            Moholy-Nagy called it the

                          Theatre of Totality,

Pauline Oliveros wrote

                    'theatre pieces;'

      Robert Ashley simply called it

                                'opera.'

I call it life itself.

---

47 The term actually originated in an 1827 essay by K. F. E. Trahndorff.

The 1966 Armory Concerts

Recognition of the many factors that create an experience is necessary in creating the 'total work.' To some, the many facets are not something to be suppressed, but rather embraced as intrinsic to artistic creation.   Öyvind Fahlström, in his 1966 essay "Take Care of the World," wrote:

> Consider art as a way of experiencing a fusion of "pleasure" and "insight." Reach this by impurity, or multiplicity of levels, rather than by reduction. (The fallacy of some painting, music, etc.; satori by mere reduction.The fewer the factors, the more they have to be "right," "ultimate.")[48]

Fahlstrom, a multi-media artist, participated in the famed 1966 *9 Evenings: Theatre and Engineering,* a series of concerts at the 26th Street Armory in New York City; these concerts were one of the great flowerings of the post-war avante-garde, and still inspire today. In fact, they were perhaps my greatest inspiration for *Creative Anxiety*.

For the concerts, 10 New York artists collaborated with 30 engineers and scientists from the renowned Bell Labs created new performative works incorporating new technology. The boundaries between music, theatre, technology, and high art were indistinguishable. In Robert Rauschenburg's "Open Score," Mimi Kanarek and Frank Stella played tennis, with each hit of the tennis ball triggering an overhead light bulb to turn off; during the second half of his piece, 500 audience members gathered on the now darkened stage, where infrared cameras filmed the audience members acting out an event score, which instructors the women to "brush their hair," and to "sing a song loudly."   Is it music?   Art? Theatre?   All of the above, perhaps.

Other artists involved with *9 Evenings* included: John Cage, Lucinda

---

48 Manifestos, 1966, p. 11.

Childs, Alex Hay, Deborah Hay, Steve Paxton, Yvonne Rainer, Robert Rauschenberg, Robert Whitman, and David Tudor. Notable engineers involved include: Bela Julesz, Max Mathews, and Fred Waldhauer. Entire encyclopedia volumes could be written about the artistic and engineering prowess on display, a remarkable confluence of art and technology. The concerts were a resounding success.

Of particular interest to me was David Tudor's *Bandoneon!: A Combine*. Watching a recently issued DVD (available via ArtPix / directed by Julie Martin and Barbro Schulz Lundestam), Tudor's performance felt like a revelation -- the perfect intersection of theatre, technology, and music. His performance quite literally changed my view of music and composition in general.

From an interview with Bruce Duffie, Tudor explains *Bandoneon!* and also the 9 Evenings:

> ...that was the second piece I wrote as an electronic composer, and that's a very complicated circumstance... a group of artists were solicited by Billy Klüver, who was working for Bell Laboratories, who loved the New York art scene very much. So he wanted to make technology available to them, and through the cooperation of many engineers from Bell (Labs), he created this festival called **9 Evenings: Theatre and Engineering**.
>
> Basically we arrived at a system of great flexibility amongst the artists... I was working with the electronic end of it, so I noticed how the whole system had been created because each artist wanted certain things to happen, but they required different components. Then, in order to make the whole thing sonically work, we had to have a generalized sound system.
>
> I noticed that nobody was really using a lot of the features of the system, so I set out to put everything into this. So I made Bandoneon ! One engineer gave me a rather antiquated but very beautiful device that would act as a microphone. You could call it a complex microphone. It was actually a set of harmonium reeds and setting that up as a microphone meant putting the sound through loudspeakers, through these harmonium reeds so that the specific frequencies would excite specific reeds. So there I had one trigger device which could trigger lots of things. So I set out to program the whole shebang and so I ended up with three kinds of triggering devices. One through light, one through audio triggers that was proportional to the sound played by the instrument, which was the bandoneón, and

then switching, which was accomplished through this harmonium device. And then in addition to that, we had a projection TV... derived from the signals being played by the bandoneón. All I had to do was play this instrument and all things were set in motion.

The first time it didn't work, and that was one of the biggest fuckups of the century. But nobody knew about it until after it happened.

It turned out to be a very simple mistake. It was the fact that many circuit boards had to be made to put into the programmer, and there was one engineer who was in charge of doing that. But there were so many to be made that people who had come there to observe or to help as they could, set to work soldering these circuit boards, and nobody told them the back of a circuit board is the reverse image of the front. So the whole wiring was done backwards, and that was only discovered because my piece was on the second day. [laughter] The second time the piece was done, it worked perfectly.

His idea to use all available technology in a single work actually reminded me of the first time I visited the audio/visual services department at Mills College. Seeing the dozens of speakers, televisions and interfaces, I wrote a composition entitled "A/V." Here is a copy of that original score:

```
A/V

for one performer

use every single item in A/V.
every speaker, every television,
every mixer, every cable, every camera,
every adapter, every projector.

plug them all into a single source.
make them all inter-dependent.
potential source materials:
moon landing, Walter Cronkite,
video feedback loop,
Charlie Chaplin,
video cameras pointed at dancers' feet,
college graduation ceremony.
set up all
equipment in a highly visible area.
attempt to make the equipment looks
as much as possible like a
disorganized 'pile,' while
still maintaining control
over the proceedings.
```

Bill Baird

Perhaps unrealistic, but still stemming from the same playful inclusion David Tudor used in *Bandoneon!* My unrealized composition *A/V* eventually melded with Creative Anxiety, in a sense – my performance used every single flat-screen from A/V and every miniature speaker available for check-out. A pared-down version of the piece.

Bandoneon was among many genre-busting works from the 9 Evenings. Also worth mentioning: John Cage's *Variations VII*, in which, during a performance, the electronics all around him caught fire to his pants, but Cage was so enraptured by the proceedings that he didn't even notice.[49]

Spurred by the success of these concerts, Experiments in Art and Technology (E.A.T.) was formed -- an organization facilitating further collaborations between artists and engineers. The group was founded by 9 Evenings alums Billy Kluver, Fred Waldhauer, Robert Rauschenburg, and Robert Whitman. In their use of technology and 'total theatre' approach, their work feels like a direct predecessor to mine, at least where I want my work to be.

---

49 As heard on the *Variations VII* DVD commentary.

'Creative Anxiety' Bibliography

Ashley, Robert. Interview. http://requitedjournal.com/index.php?/essay/an-interview-with-robert-ashley/

butch morris:

http://www.nytimes.com/2013/01/30/arts/music/butch-morris-dies-at-65-creator-of-conduction.html?_r=0

Bayle, François (1993). *Musique acousmatique, propositions ... positions.* Paris: INA-GRM Buche/Chastel.

Sontag, Susan. "Against Interpretation."
http://www.uiowa.edu/~c08g001d/Sontag_AgainstInterp.pdf

http://arthistory.about.com/cs/glossaries/g/g_golden_ratio.htm

Hunter, James. "Orpheus" - http://www.pantheon.org/articles/o/orpheus.html

Manifestos, something else press, 1966.

Taycher, Leonid. "You can count the number of books in the world on 25,972,976 hands." 2010.

http://googleblog.blogspot.com/2010/08/you-can-count-number-of-books-in-world.html

www.ingramcontent.com/pod-product-compliance
Lightning Source LLC
Chambersburg PA
CBHW032122160426
43197CB00008B/481